Inquests: Living With the Dead

by

Judge Thomas Mitchell Shamburger

FORTHCOMING, FROM THE AUTHOR OF
INQUESTS: LIVING WITH THE DEAD
Weddings, Music, and Funerals
By Judge Thomas Mitchell Shamburger

The middle act of life's play is the wedding. A bachelor(ette) party or a family gathering is a celebration, putting single life to rest. This is followed by a solemn ceremony, often with special music. The wedding is an act that lasts forever, or at least "until death do you part." Often, a vast amount of money is spent on food, ornate cakes, special wardrobes, fancy cars, a chapel, and even expensive jewelry. Family and friends dress up and join together to make the send-off the best it can be. Usually, a minister will officiate the wedding, but often it is a justice of the peace.

The final act of life's play is the funeral. A wake or other family gathering is a celebration of a life as it is put to rest. This is followed by a solemn ceremony, often with special music. The funeral is an act that lasts forever; in death we did part. Often, a vast amount of money is spent on food, ornate cakes, special wardrobes, fancy cars, a chapel, and an expensive casket. Family and friends dress up and join together to make the send-off the best it can be. Usually, a minister will officiate the funeral, rarely is it a justice of the peace.

Life is music, each person a song, each child a verse.

Weddings, music, and funerals are the fun parts of my professional life.

A male's view of a wedding is different from the female perspective. A hint of a wedding story is found in Carrie's tale in Inquests: Living: With the Dead. If you have a son or daughter, or have ever considered getting married, this book offers a few stories that you'll probably find both amusing and instructive.

Music has played a major part in my life. From singing in Sunday school to performing "Play That Funky Music" at the local dive, I love music. If you enjoy music, ever wanted to play music, or wondered why and how people make music, you'll love this book.

Funerals are a time for reflection. The funerals I have conducted are few and not the most traditional ones. I hope that you enjoy sharing my recollections and reflections on the deaths and funerals with which I've been involved. If you have conducted or thought about conducting a funeral, or if you're thinking about how you would like your own funeral to be conducted, you'll find some guides to your thoughts in this book.

A thread that runs through Weddings, Music, and Funerals is Todd Henry. Todd was a mentor and friend who taught me much about music. I performed his marriage ceremony, performed on stage with him, and performed his funeral, as I relate in the closing chapter. He was a teacher who was stabbed to death in his classroom. I hope that you're already hooked on buying this book, but if not, the opportunity to read about Todd should make up your mind.

✝o
Abigail, Jacob, and the Grandkids to
come.

Do not read until you are 21.
(OK at least 16)

Contents

Acknowledgments

Thanks to Mrs. Pitt, my Winona High School English teacher, and Mrs. Linda Lusk, my longtime Chief Court Clerk; they tried to teach me that what you have to say is more important than spelling and that three words are better than four. Thanks to Mom (LoLo), who thinks her son can do no wrong, and thanks also to the rest of my family, who know different. My gratitude goes out to Vicki Kay and those who read drafts of the manuscript and helped in editing. My spelling baffles the computer, so thanks to all who catch and correct the tecknekel errors!

Special thanks goes out to the firefighters, police officers, emergency medical personnel, funeral home staff, hospice workers, doctors, nurses, and the many others who face life and deal with death. This book is also for all of you.

Mitch

Foreword

In Texas, the position of justice of the peace is an elected office. A JP serves as the coroner and performs inquests in counties without a medical examiner, which includes most of the counties in Texas and the United States.

I am the Justice Court Judge, Precinct Four, Smith County, Texas. Much has changed over the three decades that I have been in office, but dying and performing inquests, are about the same as they have always been.

Many times I have been asked, "How can you handle looking at those dead bodies?" It takes a certain type of person. When you finish this book, I hope you will realize I am just a person with a job, like many who have to work and deal with the dead.

Through the words of this book you will see through my eyes what I have seen throughout the years. I do not write to disturb or upset; however, if reading this makes you lock your doors, put on your seatbelt, or think twice before you do something stupid, it could save a life. The book also may open your eyes to a situation that will end in tragedy if you do not do something.

Warnings:

Humor is the way many handle stress, and death scenes are no exception. No disrespect is intended when I make colorful observations. I have heard and made some comments that would put James Bond and Batman to shame.

Some descriptions are graphic. The descriptions could never reproduce the full impact of a death situation. The illustrations, with their smells and their views, are not for the squeamish.

If these events can happen in the piney woods of rural East Texas, they can happen anywhere. Last night I witnessed a crispy critter (burned body), two autopsies, and four fatal gunshot wounds, all this, while sitting in my den watching television. It seems that today, life often is graphic or morbid.

With thousands of inquests, how did I choose which stories to tell?

The selected inquest stories seemed to shout to me, "Tell my story!" Most of the stories are of an everyday nature: deaths that go unnoticed by everyone except the immediate observers. The homicide stories seemed to linger. I am not sure why. Were they the ones I would like to forget?

Some inquest stories are merged, and the dialogue comes from my own brain, as imperfectly recalled and sometimes made up to fill in gaps. Forgive me if you seem to recognize the tragic event that forever changed your life, and it is not presented as you remember it. This is not a reference book, and no story should be used in any fact-finding endeavor concerning any particular case. I acknowledge now that all the inquest events did not happen exactly as they are described here. Most of the names and inquest numbers have been changed. Don't sue me for anything! Much of what I have written came from unsworn unreliable sources. Add this to my unreliable memory, and there is much room for error. There are some things we will never know. These stories are as true as I can remember.

Inquests: Living With the Dead is about a bunch of dead people and the one thing they have in common — me.

Chapter 1

First Encounter

Scott and Dave, two young teenage kids, ride alongside North Bragg Boulevard on a little dirt bike at top speed, maybe thirty miles an hour. The machine is not made for paved roads but is ideal for a North Carolina sand trail, which is what runs along the right-of-way. The laughter of the two Army brats is heard even above the whining of the motorcycle. They weave like snow skiers around giant creosote poles supported by guy wires, tensioned half-inch steel cables that anchor and lend stability to the row of telephone poles. Bumps, dips, and guy wires complete the course and transform the dirt bike experience into a roller coaster ride. These kids had *guts*! This may be the best time of their lives. A twist of the hand throttle, and they are gone. Watch out for the guy wires.

~~~~~~~~~~~~~~~~~~~~~~~~~~~~

In 1973, I was Spec. (Specialist) 4 Thomas Shamburger; it would be nine years before I would be Judge Mitch Shamburger. As a medic and paratrooper in the 82nd Airborne Division at Fort Bragg, North Carolina, I was quite familiar with injuries, blood, and guts. Soldiers are proud of their injuries as badges of honor, and *guts* take on a special meaning, especially when you go "ALL THE WAY, AIRBORNE!" Having *guts* identifies a person as willing to go beyond what most would call normal, like "jumping out of a perfectly good airplane." Exhibitions of airborne guts are made in the field, on bivouac. "Airborne!" someone would yell before popping a big, juicy grasshopper in his mouth. Live bugs, caterpillars, and crawfish are favorites for displaying guts.

In survival training in the jungles of Panama, we learn what to eat and what not to eat. The humidity stays near 100%, with hazy skies under the rain forest canopy. The musty smell of rotting foliage adds to the inhospitable terrarium atmosphere. Survival class begins in a jungle clearing. The seats are logs hewn from large fallen rainforest trees.

"This fruit is EATABLE," says the instructor, holding up a green, pear-like gourd with a ruby-red seeded center, and then adds the punch line — "But if you eat it, you will die." In the span of two hours, we learn the fruits that we can and cannot eat to survive in this jungle. Actually, we learn not to eat anything we can't recognize. This would limit me to several varieties of bananas.

In another survival class, a chicken stops squawking when the instructor dangles her upside down. Her head stays in one place as the instructor swings her back and forth. She stretches her neck to look curiously at a group of men, upside down, which are looking curiously at her. The instructor calls a volunteer forward. The instructor grips Ms. Chicken's head with his right hand and pretends to bite the neck while pulling off the head. Tossing the head to one side, he assists the volunteer in turning her right-side up, and then orders the volunteer to drink. The volunteer follows the order and tosses it back like a jug of milk; after all, he has *guts*. The blood comes out faster than the soldier can drink, making a bloody mess.

The instructor then demonstrates how to rip the skin off the chicken, which is much faster than plucking the feathers. The insides, the real guts, are then laid out for inspection, and a delicate yellow kernel about the size of a pea is found. This would have become an egg if Ms. Chicken had not met the 82nd Airborne Division. The instructor tosses it in the air and catches it in his mouth like a piece of candy.

"This will always be OK to eat. Now we must check for diseases," the instruction continues.

Ms. Chicken passes inspection and then gets ripped to pieces and passed around, part by part. She is consumed by the troops in a demonstration of survival in the jungle and *guts*. Not everyone is meant to be an Airborne Ranger, and a few of us do not eat chicken that day.

My wife, Fae, and I lived in a mobile home community close to Fort Bragg. Military or "on post" housing is limited, and a mobile home answers the needs of many soldiers with limited income. The trailer house was much like one of the thousands that surround military bases across the United States and even around the world.

The small trailer park where we lived was pleasant enough. Across the main highway is an evergreen forest of giant pine trees. The mobile home was old, but comfortable to a still newlywed couple. Once, while showering together, we felt a shift beneath our feet. Seconds later, the tub fell through the floor! All of a sudden, we were standing in the bathtub on the ground. We laughed as the water continued to run over us. We celebrated our leather (third-year) anniversary apart, Fae in the trailer park and me in Puerto Rico for more adventure training.

That summer Fae's youngest brother came to North Carolina. Tim was twelve years old and curious. He loved to explore the neighborhood and the woods across the highway.

One day as I watch television and polish my jump boots, the front door bursts open and a very excited Tim runs in.

"Two kids on a motorcycle had a wreck across the street!" he says with a puzzled expression. "There is a head lying in the sand, but I don't think it is real."

Launching from the chair, I grab the medic aid bag, then head out the door. A few cars are stopped along the road, but there is no motorcycle or evidence of a crash or an accident on the roadway. Beyond the vehicles, next to the forest, a small motorcycle is sputtering, lying on its side, its back wheel turning, jerking with each sputter of the motor. People are gathering, not at the motorcycle but twenty feet away, beside a telephone pole. More people stop, and the crowd grows. I work my way through the throng. People see the medical bag and give me room.

"I am a nurse!" a lady shouts as she also works her way into the heart of the excitement.

~~~~~~~~~~~~~~~~~~~~~~~~~

"Good Samaritan laws" now protect those who try to help others in this kind of situation. For a period of time a liability issue existed when someone stopped to lend a helping hand. People just trying to help ended up in lawsuits. Even if exonerated, they were out the expense of a lawyer and the hassle of being run through the justice system. Worse, as in this case, a jury panel might take the words of a slick sounding lawyer and twist good works into a mistake. "This poor child will never have the full use of his arm because she, a nurse, who should have known better, did not do this or that and SOMEONE MUST PAY!"

~~~~~~~~~~~~~~~~~~~~~~~~~

"Over here!" someone yells. A child lies on his back screaming. He waves one arm in the air, and there is a bloody stump wiggling where the other should be.

Calls are made, and activity surrounds me. Then, all is quiet. As in slow motion, I focus on something lying on the ground a few feet away in the sand. A head sits there, tilted. It looks as though the rest of the body might be buried below the earth, like someone buried in the sand at the beach, except for the eyes, they are half closed, and half open. The skin is without color, beyond pale. The head blends in with the light-colored sand. The face shows no expression. No pain. No anything. It does not even look as though asleep. As Tim had reported, "It did not look real." People continue to move around it as though the head is not there.

My eyes lock upon the sight, which others cannot see. This picture did not fit or could not fit into the average mind. The brain has a way of filtering out what we do not want or need to see, and things that just do not fit — like the extra extra word in a sentence, the shortcomings of our children, the abuse of a spouse or parent, the fat we accumulate over the years, or even a pale head lying in the sand.

Pointing to the head, I say to a soldier in uniform, "Cover that and guard it!" Subconsciously, even I had separated "that" from the life that was. I go to the other child.

On the ground is a young boy with his arm torn off at the shoulder. A lifeless, bent, and broken arm lies a few feet away. It is the same pale color as the head and the sand. An off-duty nurse is applying pressure where the arm used to be. She is performing as she had been trained, probably, like me, in the Army.

"All right, people!" I order. "Let's make some room here." I treat the scene as though setting up a battleground triage for clearing and evacuation.

People tend to move when they think they are helping and to listen when someone takes charge. Army medics may not have high rank, but they often are in a position to give orders. Once, a lieutenant asked me why I was walking with him and not crawling in the ditch with the other troops during a war game training exercise. I answered that I did not want to get dirty. Then I explained that when I go to work, the game is over. What the medic does is for real. In training or in combat, it can be a matter of life and death.

People back away, creating a human fence surrounding an oblong ring of cleared ground extending from the motorcycle to the injured child. In the middle of the ring is a headless body. The decapitated body of a teenager lies on its back, facing the sky.

~~~~~~~~~~~~~~~~~~~~~~~~~~~

The human heart pumps more than a gallon of blood each minute. Unlike most of the other organs of the body, the heart has its own set of neurons and nerves that tell the muscle to contract and pump, even when the signal from the brain is no more. Much of the blood is dedicated to bringing oxygen to the brain through the carotid arteries. With unbridled carotid arteries the body was drained, in seconds.

~~~~~~~~~~~~~~~~~~~~~~~~~

The blood had pumped out faster than the sand could absorb. A dark red clot had formed where the boy's head should have been.

"Ambulance on the way!" someone shouts. The siren takes forever to arrive. Traffic crawls by on the road as rubbernecks strain to see what is happening. The ambulance finally worms its way through the traffic with lights flashing. The emergency crew bails out of the ambulance and goes to work, taking over the situation. The surviving child no longer is moaning. He is going into shock. He is still alive, thanks to the nurse, someone who saw a need and met the challenge. The emergency crew places the boy on the litter and loads him into the ambulance. The doors start to close.

"Wait!" I yell, and quickly, but gently, retrieve the arm from the ground. It is soft and relaxed, broken and flexible. It feels like my own hand when it is asleep and numb, when I can feel it with my other hand but it won't move; it appears lifeless, like the arm in my hands. I carry the arm to the ambulance. A paramedic takes it, the siren screams, and the ambulance is gone.

"Well, Officer," I hear someone say, "it looks like the driver of the motorcycle didn't see the guy wire. The passenger leaned to the side and somehow his arm got caught in it."

"It's all over," the policeman says. "Let's clear the area. Don't move anything. The judge has been notified."

Tragedies continue with the living.

The fathers of both children are notified and go directly to the hospital. One father paces the halls of the hospital as his child went straight to surgery.

"Scott might lose his arm. We are doing the best we can," the doctor says.

"What could be worse?" the father thinks. "My son without his right arm?" He bows his head and begins to pray.

The arm is reattached successfully, probably the work of a Vietnam Veteran Doctor at Womack Army Medical Center. War creates great helicopter pilots and surgeons. Doctors learn the hard way by piecing together broken soldiers in meatball surgery.

The other father arrives at the emergency room to discover that his son is not there. His son did not arrive in the ambulance. He did not know that he was in a hearse, on his way to a mortuary. The father calls his wife from the emergency room with a sigh of relief. "Thank God!" he tells her. "Dave must not have been hurt too bad; they did not even bring him to the hospital."

~~~~~~~~~~~~~~~~~~~~~~~~~~

A friend of mine calls a motorcycle a donor-cycle. From monster choppers or big classic cruisers to crotch rockets and mini-bikes, it's hard to deny they are more dangerous than their four-wheeled brethren.

When I was thirteen I asked Dad if I could get a motorcycle. He said, "Sure." When I asked him to pay for it, he said, "No." I bought a Honda 90 and paid for it by working at Dad's gas station. (The Justice Court Center, Precinct Four, is next-door to T.J. Shamburger's old gas station.) I have been riding motorcycles ever since, and it has almost killed me several times. Fae spent several months in the hospital with a concussion because some idiot did not use a turn signal. Like getting bucked off a horse, we still climb back on.

When a motorcycle competes with anything (a drunk driver, car, truck, train, wall, bridge, rubber tread, deer, tree, pig, sharp curve, cow, guide rail, mailbox, telephone pole, pedestrian, guy wire), the biker will lose.

Anyone who straddles an engine and drives on two wheels will someday have an accident. The goal is to get away with as little damage as possible. Do not trust any motorists, drive defensively, and always look for "an out."

Two kids were on a motor bike. One moment they were laughing and riding, carefree and indestructible. Pushing that cycle to the limit, they had *guts*. The driver did not see the guy wire. Did he have a helmet on? It would have made no difference. Going fifteen or thirty miles an hour, the result would have been the same. His head was plucked off like a grape. Life ended.

I wondered how this would affect my brother-in-law Tim. Years later, we talked about what happened in North Carolina. Our lives are shaped by the events that surround us, and some tragedies have long-term results. He remembered it as "just part of growing up." It did not negatively affect him. In high school he became one of the youngest members of the Winona Volunteer Fire Department. He continued to volunteer as a fire fighter until cancer took him at the age of twenty-seven. Tim was loved by all. He was a great fire fighter and a great brother-in-law.

As for me, I had no idea that looking at dead bodies would become a part of my career. This event was one of many that prepared me for things to come. Being a nurse or medic is not a prerequisite for being a justice of the peace, but it certainly has been helpful. People who are rich in life experiences make the best judges.

Chapter 2

How Did I Get Here? What Am I Doing?

"You will be in jail for the weekend," the jailer said to a seventeen-year-old prisoner, smiling as the heavy, barred door clanged shut. The dark, gray paint on the heavy steel bars was thick from coats accumulated during years of community service. The boy, wearing a black and gold Winona High School letter jacket, looked around the cell. Criminals of various shapes, sizes, and colors grinned back.

Everyone in the cell looked happy, everyone except that seventeen-year-old kid — me. They did not know or care that I was a "good kid," really, a good kid — only stupid that night. They laughed when I said, "I'm not staying here."

Once in a long while, I get a gut feeling that predicts the future. I can't explain this prophetic ability, and I've experienced it less than a dozen times in my life. I knew that night that I was not to stay in that dingy jail cell for a weekend, or even for the night.

My friends regularly shoplifted eight-track tapes. (A history lesson for you younger readers: Before the digital age of music, there were vinyl records, which were replaced by eight-track tapes, which were replaced by cassette tapes, which were replaced by compact disks, which are being replaced by digital recordings and devices.) While they engaged in their petty larceny, I would not steal anything. That Saturday night, I forgot to wear a belt. With my friends urging me on and supposedly standing guard at a department store, I stuffed a belt inside my shirt.

A few moments later, I was thrown up against a wall

and searched for that $2.50 belt. My friends, shocked, watched the proceedings while they held more than $20 worth of tapes stashed in coat pockets and pants. The experience scared the hell out of them and ended their criminal careers, then and there. It also changed my life.

My one and only phone call went like this.
"Hello."
"Dad, I am in jail."
"I'll see what I can do." Click.

The jail cells occupied the top two floors of the Smith County Courthouse. My cell held eight prisoners, myself reluctantly included. Five of them played cards around a steel picnic like table. One of the card players had wrapped a leather belt tightly around two of the one-inch steel bars. Periodically, he got up to pour small amounts of water on the leather, having seen in a movie, or otherwise heard about, the strength of shrinking leather. The other two prisoners just sat on steel beds and benches looking dangerous. I shrank back in the corner and would not even take off my letter jacket.

After three hours of incarceration, my gut-feeling prophecy was fulfilled. Justice of the Peace James Cashion led me by the arm down the steps and out of the courthouse. He knew me from church; occasionally, he would stop by the gas station to talk politics with Dad.

With a stubby, chewed cigar two inches from my nose, he exclaimed, "The complaint will read, 'The State of Texas vs. Mitch Shamburger.'" The stubby cigar went up and down with every syllable. "Boy, when you take on the *State of TEXAS*, you'd better get ready. They have unlimited resources to put you away forever. You can bump heads with the state of Texas, or you can be a responsible citizen and maybe do some good in the community. The choice is yours." He paused to adjust his jaws' clamp on the cigar. "The choices you make now can affect you the rest of your life," he finished solemnly.

I said nothing.

It could have been the decaying cigar, but I thought I

caught the scent of Jack Daniels on his breath. I guessed that the judge and Dad had shared a nip or two on the way to the jail.

Some kids you have to whip, yell at, or take other extreme measures with to get their attention. My attention was "got."

That night I lay down in the comfort of my own bed and reflected on the foolishness of the act, the embarrassment of being arrested, and Judge Cashion. I came to the conclusion that judging is one neat job. To be able to help someone, offer guidance and direction, and have the power of the gavel to put criminals away — forever! That was awesome.

I never knew if it was my distant kinfolk in the district attorney's office, the store, or Judge Cashion, or if my case just fell through the cracks, but nothing else happened, and Dad never mentioned it after that night.

I have related this story to hundreds of kids and have been known to chew a cigar or two.

~~~~~~~~~~~~~~~~~~~~~~

Eight years later, I tossed my hat into the political ring for the position of justice of the peace for Precinct Four, Smith County. The votes were counted, and I lost. I was beaten by a dead man!

Judge Cashion had died in his courtroom with his name already printed on the November general election ballot. I had to run as a write-in candidate. It was my first campaign for public office.

My living opponent was Ray Day, a butcher. He was well known and for years had cut meat at Kay's Food Store, the local grocery market, which was just across the street from my dad's gas station. We were acquaintances. He rode in a pickup truck on tires he got on credit from dad. He still owed money on the tires. He stopped coming around when the payments were due. We both ran as write-in candidates. Thomas Mitchell Shamburger has twenty-four letters in it, while Ray Day has six. It was much easier to write his name and easier still to check James Cashion or vote a straight Democratic ticket. I could see I had a mountain to climb, but climb I did. We had public debates, put up yard signs, and ate at every church gathering and meeting. Although I was half the age of Day, I tried to campaign on my maturity, life experiences, and military history of public service.

The election was close. After a recount, Ray Day received almost one third of the votes, and I received almost one third. The late Judge Cashion received *more than* one third. I think some people voted for Judge Cashion simply because they knew it would be the last time his name would ever appear on a ballot. Others voted for him out of respect, and may have experienced the saving grace of that stubby cigar instructing them to a better way of life.

The election result required the Smith County Commissioners Court to appoint a justice of the peace to fill the unexpired term. Ray and I applied and presented ourselves, expecting one or the other to receive the blessings of the Court. The Court, in its wisdom, appointed someone who did not even run, but who was very active in the Democratic Party.

I learned several political lessons that year: one, the difficulties of a write-in candidate; two, politics and reason are often two different things; and three, never underestimate your opponent, even if he is dead.

This cloud did have a silver lining. Losing the election and not getting the appointment meant that I had time to get my associate's degree from Tyler Junior College and my bachelor's degree from the University of Texas at Tyler.

I ran the station for Dad during the summer and went to college in the spring, winter, and fall. With the G.I. bill and the service station, we managed comfortably.

The year after I started junior college, I was elected to the Winona Independent School Board. While I was on the school board, the town built a new K-12 campus. Noah, my son, walked into the kindergarten classroom when it was brand new and later graduated from the new Winona High School (like the three generations before him, at the old high school).

A year after the election, the appointed judge vacated the office under a cloud of suspicion. My old opponent, Ray Day, took his place. Judge Day seemed to do a good job, and the electorate seemed happy. When election time came around again, I was extremely busy. Professionally, I was completing college, working at the station during the summer, and nursing on the side for extra money. Privately, I led the music at church and attended school board meetings.

The "Honorable" job honored the judge with only $16,000 a year. Fae was pregnant, ready to add another Shamburger to the Winona population. I was not sure we could survive on county pay. With so many irons in the fire, I decided not to throw my hat into this political ring. Despite the decision, God or fate had different plans for me.

Judge Day ran unopposed. He apparently had perfected an excellent technique to make the voters happy by not reporting traffic convictions to the Texas Department of Public Safety. What made Smith County unhappy was Judge Day not reporting all the money collected for the associated fines. Four years after Ray Day's appointment, he was indicted and convicted for supplementing his salary with fine money.

With my college degree in hand, Fae settled in as a U.S. postal rural route carrier. With son Noah attending school and daughter Lena out of diapers, the time seemed right for me to try again for the judgeship.

I applied for the appointment and was selected. One county commissioner, Jerry Shamburger, abstained from voting. At the age of twenty-nine, the job was mine.

During my first few years of Texas Justice Court schools, conferences, and seminars, I heard stories about Judge Cashion; his antics and activities lived on at such events. Even though he had been dead for five years, his shoes were hard to fill.

In Texas, the Justice Court judges have the

responsibility of determining the cause and manner of death in cases for which a medical examiner or a physician cannot sign the death certificate. They do this by compiling information from witnesses, law enforcement officers, firefighters, and medical personnel, as well as test and autopsy data, and then draw conclusions. An inquest can be done formally, with a jury panel presided over by the justice court judge, another name for justice of the peace. Usually, however, the inquest is done informally by a justice of the peace.

In the olden days of the 1980s, inquest laws were scattered throughout the law books, and some laws were even contradictory. Like Judge Roy Bean, "Justice of the Peace, Law West of the Pecos," I had to pick and choose which laws I wanted to use. The Legislative Committee of the Justice of the Peace and Constable Association of Texas took on the task of codifying the inquest laws. I am proud to say I had a hand in writing these laws. Texas Code of Criminal Procedure Chapter 49 makes some pretty interesting reading.

What Is an Inquest?

Chapter 49 of the Texas Code of Criminal Procedure includes this definition: "Inquest" means an investigation into the cause and circumstances of the death of a person, and a determination, made with or without a formal court hearing, as to whether the death was caused by an unlawful act or omission.

"Inquest on a dead body," simply put, means determining the cause and manner of death. It is actually a small part of my daily duties, but highly visible and important.

Most people think inquests are emotionally difficult, and some are, especially those on kids. A county commissioner once told me at budget time, "You could not pay me enough to go out and look at those dead bodies." I replied, "You're in luck. You *can* pay me!"

In the movies, you may see someone get shot, or put a gun to their head, and splatter the wall behind them. Somehow, the mind filter is at work, and we know that it's not for real—it's just the movies. The filter does not work if you are standing in a room with the distinct smell of blood and gunpowder, and you see a .357 Magnum handgun lying in the relaxed grip of a lady's hand, her body laid back on the bed with her face and scalp spread out like a rubber mask, her eye sockets hollow, looking up to the ceiling, where fractured bits of skull stick out at various angles, and lumps of gray matter are splattered about the room—the same gray matter that once carried her thoughts. I had met this lady before, and I knew her respectable family. In another time and place, she was a real lady, a really nice person. You try to compartmentalize this part of your job (putting those scenes and circumstances in a box to be stored away in your mind), but seeing things like this will affect other parts of your life. Movies that show death scenes or murders, for example, come across markedly different to me than they do to people who have not experienced such events.

Actually, dead people are pretty easy to get along with. They do not complain or argue. They do not ask the same question over and over, struggling to get the answer they want. Once a dead person is found, you usually know where they are and where they are going. Also, coroners, like undertakers, "bury their mistakes."

Some think inquests should be done only by doctors or medical examiners who are forensic pathologists. An inquest, however, is more than a medical operation or an evaluation that someone is dead. The justice of the peace makes a ruling about cause of death based on information acquired from multiple sources and has the power to order autopsies and tests, as well as to review information from forensic pathologists and doctors. The judge also may seek evidence from additional outside sources, which may include law enforcement officers trained in accidents and homicides, investigations by police detectives, and testimony from witnesses at the scene or expert witnesses.

Where the body or body parts lie determines the site of jurisdiction. If someone is killed in Winona, Minnesota, but is found in Winona, Texas, the inquest will be in Justice Court Precinct Four, Smith County.

Smith County is blessed with three hospitals with level advanced trauma centers. Patients come by ambulance and helicopter from all over East Texas, and not all survive. Bodies end up at the hospital with little or no information, sometimes without even a name. Often a call from a nurse will turn into a sleepless night, with the judge tracking down the who, what, when, where, and why of a particular death. Part of an inquest is working closely with nurses, medical personnel, law enforcement, dispatchers, and the family. At times, information is limited and the window for ordering an autopsy is critical. Although the justice of the peace can exhume a body, valuable evidence is destroyed when the body is embalmed or as it lies in the ground.

The funeral home or mortuary service completes most of the death certificate and files the document with the Texas Department of State Health Services Bureau of Vital Statistics. The "Certifier", doctor or judge, fills out cause and manner of death.

When someone dies of natural causes (heart attack, cancer, old age) and is under a doctor's care, an inquest usually is not necessary. The doctor will certify the death certificate. When the death is unattended, or not a natural death, or if the doctor cannot or does not determine the cause of death and there is no medical examiner, then an inquest must be completed by a coroner. In Texas, that is the justice of the peace.

The power to "formally pronounce" someone dead is an awesome one. One justice of the peace ruled a particular death a suicide, even though the cause of death was stab wounds to the back. The ruling in that case still stands. Regardless of any court ruling, the county attorney or district attorney can pursue criminal charges.

How to Determine Someone Is Dead

The telephone of the justice of the peace rings twenty-four hours a day. Calls come in from dispatchers, private citizens' residential and cell phones, hospitals, firefighters, and police officers, all with the observation that someone is dead. My policy is, "If the victim is not dead when I am called, he will be by the time I get there!" That means that if someone has not taken a breath in fifteen minutes to an hour, they probably have "left the building."

~~~~~~~~~~~~~~~~~~~~~~~

While I was attending mandatory Justice Court training, an older lady called me aside. This petite lady, in her seventies, recently had been appointed justice of the peace by the Commissioners Court. They probably had the attitude that she was wise with age and would work cheaply. It used to be a common practice to appoint the widow of a local elected official to any unexpired term. This woman asked me if something her county judge had told her was correct:

"This is how you determine if someone is dead," said the county judge. "Clear the room or area where the body is. While you are all alone, take a ballpoint pen. Slowly touch the ballpoint to the white of the eye. If there is no movement, the person is deceased."

I could only imagine . . .

~~~~~~~~~~~~~~~~~~~~~~~

"Would everyone please leave the room?"

All is still. I am all alone, or am I? Is there someone else still alive? In front of me, lying in a bed, is either a live person or a dead body. I must make that determination. I am vested with the power to determine life or death. The eyes are half closed, half open. The pupils are fixed, and the stare is constant, but not dull. "Are you dead?" I ask. No response.

The skin is pale, but not cold. The room is hot. I am sweating; the body is not. Quietly, I extract a ballpoint pen from my shirt pocket. It is the same pen I paid bills with earlier that morning. I hold the pen in my hand like a knife, except the soft, flesh part of my thumb goes over the top. I push the chrome button to click the brass point containing the minuscule round ink ball out from the barrel. It is no longer a simple ink pen; now, it is a precision instrument, a death indicator, able to determine the ultimate question of life and death. Carefully and slowly, I bend over and get close to the body to make sure that no movement will be missed. The instrument is only as good as its operator, and I must see any movement. A mistake here could cause a live someone to be buried alive, or suffer the injection of formaldehyde or (God forbid) the fiery furnace of the crematorium. Guided by a steady hand, the death indicator creeps to the white of the right eye to make the confirmative contact. No movement. All is still. But wait! The white of the eye lacks the confirmation dot to be left by the instrument. There must be one more nudge, maybe a little more forceful, just to make sure and to leave proof, by way of that tiny dot, that I have done my job. Again, contact. "WOULD YOU PLEASE STOP THAT?" someone yells as they open the door. I fall over dead, and now two inquests must be made.

"That is not the way!" I explained to the new justice court judge.

~~~~~~~~~~~~~~~~~~~~~~~~~

Before an inquest is requested, someone must come to the conclusion that someone is dead: medical personnel, law enforcement, or a family member.

It really is not that difficult to tell if a person is dead. If someone is not breathing, does not have a pulse, and has fixed pupils (they do not respond to light), the person most probably is dead. Still, there are true stories of people being buried alive or awakening on the mortuary slab. (The terms "dead ringer" and "graveyard shift" arose because at one time, people sometimes were buried with bells attached to their caskets that could be rung from inside in case of accidental live burial, and cemetery workers listened for those bells.) Twice I have arrived to do an inquest only to see the "not dead yet" roll by on a gurney headed for a helicopter that will fly them to the emergency room. Both times, the inquest was completed at the hospital.

Frequently, I am called to the hospital to find the patient on an artificial respirator. The white bellows are going up and down, moving air, breathing, and providing oxygen to a body that is lifeless, if "lifeless" is defined as meaning that life ends when the brain ceases to function. Surgeons and harvest teams are waiting for me to make the death official so that the skin, tissues, corneas, bones, and organs can be harvested. Those parts will continue to live in someone else.

Continuing judicial education includes inquest training. Classes often are given by a forensic pathologist and may include gruesome pictures and graphic descriptions. These often are displayed just before lunch.

~~~~~~~~~~~~~~~~~~~~~~~~~~~~

When people who do inquests get together to eat, the table conversation usually is not about the weather. The casual listener or visitor may wonder what he has gotten into.

Several times I have caught myself in the middle of a story and noticed that someone definitely was not enjoying the conversation. We tell our stories like old war veterans, maggots and all.

One story was told by the late Judge Hicks, my mentor and a friend. She stepped up on the porch of a house containing a decomposing body. She walked up to the open door, sniffed a couple of times, and announced, "Yep, he's dead. Send me the paperwork."

~~~~~~~~~~~~~~~~~~~~~~~~~~~~

The long handlebar mustache of a tall, lanky judge out of West Texas bounced up and down as he told the story of a particular *crispy critter*. You might read this story in three or four minutes, but it took him twenty minutes to tell it. Words last longer when they are spoken in a West Texas Ack . . . see . . . an . . . t.

"It was an automobile accident on the interstate," the judge began. "A crash with an eighteen-wheeler left a crumpled car burnin'. A man and woman and a baby were dead at the scene. They flew the truck driver in by helicopter in critical condition. You see out in West Texas, most of your travels lead to the middle of nowhere. If you depend on an ambulance to get you to the hospital, you'd probably die of old age 'fore you get there.

"You know how hot them car fires get." He looked around to nodding heads, and continued. "When the Volunteer Fire Department arrived, it was in full flame. When they poured the water to it, it hit hot melting metal. The steam and smoke looked like a nuclear explosion.

"While I was headin' that-a-way, I could see a mushroom cloud of smoke. I was dread'n this one. They done told me about the baby in the back seat. I hate doing them kids and especially babies." He gave us a moment to reflect.

"The firemen was all decked out in their bunker gear. They had already quenched the fire, but it was still hot. I looked in what was left of the car. On charred black springs of what used to be a back seat was the little thing: black, shriveled, charred beyond human existence, much less recognition. No arms or legs, just a charred little stump-like figure. There was one little spot oozing red and kinda pidgin' out, draining. It was the quietest I had ever seen that bunch of firemen.

"'OK, call the funeral home and get 'im out,' I said, tryin' to act like I was all under control. The firemen figured the best way to get the baby out was for several of them to get their hands under him or her and gently lift the body up. Then they would carry it out and gently lay it on a bed sheet. I thought it was a pretty good plan and got myself out of the way. The Jaws of Life started to work. Jaws of Life are like a hydraulic pair of scissors. They ripped off one back door. Then they ripped off the other back door. Then they ripped off the front doors. Then they went ahead and peeled off the top of that car like opening a can of sardines. Them firemen love them Jaws of Life. Next they came out with them fancy latex gloves, like you see on them hospital TV shows.

"Now the car had cooled down, but the poor little thing inside was still hot. They carefully picked it up and took it out of the car. Four firemen supported that little body with eight hands. Now them latex gloves might be good for keeping your hands clean, but they ain't no good for protection from heat. The hands got hot. About halfway to the landing point the hands began to shake.

"And then it happened! Some say it exploded in mid-air! Others say it hit the ground! Some saw nothing but red. Watermelon seeds went everywhere!" he jeered, laughing and slapping his knee. "It was a dammed burnt watermelon!"

We joined in his laughter, partly because of the way he told the story, partly because most of us have seen the zeal of volunteer firefighters, and partly because so few inquest stories have a happy ending.

~~~~~~~~~~~~~~~~~~~~~~~~~~~~

You might think it impossible to mistake a watermelon for a person, but you probably have never seen a *crispy critter*. I have seen several. One was a professional football player for the Miami Dolphins. He literally flew his Mercedes through downtown Winona, breaking several electric poles and signs, and landed on the regular gas pump at Dad's station. He burned up then and there.

With this, I have to stop typing. I get up from my chair and count the steps I take to the front door of my office. Then I walk to the station next door, counting those steps and then multiply the number by three.

It happened 140 feet from my desk, where I am now writing.

Chapter 3

The Christmas Day Murders

Inquests #726, #727, and #728

I wrote the following piece for *The Winona Times,* for December, 2010.

> I know this is not a subject we would like to talk about during the holiday season, but it could save a life. The holidays bring joy to most of us, as families get together, feast together, and even worship together.
>
> On the other hand, for many it is different. The joy is gone, usually because someone is missing or economically they are unable to do what they would like. People drink alcohol or take drugs to numb the pain, which makes the situation worse.
>
> Usually I see a rise in homicides and suicides around Christmas. This year it started before Thanksgiving. People who commit such acts do not realize the devastation they cause, especially around the holiday season. In fact, they are thinking mostly of themselves without realizing there are people out there who really care—people who will not understand, and will wonder why or "what could I have done?" for the rest of their lives.
>
> In most cases, serious depression

precedes the action. When clinical depression hits, logic goes out the window. One feels down, maybe without any reason. The feelings are real, and it is only natural that someone would look for a reason for "feeling" this way. That is where the danger comes in. Without outside help, people focus blame on someone else or on themselves. Often, they feel alone, and finally come to feel that the world and themselves would be better off if they were dead.

We need to be aware of the feelings of others and ourselves. If you are harboring such feelings, or if someone you know even hints at such, take it seriously. Depression can be dealt with much more easily in its early stages. Most of us live through some depression during our lifetime, without professional help, but help is there.

There are family and friends, and if all else fails, there is even me. Call somebody.

Don't mess up my holiday!

Finally, remember the good times of Christmases past, and plan on making this one a pleasant memory!

-Judge Mitch

As far back as I can remember, Christmas was the biggest and most memorable day of the year. Growing up, Christmas was not only the birthday of the church; it was bigger than my own birthday. Bigger parties and bigger presents! A real tree, probably stolen from a country fence row, moved into our living room, and we strung ancient lights in its branches. The bulbs on the oldest string of lights were shaped and painted angels, Santa, reindeer, and manger animals; one light was a white snowman wearing a black top hat and red scarf. The painted snowman was so old and scratched that bright light would sparkle through the cracks in his paint. If Frosty was real, I knew he would look just like that old light. Every year, some of the shaped bulbs would die, to be replaced with regular Christmas lights. In that way, Christmas would change a little every year.

The lights reflected gloriously off the thousands of strands of individual icicles delicately draped from the top to the bottom of the cedar tree. Glass balls of various sizes and colors added even more reflections to the visual effect. Sound effects also played a role; occasionally, a thin ornament hit the wood floor and popped. The cat also enjoyed the tree.

What Were You Doing on Christmas Morning, 1999?

The telephone rings just after 6 A.M. on December 25, 1999.

"Judge, I'm Casey, a nurse at East Texas Medical Center emergency room. I need to notify you of a death."

Being awakened from a deep sleep by a call from a hospital would alarm most people, but not me. I've become accustomed to it; it happens all the time. In Smith County, a judge must be called any time a trauma patient dies in a hospital, and hospital policy dictates a call for everyone who dies within twenty-four hours of admission. The only twist to this call was that it came on Christmas morning, but then again, I had done four inquests on Christmas Eve.

"You know it's still dark outside," I say into the receiver as I climb out of bed. I gather my thoughts and prepare mentally for what is to follow. "Hold on. Let me get my paperwork." In the darkness, I slip on yesterday's pants and retrieve the inquest paperwork lying on the headboard of the waterbed. The kitchen serves as a temporary office this early in the morning.

~~~~~~~~~~~~~~~~~~~~~~~

Walking down the long hallway, I think about my childhood and the many Christmas mornings on which I awoke before the sun came up, with great expectations of what I would find under the tree. All alone and being as quiet as I could, I would sneak into the den, illuminated by the colored lights on the tree. The cookies we had left out for Santa always were gone.

I would check my stocking first. It was cheating, I knew, to use one of Mom's nylon stockings, but their size relative to that of my own socks made them irresistible. A recycled women's stocking can hold an amazing amount of fruit, firecrackers, Matchbox cars, sparklers, bottle rockets, harmonicas, toys, and candy. One year, Santa must have been as poor as we were, because I saw only a few gifts under the tree, most of them wrapped. Wrapped presents meant gifts from people. Our Santa wasn't much of a gift wrapper.

After a quick survey of the situation, nine-year-old me decided to look further around the tree. Behind it, I found a gift-wrapped box with my name on it, three inches thick, six inches wide, and four feet long. I shook the package, hefted it to guess its weight, and puzzled over what might be in the box. I knew it would be dishonest and wrong to open it, but curiosity and the magic of Christmas morning got the best of me. I decided to open the box just enough so that I could figure out what was inside. I peeled back the cellophane tape and unfolded the wrapping paper on one end of the box. I could see "Montgomery Ward" written on one end of the box. That was all I dared to see. I folded the wrapping back the way it had been, to hide my deception. I had a good idea of what was in the box. My curiosity satisfied somewhat, and my appetite for adventure lessened, I tiptoed back down the hallway to my bedroom.

The next morning, the family gathered in the living room to open gifts.

"Here is one for Mitch, from sister Perry," my sister Suzie announced as she pulled the long box from behind the tree. I felt a moment's regret; I knew I shouldn't have peeked under the wrapping. There would be no surprise for me. I felt guilty, even though the only person I had harmed was myself. That little voice we used to call the conscience told me I had done wrong.

"You should have listened to me!" my conscience admonished me. "You cannot change what you have done, but you can stop the deception."

Sheepishly, I confessed. "I know what it is." Everyone looked at me. "It's a *maternity ward!*" Surely, confession is good for the soul. I looked around, only to see a group of adults staring at me as though I had come from another world. Even with the benefit of hindsight and experience, I can only imagine what they were thinking. My thoughts were on the contents of the box: perhaps a stethoscope, medical tools, maybe a surgical mask, and other tools of the doctor trade.

I expected that opening the box would be anticlimactic, but I received a most welcome surprise when I opened the box to reveal a wonderful bow and six metal-tipped arrows.

So maybe I'm a little dyslexic.

~~~~~~~~~~~~~~~~~~~~~~~~

Sitting down at the kitchen table, I ask the nurse, "What do we have?"

"Randi Burton, a twenty-five-year-old white female, was in an MVA this morning," said Nurse Casey, using the common abbreviation for motor vehicle accident.

"Middle name?"

"Raye."

"Date of birth?" I proceed from there to get identification information.

"Where did the accident happen?"

"Somewhere around Carthage."

"Carthage is seventy miles away. Send her back," I said joking. "Do you know any particulars?"

"No on both. She was transported by Air One from the Carthage hospital, and there is nothing in her medical chart."

"Don't pull any tubes or clean her up until I call you back," I instructed. My search for information begins.

"Department of Public Safety, can I help you?" the DPS dispatcher answers.

"Merry Christmas. This is Judge Shamburger."

"So nice of you to call so early in the morning!" she said mockingly.

"I wish. Fatality out of Carthage. Happened this morning around five."

"I think I heard something about it earlier. Let me see what I can find and call you back."

Decision time: Do I go to the hospital? Do I go back to bed? Do I wait for a return call? Do I eat more of Santa's cookies? I wait ten minutes, and the phone rings.

"This is Trooper Walker, Carthage DPS. I understand Mrs. Burton passed away."

"Correct," I respond. "I need details."

"Single car rollover. Happened approximately zero five fifteen this morning. It was on State Highway 149, 2.5 miles north of Beckville. She was the passenger."

"Seatbelt?"

"No."

"Alcohol?"

"Yes."

"Do you think charges may be filed?"

"Judge, there is a strong possibility. The driver tested positive for alcohol."

"Autopsy?"

"Please."

"Do you think Panola County will pay for it?" Sometimes the requesting county will pay for the autopsy, but usually it will not. Most people don't think about $2,500 of their tax money going for an autopsy. I do; it comes from my budget. I fret about it especially when I know the results will be "blunt force injuries." Or "Gunshot wound to the head." Autopsies with those results don't tell much of anything beyond what could be seen with a casual glance at the body.

"Judge, that question goes beyond my pay grade."

"I'll handle it. Can you fax me an accident report when finished?"

"No problem, Judge."

"Merry Christmas." I say as I move on with the inquest.

Because there will be an autopsy, it is not necessary for me to view the body. The pathologist will make a much better witness than I would. Outside, it's a brisk sixty degrees, typical for an East Texas Christmas.

I hop into the car and drive three blocks to my office and coordinate releasing the body, transporting it, setting up an autopsy, and finish the paperwork.

SOUTHWESTERN INSTITUTE OF FORENSIC SCIENCES

CONCLUSION: It is our opinion that Randi Raye Burton, a 25-year-old white female, died as the result of blunt force injuries.

The family of this college student will remember this Christmas Day, 1999.

~~~~~~~~~~~~~~~~~~~~~~

The Christmas after the "maternity ward" incident, I was ten years old. My double-digit age meant I was growing up, able to face new responsibilities—and receive more complex gifts. With everyone still soundly asleep, I went again into the den. Under the tree, I found a shiny chrome air rifle, a pellet gun, with just a ribbon and gift tag on it for decoration. I already had a BB gun, but this weapon was twice as heavy. It had a bolt action, which I pulled back with a click, then looked into an empty chamber. It was a single shot. It required one pellet, or in a tight spot you could use a BB, to be placed into the chamber. I had no pellets or BBs, but I figured Santa would take care of that later. I sat on the floor Indian style with the gun in my lap. I caressed the cold steel framework of the rifle and grasped the wooden stock on the pump handle. An air rifle can be as powerful as the pumper. The stronger the person doing the pumping, the more deadly the weapon can be. I gave it one pump, just to get the feel of compressing air. I shouldered the wooden stock into my bony clavicle and put my cheek against it. Looking down the sights, I aimed at a large red ornament on the tree. Then I moved the bead and took aim at the little angel sitting on top of the tree. She was lit up from within, and she was within my sights. I pulled off!

Who would shoot a Christmas tree! That is almost sacrilegious. (That's a big word I heard the preacher use.)

The room's main lighting fixture hung from the ceiling, centered in it. The round glass fixture, white with clear trim, was about two feet across and held in place by a centered two-inch circular brass cap, my new target.

I knew the gun was empty; I had just looked into the chamber. I pumped the gun only once, so it shouldn't make that much noise. I did not want to wake anyone at three o'clock in the morning. That brass ring fit *so* well within my sights. I slowly squeezed the trigger. I was right; the gun made only made a little "poof" sound. Things seemed to slow down. I saw an indention appear in the brass cap, and I heard a click sound. Maybe it was not a single shot.

The glass light fixture split into half moons and began to fall away, with a gentle roll to the outside. Like when the coverings of a rocket or satellite fall away in outer space in slow motion. I could only sit and watch as the pieces completed a rotation and flatly hit the floor. The silence broke with a crash, as real time returned. My family gathered quickly, all of them standing in the large opening to the den viewing me, sitting on the floor in the middle of thousands of pieces of broken glass, my new pellet gun resting across my lap.

"Are you all right?" they asked as someone with shoes on lifted me up and carried me to safety.

"I didn't think it was loaded!" was my only explanation.

"It is unloaded guns that kill people," said Dad. It was not the first or the last time I would hear that statement.

"To bed now," said Mom.

We all went back to bed, where I stayed until I could smell the bacon cooking.

~~~~~~~~~~~~~~~~~~~~~~~

By 6:45 A.M. I am back home, shucking off my clothes, hopeful for another hour or two of shuteye.

The telephone rings again at 6:50 A.M. So much for going back to sleep.

"Judge, we have a bad one." This time it's Tammy, the dispatcher from the Smith County Sheriff's Department.

"What's up?"

"Looks like a double homicide. They need you in Chapel Hill."

I gently roll out of the waterbed, but not gently enough. Fae is early to bed and early to rise and sleeps like a rock in between. Her normal day starts at 6:00 A.M.

"Didn't you just come in?" she asked.

"Yep, and now I have another one. Sounds bad."

"You want me to fix you a coffee to go?" We live on coffee in the morning.

"I'm going to try to make it quick," I said, putting on yesterday's clothes. "I'll try to be back before everyone gets up."

"That's not going to happen," said Fae. She knows how long my "quick" trips can be.

Sunrise is approaching. It is twelve miles to the scene. I think about how "not Christmas" it is, to be murdered on Christmas Day. A double homicide usually means a man and a woman; one shoots the other, and then commits suicide. It happens far more than I would like, and often around Christmas.

I notice several homes with a lighted tree in the window and some with outside Christmas lights burning, some extravagant and some simple, all with a message of hope and joy. Several police cars are parked in the yard of the double-wide mobile home that is my destination. Their red and blue lights twinkle much brighter than the Christmas lights. Yellow crime tape marks the boundaries of hope and joy.

The house is located in the countryside and sits close to another house.

"That house belongs to the parents of one of the victims," says an officer pointing at the house next door.

Besides the police cars, the yard holds several vehicles including a dark pickup. The yards of both houses appear neatly kept. Indoor lights shine from the windows of both houses, but Christmas lights adorn neither house nor yard.

"Judge, this is a strange one," Detective Rasco tells me. He has been here since 4:58 processing the crime scene. "Looks like someone tried to cut the phone wires, but the phones still work. No sign of forced entry. The story is that their teenage daughter heard gunshots and footsteps in the house. She escaped to run over to her grandparents' house and call 911."

We walk over to a telephone pole. An officer shines his flashlight into a plastic box of color coded spaghetti wires.

"Did she go there because she thought the phone did not work?" I ask. "If so, she thought wrong and knew the wires were cut. Let's see what we have," I say as we walk toward the front door. "I smell smoke."

"Yeah, looks like they had a bonfire. A couple of beer cans are on the tailgate," Rasco says, pointing to the pickup.

As a rule, activity is kept to a minimum at crime scenes, the fewer footprints and fingerprints, the better. I want to see the area frozen in time in order to reconstruct just what happened. Some crime scene investigators are overly ambitious in bagging evidence and moving things. They forget that the coroner also has a job to perform.

The first thing I notice is the complete absence of Christmas decorations. This could mean they had a different religious belief than me, or maybe that they just don't believe in decorating. Some Christian religions reject the "pagan rituals" attached to Christmas. Then there are the Muslim, Hindu, Jewish, and other religions, and even nonbelievers, who do not recognize Jesus as savior, but in the United States, many of them celebrate Xmas on the side.

"Bodies are back here," Rasco says. We walk through the living room and down a hallway.

Like most families, Fae and I created our own Christmas traditions, usually beginning with a saw, axe, or hatchet and a ride to Mom and Dad's ranch. Even with twelve-foot ceilings, we would sometimes have to cut the tree down to size. Some trees were a little spindly, and one year we even had a long-leaf pine, but they were always real trees.

Lights, ornaments, tinsel, and icicles filled in the deficiencies and deformities. Homemade stockings hung across the fireplace, with felt letters spelling out the names Amy, Lena, Noah, Mom, and Dad. These stockings would not hold as much as the nylon hose I grew up with, filled with fireworks, toys, and other goodies. The chilly formal living room warmed up during Christmas. Early Christmas mornings were quiet around our house. Fae would have coffee ready before anyone else got out of bed.

Family traditions often clash. "Didn't we go to your family's Christmas day last year?" "But we spent Christmas Eve with your family." "And we had Thanksgiving at . . ." To accommodate as many as possible, we run from house to house, family to family, and meal to meal to meal to meal, loading and unloading presents all along the way. Sure, it was fun watching Aunt Ditty scream at the Dallas Cowboys on TV, and the food is different and delicious everywhere, but all the kids want to do is go home and play with their new toys.

~~~~~~~~~~~~~~~~~~~~~~~~~~~

"Anything missing? Besides Christmas?" I ask.

"No," Rasco answers. "In fact, there is money, guns, and plenty of stuff to take, but I don't see any signs of a burglary or robbery. The girl's story won't hold water."

The bedroom door opens to a good-sized bedroom dwarfed by a large bed with a turned maple headboard. A bullet hole pierces the window above the supine body of a woman lying in bed.

"Daughter said she heard four shots," says Rasco,

pointing to the window. "The shooter was not the best shot in the world."

Two small dogs stand guard over the mother, lying on her back, and the covers still in place. A light tan Chihuahua sits on the pillow next to her head, and a dark, long-haired dog is curled and nestled between her right arm and torso. Her light-colored nightshirt is stained with blood. She and the dogs are the only ones on the bed.

"We decided to leave the dogs alone for now," Rasco says. "We don't want them to contaminate the scene by running around or trying to catch them. They're not barking. In fact, they haven't moved since I've been here." The longhair just lies there, like he wants to go to sleep. The Chihuahua looks around nervously but doesn't shake, like Chihuahuas sometimes do. "Just look at them. They know something is wrong."

Pathology Associates of Tyler, P.A.

The body is that of a slightly heavy-set white woman whose appearance is consistent with the given age of 43 years . . .

Final Pathological Diagnosis
I.   Gunshot wound to the head.
II.   Gunshot wound to the arm
III.   Status post resection of the neurilemmoma (remote).

Opinion: In my opinion, the cause of death is gunshot wound to the head.

~~~~~~~~~~~~~~~~~~~~~~~~~~~~~

At one side of the bed, on the floor, sitting in his underwear, is the father, his left hand reaching toward a gun under the bed. He is overweight, but so am I — most of us are. What could anyone do to deserve this? He did not die in his sleep. I wonder how secure he felt going to bed, with several weapons within his grasp. How many nights did he go to bed with the thought that he may have to protect himself and his family, with protection meaning quick access to a gun? Then the nightmare happened. A gunshot, or was it gunshots? He knew something was going down. He rolled to his right sliding off the bed, just like he had planned. Just like he had done, in his mind, so many times before. He reaches under the bed, feeling for the pistol. Then, four inches from reaching his security, he looks up. Did he see his killer and hesitates? BOOM, and it is all over.

Pathology Associates of Tyler, P.A.

The body is that of a trunkly obese white man whose appearance is consistent with the given age of 44 years . . .

Final Pathological Diagnosis
I.   Gunshot wound to head and neck.
II.   Obesity.
III.   Mild arteriosclerotic heart disease.
IV.   Prostatic hyperplasia.

Opinion: In my opinion, the cause of death is gunshot wound to head and neck.

~~~~~~~~~~~~~~~~~~~~~~~~

"We found something in the girl's closet." That observation comes from Special Agent Slagle of the FBI. When it comes to murder, we take all the help we can get. Law enforcement personnel may complain about their jobs and the hours they work, but they live for moments like this, especially when a possibly long, drawn out investigation becomes focused in the few hours just after it happened. Solving a murder is like putting a puzzle together. It is a rush when the pieces seem to fall into place, creating a picture of the murder.

The bedroom at the other end of the house belongs to

the daughter, Daphanie. The glow of a computer monitor lights the room and part of the hallway. I wonder if the modem is still connected on the computer or if it was cut at the wires outside. Computers seem to be showing up more and more at crime scenes.

Sheriff J.B. Smith enters the front door and meets us in the hallway. Quiet does not describe the sheriff, and he is asking questions in a booming voice. He has survived Smith County politics longer than I have. He does not restrict himself to administrative matters, although with more than 200 employees and one of the largest jails in the country, he has plenty of administrative matters to worry about.

"Judge, don't you have better things to do on Christmas morning?" asks Sheriff Smith, extending his hand.

"I'd probably just be sleeping," I answer, taking his hand.

"They're tellin' me we got a damn double homicide on Christmas Day. Aw, shit. Ain't there nothing sacred anymore?" We walk down the hall, Sheriff Smith obviously agitated.

Daphanie's room looks like a typical teenager's room, with pictures taped to the wall, a messed up bed, and a few items of clothing scattered around the furniture and floor. On the open closet door is written "I ♥ dinario." "Does this mean she loves money?" I ask.

"Probably a boyfriend," the sheriff says, "and he is probably in these pictures." He points at several pictures. Most reveal a white teenage girl, grinning among several black kids, all giving gang signs. "I bet you will find Dinario in these pictures." He is right.

In the closet, a sweater hangs lopsided, a .38 revolver in one pocket.

"Recently fired," says Rasco as he smells the weapon. In the bottom of a clothes basket, we find a laser sight.

"Maybe they were planted," I suggest, looking at an older framed picture, maybe a school portrait, of a smiling young teenager. I find it hard to believe that the contented face and smile I am looking at belongs to the person who could or would do such a thing. I know what kids can do, however. I have seen it before and have seen it since.

"We will look at all the angles," says detective Rasco. He knows that criminal cases are lost or go unsolved and killers escape punishment because possibilities are overlooked. Prosecution often requires not only proving what happened but also often proving what did not happen.

At 9:30 A.M., I make some notes. Estimated time of death, 4:00 A.M. Pronounced dead 9:30 A.M.

I go to the office to finish the inquest.

"Come on," said Fae on the phone. "We're at mom and dad's, about to open presents."

"Any coffee?"

"Just made a fresh pot."

"I'll be there shortly."

"Yea, quick," she said.

Years later, Sheriff Smith wrote a book titled *The Christmas Day Murders: A True Crime Chronicle, Texas-Style.* I will let him tell you about the investigation, the conviction, and the "who done it part" of this story. I didn't even get a footnote in his book. There are always people on the sidelines, making things work. Someone answered the 911 call, someone made the original response, emergency medical personal responded, and someone put up the crime tape, logged in names, secured the scene, took fingerprints, took pictures, bagged evidence, bagged the bodies, and transported the bodies. I did the inquests. What happened around 4:00 A.M. directly affected the Christmas Day of more than a hundred people. Team players like these all have stories like this one — too many of them. This particular story is how the family and friends of Daphanie will remember Christmas Day, 1999.

Daphanie still celebrates Christmas with inmates in one of the Texas correctional facilities. She never fully confessed.

~~~~~~~~~~~~~~~~~~~~~~~

Over the years, we replaced many lights on the antique

strand, so that it looked like all the modern ones with the little colored light bulbs. I don't think Frosty the Snowman ever burned out.

Now we use a fake tree with LED lights. We usually spend about an hour trying to find the single light that failed, killing the rest of the dinky sparkly little lights. The kids come when they can. Most of the bedrooms remain empty. On Christmas Day, the kids chase their own extended families, of in-laws and friends. With the kids out of the nest, our Christmas dreams and expectations are not the childlike ones they used to be. With the grandkids, however, I see good possibilities of a revival!

Truth be told, if you had asked me last week, "What were you doing on Christmas Day, 1999?" I would have answered, "Probably just celebrating Christmas, as usual."

Chapter 4

A Hole in One

Inquest #228

"You have an inquest," says the Tyler dispatcher at the Texas Department of Public Safety, "on the Gladewater Municipal Golf Course."

The winter day is cold, at 1:45 in the afternoon, and strangely foggy. In East Texas, comfort is determined by the humidity rather than temperature. Water evaporates from many lakes and rivers as well as from the Gulf of Mexico, 250 miles south. Yankees say that we don't even know what winter is! We do, however, get snow in East Texas. At times, it even stays on the ground for a few days. We have our hills and valleys, and it can really get cold in the low-lying places. One winter day, I rode my Honda 90 motorcycle through the Harris Creek bottom to high school, and my ski mask froze to my scraggly sophomore mustache. Now I am driving in the comfort of my SUV through that same creek bottom. Today is not that cold.

My best guess is that an old golfer, doing what he loved, took his last swing and fell over with a heart attack. Or maybe he was killed by lighting — several golfers are struck by lightning every year.

~~~~~~~~~~~~~~~~~~~~~~~~~~~

I play golf every year at least once. I bought an expensive set of clubs eight years ago; they are still almost like new. They may be in my garage or the "Hoedown Building" (now my building used for storage); I'm not really sure.

~~~~~~~~~~~~~~~~~~~~~~~~~~~~~

I wonder why the Department of Public Safety is calling me about someone on a golf course. The Department of Public Safety usually works highway and traffic fatalities. This might be a golf cart mishap. Maybe someone crashed his car or motorcycle into a golf cart, or the cart crashed after getting hit by a golf ball. The golfers have been hacking the Gladewater Country Club course since 1933. It lies between Texas State Highway 271 and Country Club Road, the latter of which provides entry into the club.

From the state highway, I see flashing blue and red lights, fire trucks, and at least five law enforcement vehicles encamped across the green on one of the holes. Being a lazy golfer and breaking the cart trail rule, I drive my car across the green to the scene.

Members of the Department of Public Safety, Smith County Sheriff's deputies, Gladewater police officers, and Gladewater and Winona volunteer fire fighters all are standing around a hole in the ground and a twisted pile of metal. I smell fuel of some kind and smell smoke that I don't see. Some of the nearby pine trees appear slightly singed and charred. It looks like a flash fire.

Flash fires occur in environments where fuel, typically flammable gas or dust, is mixed with air in concentrations suitable for combustion. The fuel combusts with a "poof," and then it is done and over. A flash fire sucks the oxygen out of the air and burns so quickly that not everything is turned to ashes.

The ground is muddy, either from the humidity, past rain, or the water from one or more of the several fire trucks in attendance. The fire hoses are still neatly rolled on the trucks, ruling out the latter.

The first challenge at a death scene is to find a person in charge. Sometimes it turns out to be you. I check with people from the various agencies represented.

"The FAA should be in charge," says the DPS sergeant.

If it's the Federal Aviation Administration, then it sounds like a plane crash.

Scattered around are the remains of what could have been a very large aluminum can. The largest mass of twisted debris shows some signs of its recent life as a small airplane. Forty feet away, leaning against a tree, are remnants of the plane's tail fin. An aircraft door lies on the green, near the cup.

"Where is the FAA?" I ask.

"On the way from Austin," replies the sergeant, "maybe four to six hours away."

"Do we have a name?"

"Don Murdock taxied off Tyler Pounds Field Airport earlier today. The control tower thinks it might be him. We are securing the area and waiting for them to make the call."

Tyler Pounds Field is forty miles southwest of our location. Gladewater Municipal Airport is two miles away and small in comparison to Tyler, but it houses many private aircraft. Planes landed on grass there before 1947, when two paved landing strips were built. It is also a favorite place for my nephew, Jeff, and his son to skydive.

Different judges handle inquests in different ways. I could have said, "Call me when the FAA gets here, and get your ducks in a row. I'm going home." I decide to stick around.

No two death scenes are the same. Law enforcement officials at inquest scenes may include representatives from county sheriffs, constables, city police, fire marshal, Texas Alcohol Tobacco and Firearms, Texas Parks and Wildlife, Texas Department of Public Safety (including the Texas Rangers), and various other agencies; this time, it will be the Federal Aviation Administration. They all pretty much get along and work together when they have to. They eat and party together at the Peace Officers Association. But they are all paid differently, have different bosses, and are trained differently. Each department has its unique set of rules. Their members live and work in the same area, but the agencies have their territory or turf. Some officers work with the judges, and some do not have a clue about Chapter 49 and the performance of an inquest. Although the law indicates that an inquest is investigative in nature, the judge is usually not the investigator. Whatever the type of investigation, an appropriate agency should be the one running it. The judge does not run the investigation but instead attempts to see that it is performed properly. We may not be the fact finders, but we do review the evidence in order to make an informed ruling or finding. In the event there is no law enforcement or other agency involved, or if for some other reason we need to, we do it all. The bottom line is that the signature of the justice of the peace will go on the death certificate, thus certifying the cause, manner, and time of death. Usually, it does not take a rocket scientist to figure out what happened. In this case, the Gladewater airport is close by.

~~~~~~~~~~~~~~~~~~~~~~~~

"Planes buzz the golf course all the time," says one witness. "This one sounded different, like it was running real fast and coming down! Then there was a pop sound. Not a big explosion, just a pop."

"Call the funeral home." I tell the sergeant, "We're fixing to move on."

"I don't know, Judge. I think the FAA will want us to wait until they get here."

"Sergeant," I say, "I would like for them to be here right now. It looks like neither one of us is going to get what we like. There are a few things we need to do. First, we need to figure out how many were in the plane. Second, who was piloting the plane? Third, notify next of kin. Fourth, send the victim or victims for an autopsy. It will take an hour for the funeral home to get here. Have you taken pictures?"

"Yes," he says.

"You might want to shoot a video. We will try to leave as much undisturbed as we can for the FAA. We don't know when or if they will get here. I don't see a fire, so it is going to get cold around here and maybe wetter." The clouds are now looming above us as the fog lifts. A mist of droplets had begun a few minutes ago. "Let's do the removal of the body and leave the scrap metal for the fly boys."

"Get the funeral home en route," the sergeant orders the dispatcher over his radio.

~~~~~~~~~~~~~~~~~~~~~~~~~

Pilots call it vertigo. When flying in fog, the pilot may become disoriented. The instruments say you are upside down, but you feel right side up. The altimeter is telling you that you are spinning down, but you feel like you are going up. The expression "You have to trust your instruments" comes from this very scenario. In any plane, big or small, if the pilot cannot see, he or she has to fly using the instruments as guides. If he or she doesn't, the result might very well be like this crash. At full throttle, he screwed the plane into the ground.

Walking around any inquest scene, I try to see things from a different angle than law enforcement. A good police officer stays focused. I think it is a reflection of their firearms training. They look down the barrel sights at a target. The big picture is filtered out; the target (human or paper) is the focus. All else is blurred as the shooter takes aim. I try to see anything and everything all around, especially looking for something that doesn't quite fit.

~~~~~~~~~~~~~~~~~~~~~~~~~

I find a small body part dangling from a low tree limb. Just a few feet away, on another limb, hangs a little square cloth bag.

"I need some help and gloves," I call to a fireman.

The body part is a testicle, which I do not touch. The cloth bag is a back pocket blown away from the victim's pants. It must have been a pretty big *pop*. Newton's first law of motion says in part that "an object in motion tends to stay in motion until acted upon by an outside force." An airplane traveling at least two hundred miles an hour was stopped by the earth in less than a second. This releases a large amount of energy, and strange things happen. Things fly apart, including bodies and pants.

The funeral home arrives, and the removal begins. Firemen are pulling limbs and body parts from the crater dug by the plane and placing them in a body bag. They've found only one head; that's a good thing — it means only one victim. Clothing was mostly burned and destroyed. The crater is half full of water. Pumps from the fire department suck out the water as the fire fighters work. The smell of airplane fuel lingers in the air.

In the pants pocket hanging in the tree is a billfold. I am proud of my find and maybe a little territorial myself.

"I'll check it out," I tell the sergeant as he reaches for *my* evidence. In the billfold is an employment ID, a driver's license issued to Clifford Peterson, and several addresses and telephone numbers. I call one of the numbers.

"Hello," a woman answers in a pleasant voice.

"Hello, do you know Mr. Clifford Peterson?" I ask. "Does he work for an airline?"

"Yes. He is my husband. He commutes to Houston and flies out of Gladewater. Who is this?" she is, starting to show concern. This confirms what the evidence is pointing to, a local resident commuting to work.

~~~~~~~~~~~~~~~~~~~~~~~~~~~

I know that when I identify myself as Judge Shamburger, she will have questions. Some of them do not need to be answered over the phone. How can you reveal to the person you're talking to, in a gentle way, that someone they love is dead? In my nursing days, the practice was not to directly tell the person on the other end of the line, but if they asked, "Dead?" we would say "Yes." This is a good method, because if they really do not want to know, they will not ask. Some people need time to prepare their minds for what might be bad news. On most inquests, someone else will notify the next of kin. Sometimes we have no choice but to be the bearers of bad news.

When asked "When would you want to know?" most people would say, "As soon as possible." But when the family surrounds the decedent, the first thing often said is, "Don't tell so-and-so! We had better wait until . . ." Then, when it is all over, so-and-so is mad because no one said anything; somebody else called, or worse, they read about the death in the paper or saw it on the TV news.

~~~~~~~~~~~~~~~~~~~~~~~

I take my phone away from my mouth and ask the sergeant, "Do you have someone in the area?"

"Gladewater Police Department is on standby," he says.

I make the decision.

"My name is Judge Shamburger. Are you at home, 1221 Bonner Street?" I had gotten the address from the decedent's driver's license.

"Yes," she says, her voice quivering. "What's wrong?"

I nod to the sergeant to get a patrol car en route. "Is there anyone else with you?"

"No! What is wrong?"

"Mrs. Peterson, I need you to relax. Are you sitting down?"

"Relax? Is this a joke?"

"No, ma'am." I pause. "This is not a joke." I pause again. "Let me know when you are sitting down." I wait, stalling, hoping the local officers get to the residence in a hurry.

"Talk to me!" she demands.

"Let me know when you are sitting down."

I hear a chair slide and a sigh as she lands.

"OK, I'm sitting. What is going on?"

"Did Mr. Peterson fly out of Gladewater today?"

"Yes." She sighs; she knows what is coming.

~~~~~~~~~~~~~~~~~~~~~~~

Husbands and wives of pilots, like those of police officers, fire fighters, soldiers, and oil field workers, all live with the knowledge that their significant other may not come home one day. It is the nature of their jobs. Today, she fixed his breakfast for the last time. Today, she kissed him goodbye for the last time. Today, her greatest fear is realized.

~~~~~~~~~~~~~~~~~~~~~~~~~~~~~~

"Did he crash?" she asks, knowing the survival rates of small plane crashes.

"Yes."

"Where is he?" she asks.

"It happened just outside of Gladewater, at the golf course."

"What do I need to do?"

"Just wait there. Someone will be there shortly. Do you have any family, or friends or neighbors, you could call?"

"Our daughter," she says. Then silence.

"Relax and breathe. There is no rush for anything. Take your time. Are you okay?"

"I will be all right," she says. "There is someone at the door."

~~~~~~~~~~~~~~~~~~~~~~~~~~~~~~

People who live on the edge take chances. It is irritating and scary when you care about or love someone who is a "risk taker." You wish they were different, but if they were different . . . well, then they would not be the same person you chose to care about or love. In fact, the relationship with you may be one of the risks that *they* are taking.

Risk takers are the ones who will take off across the street while everyone else waits at the curb for the cars to pass by. They are the ones who will climb the cliff rather than take the trail, or take that little road just to see where it goes, or jump out of an airplane, bungee jump, ride in a glider, or ride a wheelie on just the back tire of a motorcycle. They go too fast and swim out too far.

I have done them all. We push the limits physically and mentally. The reward is the thrill. The cost can be devastating. It is always sad when the adventurer goes beyond his or her capacity and ends up in a hospital or in a coffin. Still, I dare say, no astronaut leaves this earth without accepting the possibility of never coming back. Knowing this possibility, the astronaut works and waits for years for the opportunity to ride the rocket! Death is the ultimate risk that awaits us all, over the edge.

~~~~~~~~~~~~~~~~~~~~~~~~

The fire fighters went home. The wreckage remained. The Department of Public Safety stood guard till midnight. Investigators from the Federal Aviation Administration arrived around noon the following day.

Chapter 5

Getting Ahead

Inquest #332

"Judge, we have an inquest off of Sand Flat Road, at Skelly Camp."

East Texas produces much of the oil that literally drives our country. In 1931, the area produced one million barrels of oil a day. Many of the wells continue to produce. In Sand Flat, miles and miles of blacktop or oil-sand roads wind through the woods and across pastures, from oil well to oil well. Skelly Camp is one of these oil producers. The roads are private and often reluctantly shared between oilmen and land owners. A gate or cattle guard controls the people and animals that come and go. Often, gates are left open or there is no gate, and people enter, ignoring the red letters that read "Do Not Trespass."

Property owners find kids exploring, lovers parking, alcoholics drinking, workers eating, campers camping, partiers with bonfires blazing, hunters hunting, oil field workers working, and even swimmers skinny-dipping. Sometimes they find dead bodies: a car with the driver sitting behind the wheel with a bullet hole in his head, one or more dead kids around a natural gas valve, a shallow grave, or a body lying in the brush. These roads provide an illegal dumping ground for old beds and furniture, trash, and bodies. This body was discovered when Bill Johnson, the property owner, checked out a dump site. Something did not seem right with a mattress and box springs.

I drive by an oil well, the tall galvanized skeleton derrick long gone. The oil well motor is powered by natural gas. The loud internal combustion motor varies in sound and rhythm as it makes its cycle sound of strain and release, strain and release. The huge black head of the steel rocking horse goes up and down, thrusting the pump rod into the earth to suck out the black gold. The massive counterbalance goes around and around at the horse's tail. I think about high school days and the night I showed an oil well to an exchange student from Sweden.

"I noticed something stinking to high heaven," says Mr. Johnson, thumbs resting in the sides of his worn denim overalls. "I figured someone had dumped a dead dog, or skinned out a deer, or gutted a hog and left me with the guts."

There is a definite odor. We begin walking around the body and the bedding, trying to find a breathable place to stand. It is like walking around an invisible campfire; the smell seems to follow us like invisible smoke.

"I turned over the box springs." He pauses for a moment, putting what he saw and the putrefied smell together.

"Hot damn, maggots was churning. . . . I could see arms and legs and shoes, so I knew it was human." He starts to take a deep breath to continue, but decides not to. "Hell, I threw up and called 911."

"It can be pretty rough," I say, waiting to see if he will continue to talk or throw up again. "Do you have any idea how long he may have been here?"

His hands leave his sides and go to his knees. Bent over, he shakes his head. "Man, I don't see how you do this. I won't ever be able to eat another bowl of rice again."

"Why don't you go sit in your truck and turn on the air conditioner. We will call you if we need anything else." He gratefully looks at me, and then continues.

"I'm not sure. This bed stuff has been here for a long time." He points to the illegal dump. "I used to clean this mess up, but they just junk it up again. If there is a pile, they will add to it and at least keep it in one place. When they see me, they take off. I'll catch 'em one of these days."

"You might be lucky you did not catch this one," I say. "That is a full-size bed, and it would cover two bodies as easy as one."

"You think he was murdered?" he asks.

"Well, he isn't out here taking a nap."

The box springs are covered with a light brown course material with a flower print. A dark stain burnt into the fabric looks like the shadow of a human. It is now basting in the summer sun. The body, matching the shadow, is lying next to it. I estimate that the body has been there at least two to three weeks. A trip of 120 miles to the Southwestern Institute of Forensic Sciences in Dallas will narrow the time line. There, the bug people, forensic entomologists, can look at the age of maggots and beetles, and the hollow shells of insect generations, to pin down how long the body has been there.

"Judge, we cannot find any ID," says Detective Smith.

~~~~~~~~~~~~~~~~~~~~~~~~~~~

Life for me, and death for others, would be so much easier if everyone had some kind of identification or label attached permanently to their bodies, with a name and next of kin. A tattoo sometimes is helpful, except that people rarely tattoo their own name on their bodies. A tattoo would not have helped much in this case. The Forensic Center may help in identification. Dental X-rays and X-rays of bones, fingerprints, and a closer inspection for scars and tattoos are the usual methods.

Deoxyribonucleic acid (DNA) is wonderful if you have a suspect or someone to whom you can connect the genetic fingerprint. Without a comparison, its value is greatly reduced. As for fingerprints, the tough hide of the fingers lasts longer than the thin skin covering most of the rest of the body. Because the skin is loose, during decomposition, the flesh cleaves from the bone and the fingerprints can be slipped off the hand for examination.

Another method used for possible identification is to

strip the skull and jaw of all the soft tissues. Ants and animals do this in nature, leaving evidence used to determine how long the body has been lying there. A nice large cooking pot works in the laboratory. Forensic facial reconstruction (or forensic facial approximation) uses clay on the skull to create a face, based on an amalgamation of artistry, heavy on the art. Some creative busts look very good; unfortunately, some do not look much like the original.

~~~~~~~~~~~~~~~~~~~~~~~~

The crime scene investigators continue to take pictures. The body is placed, piece by piece, into a thick black plastic body bag, which is zipped from head to toe. I am headed for Winona, and Mr. Doe is going to Dallas. Later, we have spaghetti with meat sauce for supper.

Two weeks later, I receive a call from Detective Smith, with an update on the case. "We have a name for Mr. Doe: Philip Brinkman. Apparently, he had a gambling debt that was settled in the oil field. We have the suspect, and he is charged with murder. Mr. Brinkman moved here from the State of Maine. Next of kin has been notified."

Two days later, I receive a call from Mrs. Brinkman. "They will not release Philip until you tell them," she says. I fax the order to Dallas to release the body to a funeral home in Dexter, Maine, for burial in a cemetery near Lake Wassookeag. As far as I am concerned, the case is closed.

Three months later, I receive a letter from an attorney from Dexter, Maine. It reads, in part:

This is to inform you that the body of Mr. Brinkman was buried, the grave closed and headstone set. It has come to our attention that the head of Mr. Brinkman did not arrive with the body. It is the desire of my client that the head be interred with the body. The ground is frozen at present and cause additional expenses. An alternative is to wait until the spring thaw.

I need to know the whereabouts of Mr. Brinkman's head, and if a lawsuit is necessary. Who will be the responsible party?

I call the Smith County sheriff.

"Detective, where is Mr. Brinkman's head?" I ask. I know that the re-creation of Betty Bones is sitting on a bookshelf behind his desk. I hope—or maybe not—that Mr. Brinkman is keeping her company.

"Not here, Judge! We did not get anything but stinky clothing from Dallas."

I make another call.

"Southwest Medical Examiners," the operator says.

"This is Judge Shamburger from Smith County."

"Yes, Judge, what can we do for you?"

"You did an autopsy on Mr. Brinkman."

"Let me pull it up." Computer keys tap in the background. "Yes, sir, we sent the preliminary, 'gunshot wound to the head.' Do we need to send it again?"

"I am looking for Mr. Brinkman's head." Silence follows for several seconds.

"His body was released to Dexter Funeral Home," the woman says confidently.

"I know, he is buried in Maine, but they tell me he was buried without his head. Do you have it there?"

Silence, longer this time. "Please hold."

Another voice comes on the line. "This is Dr. Hartman. I understand you are looking for Mr. Brinkman."

"Well, part of Mr. Brinkman; his head, to be more exact."

"We were going to do a forensic reconstruction on him. . . ." I suppose he is reading the file. "That did not happen."

"You sent them a body. I hope it was Mr. Brinkman."

"Oh, yes, I see the release . . . one moment." Another long pause, a click, and a new voice.

"Judge Shamburger, this is Gerald Jessup, an attorney for the forensic center. I understand you are looking for Mr. Brinkman's head."

"That is correct."

"The good news is, we have the skull," he says.

"That may or may not be good news," I reply. Whenever someone says "the good news," chances are it will be followed by the bad news.

"We are going to release the skull to your investigator in the District Attorney's office. He wants to use it for evidence."

"Evidence?" I ask. "Does he plan to exhibit the victim's skull to the jury?"

A call to the District Attorney reveals just that.

~~~~~~~~~~~~~~~~~~~~~~~~~~~

Now imagine the impossible. Somehow, you are accused of Mr. Brinkman's murder, of which you are totally innocent. You have been indicted by a grand jury because the District Attorney told them you did it. You feel confident because there has been no real evidence presented to the jury to link you to the crime. In final argument, your attorney says, "There is no evidence; my client is not guilty."

The prosecutor points out, "YOU the defendant cannot explain your whereabouts on the day of the murder." It happened six years ago. "The defendant admits to having the same interest as Mr. Brinkman." You like to play cards and bingo. The difference is that Mr. Brinkman bet heavy on his interest. "We are in this courtroom for one reason — because you," he says, pointing at you, "took Mr. Brinkman into the woods." His eyes focus on you as he walks over to the evidence table. He turns and picks up Mr. Brinkman's skull, and as he walks back toward the jury and says, "Where you MURDERED Mr. Brinkman!" He pauses for dramatic effect.

"This skull once belonged to a breathing, living, human being: Mr. Brinkman." He walks back and forth, individually looking at each and every person in the jury box and then looking at the skull he holds up in his hand. He holds the skull from behind, at the base, like a hand puppet, and he moves it so that it also appears to be looking back and forth.

There are two distinct holes on one side, in the temple area, each the size of a dime; on the other side is a hole the size of a small coffee cup. "This skull is the only voice left for Mr. Brinkman. He cries for justice. You notice three holes." He turns the skull as though it is looking at them, and then turns it to look at you, the accused. "They show the violent act of point-blank gunshots, done by the defendant's own hands." Now the jury, the prosecutor, and the empty eyed-skull of Mr. Brinkman are all looking at you. "These two holes are where the bullets entered." He turns the skull to face him, as though he is now facing Mr. Brinkman eye to eye. He lowers the skull so that each jury member can peer into the skull through the entry wounds and out through the larger exit wound. He aims the skull so the jury looks through the holes like a telescope. Each of them will see you, the accused murderer, on the other side.

Each trial begins with a presumption of innocence. We all want to believe that law enforcement, prosecutors, and courts are all doing the right thing. We assume they all know what they are doing and strive for justice; I believe that they do. Justice and fairness are two different things. Fairness is a gray idea in the eye of the beholder. What is fair to you may not be fair to me. Justice is more black or white, guilty or not guilty. It deals in law, which may or may not be fair.

Whether it is a traffic ticket or a murder, the burden of proof is the same, "beyond a reasonable doubt." The jury is admonished, "If you have a reasonable doubt, you will find by your verdict not guilty." Still, I have had jury after jury say, "we were not sure about this or that, but we unanimously voted guilty."

I find disturbing two common sayings that make their way around the criminal justice system. The first is that "A good prosecutor can convict a guilty person; a really good prosecutor can convict an innocent person."

You may think it absurd to find yourself in the position of being mistakenly charged with murder, or anything else, which brings us to the second saying: "You can indict a ham sandwich." That is to say, anyone can be accused of anything. It's another thing to prove it, beyond a reasonable doubt.

~~~~~~~~~~~~~~~~~~~~~~~~~~

After a lengthy discussion with the District Attorney, I decide they have all the pictures and physical evidence they need. I send a letter to Southwest Forensic Center:

> In the matter of Mr. Philip Brinkman:
> When I order a body to be released, it includes the whole body, which includes arms, legs, and head. Except for tissue or fluid samples needed for further investigation, the total body should be released for interment.
>
> cc. Attorney in Dexter, Maine

With this order, the rest of Mr. Brinkman headed to Maine.

Chapter 6

A High Roller, or Let It Ride

Inquest #21 or Bust

There are NO casinos in Texas, at least no legal ones. Our "Bible Belt" heritage and the zeal of the State of Texas Attorneys General, present and past, have managed to spurn the evils that have beset the lands that surround us.

Just twenty years ago, the closest place you could find a casino was Las Vegas. My dad said he knew someone who went to Las Vegas in a $10,000 car and came back in a $150,000 Greyhound bus. He also told me how to come back from Vegas with a small fortune: "Go there with a big one!"

Our neighbors (Old Mexico, New Mexico, Oklahoma, Louisiana, and even Colorado) now all have casinos. Their parking lots are stuffed with Texas tags. North and west, casinos rise out of Indian reservations, huge colorful neon temples surrounded by deserts, hills, and plains. This is where the Indians get their revenge on the white man.

A couple of ships will take you from remote Texas ports out into the international waters of the Gulf of Mexico. There, you can feed slot machines until you run out of money, or you can build several small fortunes on the numbers of the craps table, until the stick man yells "Seven out!" and they rake it in. Most gamblers say they go for the food, the trip, and the music. Most gamblers do not tell the truth, at least not all the time.

In Shreveport, Louisiana, casinos are on boats — boats built to go nowhere. Some were dragged up the Red River from failed gaming endeavors. Some are leftover boats from New Orleans, where they were replaced by bigger boats. Some were built on the site, moored with huge metal rings to allow for the rise and fall of the river, but still going nowhere. The miles these boats will "go" will be up and down as the river rises and falls, rather than up and down the river. On the other hand, miles and miles of river water will flow by these casinos every day.

Gangplanks have been replaced with long enclosed walkways that go uphill or downhill according to the tide of the river. The walls display pictures of people holding huge checks: checks two feet tall and four feet long, written for thousands of dollars. One casino displays a wall papered with hundred dollar bills, a million dollars worth. A couple of those hundred dollar bills look familiar.

Once upon a time, these gambling boats were all "decked out" like their historical brothers that long ago spread their treasure up and down the Mississippi and Red Rivers. Now, unless you go outside on one of the decks, you might think you are in a multistory earthbound building. The difference is felt mostly in the wee hours of the morning; the rumble of the ships' engines vibrates the floor as the big diesels make the required daily startup. These "ships" each have a captain, but the captain will never guide the ship anywhere. I am certain that "El Capitan" has other duties, but I would bet the government requires an able seaman with proper training and required continuing education, and of course docking fees, floating fees, and whatever other fees they may come up with, as if the ships ever would leave the dock. If I am wrong, it will not be the first time I have lost a bet on the boats.

Shreveport is about 200 miles east of Dallas/Fort Worth on Interstate 20. About halfway between Dallas and Shreveport, on that same interstate, is Winona.

Every now and then, my friends and I "go for a boat ride," "head east," "go to the boats," or "go fishing over on the Red River." At times, most of the traffic on the interstate is headed to or from Shreveport, for either the boats or horse races. Busloads of gamblers come from all over Texas, some too old and feeble to drive but strong enough to climb or utilize the handicap apparatus. Once, returning from Shreveport to Dallas, a bus was robbed on the interstate. The gun-wielding thieves would have taken a lot more money if they had planned it better—they should have planned the theft on the way *to* the boats. Few people carry those big checks, or much cash, home.

~~~~~~~~~~~~~~~~~~~~~~~~~

Gamblers are usually in a hurry. Sometimes, the first bet they lose is to the traffic cop just over the hill; red lights flash and next they get to visit me. The justice courts handle traffic tickets. Sometimes the drivers go too fast, drink too much, or maybe are just fatally unlucky that day; for some, red lights flash, and I go to see them. The justice courts do inquests. Betting on traffic is the last time the gambler will lose. People really gamble with their lives when they do not put on their seat belts. Most accidents involve alcohol, speed, and/or fatigue. Most people who die in traffic fatalities were not wearing a seat belt.

~~~~~~~~~~~~~~~~~~~~~~~~~

"Judge, we have one on the interstate," says the Department of Public Safety dispatcher. It is Saturday, and I am having a late supper and am hungry. People do not conveniently die between nine and five, Monday through Friday.

Fatal accidents on the interstate usually involve at least one of the following: a head-on collision, a rollover, a truck, a bridge, a fire, or a tree. I figured it was one of these, or maybe a pedestrian. The interstate is 6.8 miles from my house.

~~~~~~~~~~~~~~~~~~~~~~~~~

As a child, I had been on this stretch of Interstate 20

when it was a dirt road and a dream. There was no traffic. Only heavy machinery sat parked that Sunday afternoon: bulldozers, dump trucks, maintainers, and other equipment needed to change forest, pastures, creeks, and wilderness into a highway. The interstate was a vision in progress, complete only in the eyes of engineers and construction workers.

I was eight years old. My uncle Curtis took me for a ride on an earth mover. This was beyond my wildest dreams. An earth mover is a machine that looks like a giant crab with four giant wheels; each wheel is as big as a car. "Uncle Curt" sat me on level after level as we climbed up to the control area of the vehicle. In the cockpit were levers and handles that all worked with clicks and bells. When the first engine started, I thought the whole machine had started. The earth mover is so big that it takes a little engine to start the big engine.

Then the real engine started! Black smoke billowed from the exhaust stack, which was as big around as I was. This massive beast shuddered with power, and with a click and a ding, it began to move.

I had ridden many miles in an eighteen-wheeler, but it was nothing like this. The wheels were so big that although they were turning slowly, we were zooming along. Uncle Curt hit a lever, and the belly of the containment area dropped and began swallowing earth. Soon, the dirt, enough to fill ten dump trucks, was scooped into the bed. Eight-year–old boys love dirt, and this was the ultimate dirt toy! We dropped the load, ending my uncle's demonstration. We rolled back next to our car, and the big diesel shuddered as the engine died. LoLo, my mom, was waiting; there was no smile on her face. While I was having the ride of my life, she had found half a bottle of whisky under my uncle's car seat. When she got through with him, there was no more earth moving.

Let It Ride

Interstate 20 has come a long way from that engineer's dream to reality. Twenty-four hours, day and night, traffic runs east to west and west to east, coast to coast. This particular evening a mother, a daughter and son-in-law head east, to "The Boats," from Dallas.

"I am going to the third floor and play the quarter machines," Mother says, driving with the sun setting low in her rearview mirror.

"I am going to MY machine on the first floor," says Daughter, sitting beside her in the front seat. If you ever win big on a slot machine, it somehow becomes "your" machine.

Hubby sits quietly on the back seat. He knows he is not wanted on this girls' night out.

Mother and Daughter talk about what they will do with one of those big checks.

"The first thing I am going to do is buy a car," says Mother, dreaming. "Sometimes I wonder if this clunker will make it to The Boats."

"This is our lucky night," says Daughter. "When I win, I am going for the big money in Vegas!" (If so, she probably will take the small fortune and ride back in a Greyhound bus worth a large fortune.)

"I'm not losing more than fifty dollars on the slots," Mother says, "and then I am going to play blackjack." She has a plan; most gamblers do. The plan usually does not make it to the gaming floor, and the night ends with, "If I had just stuck with my plan."

"I am sticking with a proven winner," Daughter says, "which is three spins, no wins, move on. If I lose, then I am going to eat. I get to eat free with this coupon." Daughter holds up her reward for playing in the past. "It's for two buffets," she says, making sure Hubby can hear her. "Me and Mom."

~~~~~~~~~~~~~~~~~~~~~~~~~~~

Eating at The Boats is different from just dining out. Each boat sports a buffet that competes with those on the other boats. From crawfish and king crab legs to steak and potatoes, from pizza to Chinese, there are all kinds of food. And the desserts! Once I was greeted by plates piled high with whole lobsters, bright red lobsters so big only two or three would fit on a plate. Lobster, on an "All You Can Eat" buffet! Paying for the food is also different. Before you hand over your hard-earned money for food, you can get a player's card; if you play the machines, you get a free meal. That "free meal" usually costs me about $300.

~~~~~~~~~~~~~~~~~~~~~~~~

"I need to borrow some money," Hubby says.

"Borrow" sounds better than "Give me." "Borrow" at The Boats means "If you give me $100 and I win a thousand, I will give you your $100 back. If I lose, WE lose!"

"What! No way!" says Daughter, turning to look at him with flaming eyes. "You begged us to let you come, and you didn't bring any money? I don't want to hear it. You are not going to wart me and follow me around all night like a dog waiting for a bone! You knew we were planning this trip. You knew it would take money. You are on your own!" She jerks back to her seat with a huff. Then she reaches forward and turns up the radio. "I don't want to hear it," she says, trying to close the subject.

"Well, don't worry about it," Hubby says. And he did not say anything else about the matter . . . ever.

The music drowns out the road noise in the older model four-door Chevy. The pavement runs under the car at seventy miles an hour. A few moments later, there is a new sound, the sound of air rushing through the car, like someone opened the car window or a door. A swish, a slam, and all is quiet — deathly quiet. Hubby is gone.

~~~~~~~~~~~~~~~~~~~~~~~~

One day while I was in high school, I took Jackie Globe on a motorcycle ride around the parking lot. She wore a miniskirt and sat sidesaddle behind me, holding tight, to my delight. The little Honda was not made for sidesaddle; I don't think any motorcycles are. We started out laughing and riding. The already short skirt rode up higher with every bump and turn. She had some mighty fine legs, and the rest of her bounced around great in my rearview mirror and my teenage mind.

"I am getting off," Jackie announced while we were going twenty miles an hour.

"Not yet!" I yelled, but too late.

She rolled twenty feet, got up, and cussed me up one side and down the other. It was a miracle she was not seriously injured.

Some people seem to think you can just jump off something moving, and everything stops when you hit the ground. An old "Airborne" joke was that to avoid injury in a crash, all you had to do was jump up in the air just before the plane made impact. As a paratrooper, I felt that weightless feeling, like jumping up when an elevator reaches the top or starts down. Roller coasters and other amusement park rides offer even more of the same feeling. Many other people do not seem to appreciate that weightless, slow-motion feeling, especially in elevators when 210-pound me is jumping up and down.

When a person is in an accident, things seem to slow down. This is because the mind shifts gears into high speed. "My life flashed before my eyes" is how people commonly express the feeling. The mind is working quickly. If you have ever been in a tumbling automobile, you know the feeling; you see the dash, then the seat, then the headliner, all in slow motion, as you become weightless, spinning out of control.

~~~~~~~~~~~~~~~~~~~~~~~~~

Hubby makes a decision, and things seem to stop or slow down. He reaches for a slick chrome door handle and pulls. The door unlatches with a click, but the door opens only a little. The air rushing along the side of the vehicle does not let the door fly open. He puts his shoulder against the door and begins to push and shove, using his feet and legs. Finally, the door opens; then, with a rush of wind, it slams shut again.

Hubby is not in the car. Like an airborne trooper, he slips into the abyss, a near vacuum sucking him out, into oblivion, away from all his problems. He feels like he is floating, drifting down and weightless, as though he is in outer space, suspended like a puppet, with no control of his destiny.

Maybe he will land on his feet, to walk away from the nagging situation he has endured for so long. Did he think about who and what he was leaving behind? Did he change his mind? Did he think, "Maybe I should reconsider what I am doing?" Did his life flash before his eyes?

The pavement below him appears smooth. Rocks and gravel are indistinguishable, whizzing beneath him at seventy miles per hour. As soon as his feet touch the ground, they disappear. Did he see his tennis shoes fly into the darkness as he flew, rolled, and tumbled down a road built for automobiles and not people to spin? Before he felt the pain, did he see or know that his body was breaking into pieces? Did he see the headlights of the cars behind him?

Maybe his head took a crack on the unforgiving pavement, sending him into eternity, leaving his body for what came next. What came next was another car. Then another. Then another.

It takes a minute and a mile for the ladies to pull over and stop. They look at each other, then look back to the empty back seat. They quietly sit, wait, and wonder.

Chapter 7

Choose Your Path

Inquest #1470

"Judge, you have the biggest family and graduating class I have ever seen," said trooper Barry Goins of the Texas Department of Public Safety. "Everyone we stop says they are kin to you or graduated with you." I had noticed that the number of my friends and relatives greatly increased after I raised my hand and took the oath of office.

I'm often asked, "Are you kin to the Shamburgers in (fill in the blank)? "

My answer to the question is, "The Shamburgers have an agreement. If you have picture identification, you can bum a meal. You can't spend the night, but you can bum a meal."

Shamburger is not a common name; there are only about five or ten thousand across the United States. When I lived in Germany, my landlord said Shamburger was a Jewish name. I was told the spelling was changed when two brothers migrated here from Germany. Some date that to the early 1800s, while some say we had ancestors who fought in the American Revolution.

The sixty or so Shamburgers in Smith County do not connect very often. The Shamburgers I know are not a closely knit group. They range in personality type from Dr. Shamburger, pastor of First Baptist Church in Tyler for around 30 years, to Ronald Scott Shamburger, age 30, who was executed by lethal injection on September 18, 2002 in Huntsville, Texas, for the murder of a 20-year-old woman in her home. Actually, Ronald seemed to be a pretty nice person, with no criminal history before going off the deep end.

Most Shamburgers have reputations as good citizens with a good sense of humor. The Shamburger Lakes at Belzora Crossing often see various Shamburgers, Attwood's, and other kinfolk enjoying nature and getting away from the rat race; even then, it is no family reunion, at least not like the ones on my mother's side of the family. The McClenny family gathers annually at the old school cafeteria to bring everyone up to date on our lives, get reintroduced to great cousins twice removed, and share a potluck meal. Each year, there are fewer and fewer old-timers. My ninety-two-year-old mother, LoLo, claims a seat at the head table.

I can remember when the "old" school cafeteria was built, replacing the "old old" wooden structure. I was eight years old when we moved from our two-story downtown house to a small white frame house on the hill, two blocks from the school. I remember wandering up to the construction site when they replaced the wooden screen doors on the back entrance to the school with metal and glass. The Winona School building held all the white students in grades 1-12. Two miles down the road was the Industrial School, where the black kids went. By the time I entered junior high, we went into "choice" mode, and a few African Americans started integrating into the formerly white school. During my sophomore year, integration was in full swing. The Industrial School was to become the elementary school, and the junior high and high school stayed in Winona.

If there was a big fight against integration of the schools, I did not see it. There was some discussion about bussing, and I remember a few old-timers saying, "The niggers are taking over!" But old-timers did not carry much weight with me in the 1960s.

In fact, the school administration and student body saw and hoped for the great benefits that would come with integration—mainly for the football and basketball teams! The year before joining forces, Coach Wills loaded some of us football players into a small yellow bus, and we went to the

Industrial School for our first training session. I am not sure they had ever seen a real football. I know none of them had ever played on an organized football team.

We met in an open field and playground behind the Industrial School.

"Let's make a single line," said Coach Wills. And so the first challenge began. Side by side, they lined up, and continued to line up side by side, while we tried to get them to stand one behind the other. Finally, we got it across to them that we wanted a single-file line. They did fine until a more complex coaching instruction.

"Go down ten yards and cut across," said Coach Wills to the group. Everyone turned to face him, creating another side-by-side line that expanded as they turned shoulder to shoulder causing confusion until we finally got them again facing down our pretend football field.

Coach stood with the football in his outstretched hands, pretending to wait for the snap.

"Hut one, hut two." He slapped the ball and stepped back, ready to throw the pass. To experienced football players, the slap meant "go." To the players who were the prospective salvation from a losing football season, it meant nothing, or that maybe the coach was a little crazy. "Go on!" said Coach Wills, waving his hand. The first player took off and did not look back until he ran a straight fifty yards into the open playground. Then, he stopped and turned around. Coach did not throw the ball.

"Next!" Coach yelled. "Ten yards and cut across. Now, when I slap the ball, you take off. "Hut one! Hut two!" Slap!

The next player figured the first player did something wrong, so he ran the fifty yards and continued running slanting across the field, looking back. The run changed into a trot as he circled back to the group.

"Next."

This one went twenty yards and cut across. Coach threw the ball.

"That was close," said Coach, "but it wasn't ten yards. Are you ready?" He looked at the excited future "All District" split end. "Hut one! Hut two! " Slap!

Like a bullet, he was gone. We marveled at his speed. At ten yards, he did not look back, nor at twenty or fifty. You could see the excitement drain from the coach as the kid sped away. You could see Coach's puzzlement as he wondered just how far this kid would run. A hundred and thirty yards later he stopped, a red brick wall of the Industrial School a yard or two in front of him.

Two of the new players were brothers: Charles and Earnest Prince. I never called them black, Negro, or African Americans. I just called them friends.

Just a note: When it came to basketball, *they* taught *us* how to play.

~~~~~~~~~~~~~~~~~~~~~~~~~

On the afternoon of May 13, 1999, I hear from my bailiff.

"Judge, Charlie Prince is in the courtroom. He says he is an old schoolmate of yours. It is not about a ticket."

I was born September 20, 1952, and Charles Ray Prince was born eight days later, in a Gladewater hospital. We grew up three miles from each other but never met until our first football practice. As most high school friends do, we parted ways after graduating, but we both ended up close to home in 1999.

He worked on a ranch with his father and his brother Earnest, who was almost exactly a year younger than us. The brothers were good-natured. Charles was kind of quiet, and Earnest had the big smile. It was hard to believe that twenty-eight years had passed since we had walked across the stage to receive our high school diplomas.

"Charles, what have you been up to?" I ask, stepping up on the bench from the side entrance into the courtroom.

"Aw, nothing much. Just tryin' to make ends meet." Charles grins as he looks down at the floor. His cheeks are hollowed, and he weighs about the same as he did in high school.

"It's been a long time since we played football," I say, trying to make conversation. I know why he is here. Three months earlier, he had borrowed twenty dollars. He paid it back last week, and I figured he was back for more.

"Charles," I tell him, "I have heard you have been messing around with crack. You know that stuff will kill you." I think about jail photos that I have seen. The first time they go to jail, the picture is that of a healthy man or woman, usually with a discouraged look on their face. As they are booked in again and again, usually on drug-related charges, weight loss is evident, sores appear, teeth rot, and the look on the face becomes blank. These photographs show a history of drug abuse. Now I'm seeing it live, looking at Charles Ray Prince, or what is left of him.

"I'm quittin'. I have had enough. But man, it is hard. Every time I do it, I think it will be the last."

"You are going to end up in prison or dead if something doesn't change."

"Mitch, that is easy for you to say. You got a nice place, nice job, nice family, I ain't got nothing." He looks back at the floor. "I lost it all."

"And you know why," I say, looking at him; wishing to see a glimpse of the kid in high school. There is a short period of silence as we both look at our lives. I feel blessed. He, I imagine, feels damned.

"Could you spot me twenty until next week?" he asks eventually. "Man, I need it in a bad way."

"Not if you are going to go out and buy dope with it."

"Naw, man, I just need to get some groceries. I am off the stuff now." He lies.

I pull out my billfold. "Here's a ten; that's all I can spare right now." I lie as well.

"You know I'm good for it," he says. "I'll pay you back." He never did.

~~~~~~~~~~~~~~~~~~~~~~~~~~

Four days later, on Monday morning, I hear from the

bailiff again.

"Judge, there is someone in the courtroom, Earnest Prince. He says it is not about a ticket."

"What's up, Earnest?" I say, entering the courtroom. There it was, that high school smile that separated Earnest from his brother. Even if we were losing a football game, Earnest could muster up a smile.

"I'm OK." The smile disappeared. "I'm worried about Charles Ray."

"Yeah, I talked to him the other day. He owes me ten bucks."

He forces a grin, but it disappears quickly. "He has disappeared. It's not like him not to come home. I've talked to Constable Wilson."

"Any idea where he may be?"

"You know them dope-headed dudes he hangs with. They are bad news. He got in a car with them and hasn't been seen since. He owed them money. They said they wanted him to fix a flat. Bobby Lee said he could go with them, and they stopped him; said Charles could fix a flat by himself. Charles has a good heart. I just know like something bad has happened."

"How long has he been missing?"

"Since Friday."

"That is just a couple of days. He'll probably show up." I say this more with hope than fact or intuition. Sometimes drug users just disappear for days or weeks, or forever.

"I don't think so. We are close, I can feel it. Charles Ray don't travel far from home. And, he never just disappears."

"We will find him. After all, he owes me ten dollars."

Earnest offers another forced smile.

~~~~~~~~~~~~~~~~~~~~~~~~~

My family owns an island that lies between the Sabine River at Belzora Crossing, and the Shamburger Lakes. The two lakes lie beside the river, a result of a changing meandering riverbed. The natural lake is called the Little Lake and is connected by a small channel to the larger lake, which is called (you guessed it) the Big Lake. Belzora has a long history that consists mostly of men standing by a campfire. Belzora was a ferry crossing where Texas Farm to Market (FM) Road 14 now crosses the Sabine River in extreme north central Smith County. The site was settled in 1850 and had a post office. The only thing left of the city of Belzora is Texas Historical Marker Number 5423007705.

~~~~~~~~~~~~~~~~~~~~~~~~~

On Monday, May 24, 1999, I hear from Tammy the dispatcher at 11:30 A.M.

"Judge, we have a homicide down at the river off of FM 14."

"What is the address?" I ask.

"FM 2015 and FM 14, within sight of the Belzora Bridge. It's in the woods — way back in the woods. You should be able to see a unit from the road. " A police car and driver make a unit. "401 said he would transport you." 401 is Constable Charles Wilson.

~~~~~~~~~~~~~~~~~~~~~~~~~

On our island, wood-framed two-story houses once lined a narrow blacktop road. Some had large stairways on the outside leading to the top floor. Sitting on those stairs, anywhere from top to bottom, you could look across the Big Lake and see fish ripple the water or a bass slapping the surface, or a turtle sticking his head up for a breath of air. Some houses had the stairwells on the inside, and some had both. The houses were not large, but on the river, bedrooms were not important. Beds and cots, lined up side by side, were enough to handle us campers, with one or two rooms reserved for the elders. The front of the houses overlooked the big lake, and the back was to the river. The lower story of the house was designed to allow the water to run through during the annual flood season. This worked well for the flow of water, but not for trees and other large objects tossed around and carried by floodwaters.

There Are People in This World Who Do Not Need to Be Here

It is late at night on May 14, 1999.

"Come on," says Charles Ray Prince. "I'll drive." He is sitting in the car with Lenord Ray, in the driveway at Murtis Wayne's house. Lenord is tired. He really did not want to go to Murtis Wayne's that late at night, but Charles wanted to go, and a beer is a beer.

"One more beer," says Charles Ray, chugging the beer he has in his hand. "We got a long day tomorrow if I am going to help you move."

Soon after midnight, headlights bounce as a vehicle drives toward Lenord Ray's car.

"That looks like Little Rich's Blazer," Lenord Ray says.

"Crap, I owe him," says Charles. "I owe just about everybody." He smiles and takes another drink. There are four more beers left, two for him and two for Lenord Ray.

The window of the Blazer goes down, and his concern is confirmed.

"Charlie, come on. Get in. We got a deal for ya." It is Demond Richards, aka (also known as) "Little Rich." He is eighteen years old and has the reputation of a tough guy and dealer. Charlie walks up to the car and sees the other two passengers. Bennie Ray Callaway, Jr., is white and the stepbrother of Richards, who is black. Jackie Brown, aka "Creep," is eighteen. Neither has a criminal history. In the back seat, next to Creep, is a camera. The film inside will later develop into pictures showing them and others posing with their gang signs.

A "deal" to Charles means crack cocaine. These guys may be bad dudes, but they always have some good shit. Besides, they are just teenagers, just high school kids, in comparison to forty-six-year-old Charlie Ray. "I'm broke," says Charles. He had planned on giving Little Rich his twenty dollars, but he could come up with only ten, and that bought the beer. "I know I still owe you. You know I'm good for it."

"No problem, man. We got a job for you. You change out the brake shoes on this Blazer, and we will call it even. Come on; we got everything we need to do the job."

"I don't know. Tomorrow I am helping Lenord Ray move," says Charles.

"How 'bout we provide you with the mo-to-va-tion! I have the rocks." Little Rich dangles a Ziploc sandwich bag by one corner. This makes the little cream-colored rocks settle into the lower corner. Whoever invented Ziploc baggies probably had no idea that billions of dollars of illegal drugs would go to consumers neatly sealed within them. Crack cocaine comes in a crystallized form, or "rock." When it is heated, it turns to vapor, which is inhaled into the lungs and goes straight into the blood. This sets off a chain reaction affecting the whole body, but primarily it triggers the brain into a feeling of grandeur.

Charles trusts them because he has to. They are dopers, like him. He trusts in honor among thieves, so to speak. Besides, who cares about working off the debt? The most delicious meal anyone could ever eat, the best prize anyone could ever win, the finest car anyone could ever drive, the best sex one could ever have, all seem dwarfed in the mind of a doper by the thrill that is clumped together in the corner of that clear plastic bag. Charles gets into the Blazer. It is a short drive to the Sabine River bottom.

Lenord Ray lies down in the front seat of the car and goes to sleep. He will awake the next morning, alone.

~~~~~~~~~~~~~~~~~~~~~~~~~

Some people live on the river do not take kindly to a locked up river house. We called them River Rats. Their belongings travel with them in a flat-bottom boat, often stolen somewhere upriver. They are not social people. River Rats avoid people like us: people who just visit the river. They think of themselves as part of the river, like the squirrels, rabbits, hogs, and deer. Those who come to visit the river hunt and kill the squirrels, hogs, and deer. We learned not to lock up or secure the river houses. If River Rats are hungry or need a place to sleep, they will find it, even if it means kicking in the door and breaking into the cabinets. Like the wild animals, they avoid people and houses that are occupied. They are not looking for trouble. On the other hand, if they were treated kindly (the house unlocked and food in the cupboard), we would sometimes find replaced canned goods in the cabinets and little or no destruction.

~~~~~~~~~~~~~~~~~~~~~~~~~~~

The Blazer bounces down the rough, sandy, dirt drive and arrives at an old mobile home. The grass is high, and a fifty-five-gallon steel drum serves as a burn barrel. Bennie goes into the mobile home to watch television, or so he says.

They take out a crack pipe for a quick hit. A simple glass tube, a piece of a copper Brillo pad, and a butane cigarette lighter are all that is needed to turn the crack cocaine into a vapor.

They enjoy the rush. In their mind, they go somewhere. They are not sure where, but it is better than here, and it feels good. They sit for a minute or an hour; no one is really sure.

"The brake shoes are in the trailer," says Jackie as he returns somewhat to reality. Charles knows the trailer they are speaking of. It is deep in the woods, a good place for a campfire and getting high. The logging road that leads to the trailer is just a trail. The only way to get there is by four-wheeler or on foot, and there are no four-wheelers. "Shit. Anybody got a light?"

"Torches!" says Little Rich, and they proceed to get sticks and wrap the ends with old clothing, some left over from the burn barrel. With some effort, and possibly having dipped the cloth-wrapped tips in gasoline or some other accelerant, they light the makeshift torches. The four of them stand in a circle facing each other. They are excited to be on an adventure. One will go farther than all the others.

They high-step over the grass, and go into the wild. Like African hunters in a Tarzan movie, they flash strange shadows in the brush and trees with their torches. After fifteen minutes of winding and turning, they come to a squarish clearing, about ten yards on a side. Pine needles carpet the area, making the earth feel as though it is a thick plush carpet, soft enough sit or lie down on, soft enough to get comfortable, go trippin', or pass out on.

They easily gather wood and brush and pile it on the charred remains of a campfire. Another fifty-five-gallon drum is in the middle of the clearing. Beer cans from past gatherings are strewn around, many covered by pine needles.

An old trailer, ten feet by ten feet, borders one side of the clearing. Brown rust is taking over the white paint that once covered it. The tires are gone, and it sits on the ground. How or why it sits in the middle of nowhere, nobody knows; nobody cares. It must have been towed in when the road was more than a trail; it would take a helicopter to move it now.

"I gotta pee," says Bennie. He whips out his pecker beside the trailer. It happens whenever he drinks beer.

"The brake shoes are in the trailer," Little Rich says, motioning Charles to open the heavy door.

Working on the farm with his dad and brother has kept Charlie in shape. Hay baling and hauling and tossing fifty- and hundred-pound feed bags all day builds muscles like working out in a gym. Crack has taken away all of his body fat, and his muscles are well defined. The boys have seen his strength before. Charles is friendly, but you really don't want to piss him off. Like most people on drugs, he can be unpredictable.

He turns his back to Richards to open the door. Little Rich pulls out a nine-shot .22-caliber pistol.

Charles tosses the latch open and swings open the wide heavy doors. He turns around. It is dark, but the firelight reveals a pistol leveled point blank at his chest.

Pop, pop, pop.

Charles feels the impact of the bullets hitting his chest.

It doesn't hurt; it feels more like someone pushing against him. One bullet lodges in his spine, stopping all feeling from that point down. He does not feel his legs as they fold beneath him. He collapses to the ground and rolls to his back. He is breathing but does not seem to be struggling for breath. His eyes are open, but he sees only a tunnel made of light. He knows his time is near. He hears nothing as a thousand thoughts rush through his mind. He does not think about who shot him or why. He does think about how the big problems of his life no longer amount to even a little hill of beans. He is surprised that he feels no pain. He thinks about what his mother told him about Jesus and heaven so long ago. He wonders about what the preacher said before he walked down the aisle of the Mount Olive Baptist Church. Is it as simple as a child saying, "Jesus I want you in my heart?" Is this really enough to get him through the Pearly Gates? Is this what "Amazing Grace" is all about? He will know in a minute.

Bennie hears two shots, or was it three? He quickly tucks himself back in and zips up while rounding the corner of the trailer. Four steps later, he sees Charles dropping to the ground. Charles rolls backward, to lie face up. Bennie sees Little Rich and Jackie bend over Charles, holding their torches close to his face. Their faces are also glowing. Charles's eyes are open, but he cannot see the evil faces looking down upon him. He sees only light. The others intently watch his eyes, the light of the soul, wanting to see what it is like to die.

"What do you see? How does it feel?" Little Rich asks Charles.

"Come on, man, talk to us!" Jackie implores. "Tell us what you see. How does it feel to die?"

Charles says nothing as his breath softens and the light fades from his eyes.

~~~~~~~~~~~~~~~~~~~~~~~~~~~

The real destruction to the river houses came from the river. Semi-annually, the thirty-foot-wide river would rise up the twenty-foot-high bank to spill over into the two lakes.

Some years, the spring rains would add another ten-foot rise, which would put the river into the houses, leaving a muddy mess to clean up in the summer. One by one, the old houses came down, giving way to the river, which had been traveling this course for thousands of years. It does not take long for a roof leak to turn wood into rot in the humid river bottom. Now the river is controlled by lakes and dams. Still it overflows, but not like it used to. Small wooden frame houses now sit where the majestic two-story houses of my youth stood. A campfire occasionally burns by a travel trailer sitting next to the swimming hole.

~~~~~~~~~~~~~~~~~~~~~~~

"Hot damn! We did it!" says Richards. He points the gun at the corps. "Now we're even, motherfucker. That son of a bitch is dead! We killed him." The torch flame flickers as he dances a victory dance.

Bennie only hears one word: "We!" What the hell have "we" done? Bennie has never even been close to this kind of trouble. Sure, he wanted to be a gang-banger, to fit in; he wanted to be somebody. He has been around when unlawful things have happened, but he has never even gotten a traffic ticket.

"Hell, yeah," says Brown, "we did it." The two look at Bennie, who is decidedly *not* dancing like a wild Indian. Bennie looks at the pistol, and it only takes a split second for him to realize what friendship means in the hood.

"Hell, yeah! We did it," he says. He had gone too far to turn back now.

~~~~~~~~~~~~~~~~~~~~~~~

No one enters life with a desire to go to hell in a hand basket. People just open their eyes one day to find they are sitting in their own hell, wherever it may be. To some, it is a jail cell; to others, it is a memory fog; to others, it is a broken marriage or relationship, an empty bank account, a lost job or no job at all, a pregnancy or inability to get pregnant, too little money or even too much, taxes, or even watching their kids make their own hell. Some blame God or karma; most blame other people for putting them where they are. Some will open their eyes only for a short time to look around, and then close them again. Some prefer the darkness. Some will never open their eyes.

~~~~~~~~~~~~~~~~~~~~~~~

After twenty minutes, the fever is over. Sobering up means awakening to what you have done. Charles is lying on the ground, and he is not getting up. The torches combine with other sticks and limbs to make a larger campfire.

"We gotta get rid of the body," Richards says

"They will find him, and they know we were the last ones with him," Jackie adds.

"If there is no body, they can't find him." Little Rich looks at the fire. "Let's burn him."

They put some of the burning sticks in the fifty-five-gallon drum and proceed to build up the fire inside the receptacle. When they are satisfied that the fire is large enough and hot enough, the three pick up lifeless Charles and dump him into the barrel.

"There will still be bones and shit," says Jackie.

"There are tools at Pop's old house," Little Rich says, talking of the old home that is not far away. "We can bury him."

With this, the three stumble back to the Blazer, with a half moon to guide them.

In the Blazer, Jackie speaks again. "Suppose somebody digs him up?"

"You chicken-shit," Richards says as he pulls into the drive. "It's under control. You keep your damn mouth shut, and nobody will find anything."

The house has been vacant for more than two years. The front door is hanging by a single hinge and stands half open. No one really lives there, legally. It serves as a place to crash for the gang or a holdover for when someone is kicked out of their house, and it is a good place to hide. The group makes its way to the garage, where many tools once hung on the walls.

"Not one damn shovel!" Richards says. "Pop always had shovels and hoes, and now there ain't shit. Damned thieving bastards." Richards has forgotten that last year he and his buddies hocked the equipment for dope money. "They can find a body, but if there is no head, they can't tell who it is!"

Little Rich holds up two rusty wood saws. "These will do it. Let's get it on!"

~~~~~~~~~~~~~~~~~~~~~~~~~~~

I am constantly amazed by the stupidity of criminals. Don't they know, by the third time they go to jail, that there are surveillance cameras in the stores, with people watching them? By the fifth Driving While Intoxicated violation, wouldn't you at least think about not driving when you are drinking? What part of "Don't go back on the property" do you not understand? If you hit her/him, you are going to jail. If you park your car and smoke dope in a known drug area, you will get busted. Most people do not carry digital scales, three boxes of sandwich-size self-sealing storage bags, and two pounds of marijuana for their personal use. Doctors put a phone number on prescription pads for a reason. You went through Whitehouse, Texas, after midnight with a burned out license plate light?

Some can blame drugs and alcohol for reducing their cognitive skills. Some kleptomaniacs cannot help themselves, and likewise, some people have definite mental problems that lead them to commit crimes. And some are just stupid.

~~~~~~~~~~~~~~~~~~~~~~~~~~~

Back at the mobile home, they find some large plastic bags. Dawn is breaking, and they easily work their way back down the trail. Charles is more roasted than burned and there is a lot of meat and bones. They dump the barrel and began to saw.

"What about fingerprints?" said Jackie.

"If there ain't no hands, there ain't no fingerprints," Bennie says and they continue to saw.

~~~~~~~~~~~~~~~~~~~~~~~~

"I think we have found the missing Prince," says Constable Wilson. "He's been missing ten days now." We are driving to the crime scene. We pass the closed "old high school" in Winona. The football field is now a baseball field. "I have been working on this for a few days. Earnest came by and reported Charles Ray missing."

"Yeah, he told me too," I answer.

"We have an informant at the scene. A girlfriend of one of the actors gave him up. Sounds like a bad drug deal went down."

"I can't see Charlie hurting anybody."

"Judge, you know that when those junkies get cranked up, they do crazy-ass things."

"I know," I say as we pass what was the Industrial School. The field is all weeds, with a healthy scattering of scrap metal and old cars. "What do you know about this?"

"Looks like three subjects picked up Charles, took him to the woods, and shot him."

"Crap. I was afraid something like that may have happened."

"That's not all," the constable continues. "They decided to conceal the body by cutting off his head and hands. Then they burned what was left in a fifty-five-gallon drum. They sawed his bottom jaw off in case of dental records. We have information that the head, hands, and gun are over at Moore's Lake."

"His jaw?" I ask, without a clue what to expect. We turn onto FM 2015, going toward the river.

The constable leans as we make the crooked S curves

on 2015. He is driving faster than he usually does.

"A Bennie Callaway is our informant and an actor in the crime. He said they drove down State Park Highway hanging the jawbone out the window, waving it around, kind of playing with it before they tossed it. Officers are looking for it now."

"Have they found his head?"

"We just found the remains of the body. I'm working with the S.O.," the constable says, referring to the Sheriff's Office. "They are processing the crime scene. We figured we better get you out here before we go further. Callaway is going to show us where they 'chunked' the rest."

We turn off FM 2015 onto a sandy driveway that takes us to the mobile home. Deputy Houston Ramsey is standing beside a burn barrel.

"Hi, Hugh." I say. "Looks like we have a good one."

"Yeah. I'm guarding this barrel. Look down here." He points into the darkness of the soot and ash. "All kind of bone fragments. These guys were either messed up or crazy."

I walk down a trail that appears to have been a dirt road at one time. The sand is washed out in places, and the trail winds around brush and holes. Detective Jason Waller leads the way.

"Looks like they came down here to shoot Prince," Waller says, thinking out loud. "Could have been a drug deal, but it looks to me like it was a planned hit from the beginning."

We arrive at a clearing. An old box trailer is sitting on the ground, looking like it has been there a long time. The roof is covered with a carpet of pine needles, and brownish-red rust is eating away at the faded white paint and metal walls. The trailer is slowly melting into the forest.

"They made torches for light," says Waller, pointing to some of the charred cloth bits lying around. "Allegedly, they shot him here." He points to the back of the trailer. "Then they tried to burn him up." He points to an overturned burn barrel. "Sometime during all this, they decide to saw him to pieces. We haven't found all the pieces. The animals did. We have bone fragments all over the place. We found the ribcage over there by the creek." He nods toward an orange flag on a wire that marks the spot.

Cameras are clicking, notes are being taken; the missing person case is now a murder case.

I walk around, looking at many other orange markers stuck on wires marking evidence, mostly bones. There are 206 bones in the adult human body, and more than half (106) are in the hands and feet.

"Here are some more." I point to the ground thirty feet from the barrel. An officer marks the spot with another orange flag. I can recognize many human bones; however, in these woods, there are lots of bones, most of them not human. With the skull missing and the body stripped of its flesh, a pile of bones is a pile of bones. To the untrained eye, we appear little different from any number of long-boned animals.

"Get Harmon Funeral Home en route when you are ready to transport," I tell Waller. "Be sure to tell them to bring a bag." I take my notes and head back to the mobile home.

"Wilson said they found his head," Officer Ramsey says. "I am to take you there."

Ramsey's Sheriff Unit is not much different from the constable's car: same radio, siren and light controls, radar, and flashlight with charger. A new video camera is mounted on the dash. Cars weren't equipped with laptop computers in 1999.

We drive through another wooded area to the secluded Moore Lake. It is half the size of Little Shamburger Lake. We park beside Wilson's unit and several others next to the dam. In the back seat of one unit is a kid in handcuffs who just turned nineteen. He will be as old as Charles Ray Prince before he will see freedom again—that is, if he serves his thirty-year sentence.

Halfway across the dam, Wilson is standing, waiting for me.

"Down there," he says, pointing to a clear plastic bag forty feet down the dry side of the dam. "You can't really tell if it is his hands and head, but there is a head." I climb down to get a better look. Sure enough, I can make out a nose and eyebrow against the plastic bag.

"And the gun?" I ask, climbing back up the earthen dam.

"He said they threw the head over on this side and the gun out there." He points to the still waters of the murky pond. "We have the dive team coming." They will find the gun two days later. "He said they threw his wallet, the saws, and what was left of his clothes in another white plastic bag over the spillway."

"Got your pictures?"

"We are waiting for the crime scene people to come from the other site."

"When you are done, pick up the pieces, and Harmon will take them to Dallas." The local forensic pathologist does not like to do bodies that are decomposed.

We walk across the dam to the spillway and look over the edge. It is a swamp. It reminds me of when I was lost in a jungle in Panama.

"You know, snakes and spiders thrive in that mess," I say as we both look down. "Are you sending divers down there?"

"We have a flat-bottom boat coming. Parks and Wildlife will drag it," Wilson says. They will not find anything.

I meander through the surrounding woods, looking for something out of place, thinking about how and what happened. I find a light blue pair of infant's shorts, the "Tumble Togs" brand. That strikes me as strange. They are not dirty and do not appear to have been there long. Things happen in the river bottom that we will never know about.

The game warden is pulling the gray flat-bottom boat up to the dam as I leave.

I arrive back at the Justice Court Center at 3:30 P.M. Detective Charley Baker from the sheriff's office is waiting. He has affidavits and warrants ready for me to sign.

I issue three warrants for murder. One suspect is in custody.

~~~~~~~~~~~~~~~~~~~~~~~~

I wonder if Bennie will get special treatment for his confession. He seems to be the one with regrets. He also fears for his life.

"You know, we may not have broken the case without Bennie," I tell Earnest Prince. "Don't you think he deserves a break?"

"Not at all!" says Earnest. "They went together to find my brother and to kill him. They all knew and planned it together. Any of them could have stopped it at any time. He is as guilty as the one who pulled the trigger. They are supposed to let us know when parole time is coming up. Judge, there are people in this world that do not need to be here."

~~~~~~~~~~~~~~~~~~~~~~~~

An attempted carjacking on May 27 yields suspects' descriptions that match the two remaining murder suspects. A search with dogs leads to Demond Richards II and Dorothy Richards, parents of one of the suspects. A short time later, Tyler Police Department receives information that both suspects were at a residence on North Bois D' Arc Street. Richards was arrested as he fled the residence. Brown was able to escape.

On June 19, 1999, Illinois State Police arrested Jackie Brown in Cook County. He would not tell them how he arrived there; nor would he speak about the case. On July 12, Brown was transported from a federal holding center in Seagoville, Texas, to the Smith County Jail.

All were arrested on my warrants.

All three subjects were found guilty of murder.

Jackie Brown, aka "Creep," was sentenced to thirty years.

Bennie Ray Callaway, Jr., was sentenced to thirty years.

Demond Richards III, aka "Little Rich," was sentenced to forty years.

~~~~~~~~~~~~~~~~~~~~~~~~~~~

Cops, judges, and a lot of other people get tired of dealing with people who do drugs. The value of their life depreciates with every trip to the jail, every lie, every time they steal, beg, or borrow. Many in the criminal justice system have the attitude, when two drug dealers kill each other, of "Kill them all and let God sort them out." To many of us, it really is "a war on drugs."

Charles Ray Prince was introduced to crack in 1986. "It took one time, and I was hooked," he told his brother. Even after two rehabs, he still could not put it down. While Charles was on probation once, the probation officer asked Earnest if he thought Charles was still using.

"You can test him any time you want. I know he is using. You need to do your job!" Earnest said. "It is all about money." What Earnest means is that if Charles tested positive, he would go to jail, and if he went to jail, he would not be able to send in the forty dollars a month probation fee. Earnest thinks that the criminal justice system is more interested in that forty dollars a month than in putting Charles behind bars or helping someone change their lifestyle. Besides, he will never quit, and if the drugs don't kill him, the drug business will.

I came to a doper's defense several times as we looked for bones. "Damn dopers got fried brain syndrome," one of the searchers says. "There is hell to pay when you play with the devil. Probably got what he deserved."

"Charles Ray was a friend," I say.

"Yep, you're right, Judge. Nobody deserves this," the searcher answered.

Chapter 8

Rolling on the River

Inquest #78

The college semester in Paris is over. Even though her father does not like her driving at night, Misty is determined to get home from Paris Junior College, in Paris, Texas. The nineteen-year-old drives south to Bogotá, then down through Mount Vernon. She then crosses Lake Monticello, making her way through Pittsburg on her way south through northeast Texas.

It will be twenty years before cell phones would be common, and even then there would be miles and miles of woodlands and territories throughout East Texas without bars—either bars for drinking or bars indicating cell phone reception.

Misty has to be careful traveling through the many small towns. Each one has a policeman shooting a radar gun to make the highways safe and help fill the city coffers. In Gilmer, a city cop is not quite hidden, and she almost runs a red light, straining to see him, instead of paying attention to the light over the intersection. On State Highway 155, she makes the turns and red lights in Big Sandy and continues south.

The four lanes of Highway 155 narrow ahead as she approaches a two-lane bridge. A big truck takes advantage of the passing lane and blows by, shaking her gas-saving little car and cutting in front of her as the extra lane closes. She gives the eighteen-wheeler plenty of room.

"Let him run the front door," she says to her imaginary passenger. It is an expression her father uses. If a ticket is to be given, it will be for the big rig that runs ahead. The trailer lights fade quickly as she approaches two bridges. "That truck is going way too fast."

The first bridge crosses Pump Station Lake; the next crosses the Sabine River. The river is the dividing line between Smith County and Gregg County. Five miles further south, and you are at the blinking yellow light in downtown Winona.

"Th-thump, th-thump, th-thump." A group of men standing around a blazing campfire under the bridge hear the sound of vehicles passing overhead. The Sabine River slowly flows by. The fire is energized every time one of them throws a cardboard box into it. Blues, greens, and some strange colors flame off of the boxes. It is as though the fire is celebrating the end of another six-, twelve-, eighteen-, or twenty-four pack of beer. Freedom is the feeling on the river. There is no social or age boundary within the group. The usual prerequisites for respectable living fade into the distance with the th-thumps of the vehicles speeding away. Life goes on at sixty or seventy miles an hour up on the bridge, but below it, life is "on hold."

On the river, one does as little or as much of whatever one likes. William likes a combination of alcohol and pain pills, a combination that is sometimes fun and sometimes fatal.

William spins around in a wheelchair. The firelight reflects off of the chrome that is not covered in mud. He feels that he has done all he can to get some pleasure out of life. A ruined spinal cord has kept him in a wheelchair for the last four of his twenty-nine years. His legs are nothing but dead weight, more of a hindrance than a help. He is determined to do some of the things he once did, however, including going to the river with the guys.

"This is what the river is all about," William says as he rocks back in his chair, balancing on two wheels. Then he does a 360° spin. The two small front wheels land in front of the fire, and the blaze reflects off the frame, giving it a fiery orange look. Even though he is drinking, he can still maintain his balance, rocking back and forth through the use of his hands on the big wheels. The chair has replaced his legs, and he has learned to control the wheelchair like some control a pair of skis or skates.

"There's something special about getting away from the civilized world, building a fire, and standing around telling stories with friends and strangers," William thinks. But he cannot stand; he has to sit. He cannot hop into the boat and run the trot lines. He cannot jump into the car and run back to Big Sandy for another six-pack. He has to depend on others. He has stories to tell, but his stories always begin with "Before the accident" and end with a sigh. It is as though his life ended with the loss of use of his legs, and the rest of his body painfully lingers on.

~~~~~~~~~~~~~~~~~~~~~~~~~

The Sabine River has been hearing stories since the days when Indians camped along its muddy banks. Some things have changed: There was no Highway 155 in wilderness days, of course. The Indians heard the scream of a big cat, the hoot of an owl, and the deep, rumbling, belching sound of a bullfrog or alligator, sounds still heard deep in the river bottom. Camping Indians did not hear the th-thumping sound of progress.

~~~~~~~~~~~~~~~~~~~~~~~~~

"Th-thump, th-thump, th-thump." Misty hears the sound as her tires slap against segment after segment on the first bridge. The car rocks in rhythm to the sound. Instinctively, she holds the steering wheel tighter and becomes more aware. The bridge is a hundred yards long and broken into concrete segments separated by spaces of one-quarter to three-fourths of an inch; the distance varies with the temperature. On this July night, at 11:14 P.M., the space is half an inch. A full moon reflects off the lake and provides enough light to outline a tall pine forest. The headlights make everything else appear as black and white.

~~~~~~~~~~~~~~~~~~~~~~~~~~

Up on Highway 155, the people in the cars and trucks move on, without a clue about the activity below the bridge. The people under the bridge think, "We are safe in our sanctuary here in the river bottom." The th-thumps are a reminder of the world above, but not a deterrent to the activities; in fact the sound adds a certain thrill.

Under the bridge, the fire is smothered and dimmed momentarily, falling victim to another twenty-four-pack beer box. The box discolors as it heats up to kindling temperature. Strange colors appear, as small fingers of green and blue flames caress a fading picture of mountains and words that claim the goodness of this brand of beer. Light flashes as the box ignites, sending glowing ashes up and away. The fire prevails. The concrete columns and rusty steel beams of the undercarriage of the bridge are revealed. Overhead, the shadows dance with the flames.

William sits in his wheelchair. He sees the glowing ashes drift weightlessly away, unbound by Earth's gravity. They are free to drift and fly until they disintegrate, turn to powder, and no longer exist.

"Do you remember that time the River Rat came by?" Another story begins, and attention is focused on the storyteller by all save one, William, who rolls away in his wheelchair.

The rutted dirt road that runs beside the highway would be difficult to walk by moonlight; it is a hundred yards of rough uphill terrain. William's wheelchair rocks and rolls with the battle to get up to Highway 155. The rider's hands are reddish brown from the sticky clay and dirt that now cover the wheels.

The smaller front wheels bump up as the chair hits the ridge of the asphalt shoulder of the road. The chair jerks over the edge and forward, to sit on solid pavement. William thinks of his chair as another vehicle on the highway. He is back in the modern world.

A car approaches, and the bright white headlights change the surrounding view, from the black and white of moonlight into color. William looks at his red, muddy hands. "Would I complain if my shoes were caked with mud?" he wonders. He remembers the whipping he got from his mother the time he tracked dog poop into to the house. How he wishes his legs would work again.

"I would gladly jump into a pile of shit if I could," he thinks as the car whooshes by. "Now I can't even feel the sting of mama's hand on my butt."

After fighting the muddy dirt road, the chair glides easily along the paved shoulder of Highway 155, going back toward the bridge. The wheelchair vibrates as it rolls over hundreds of tiny pebbles embedded in the black asphalt. Perhaps William is tired of looking up at his friends. From the vantage point of the bridge, he can look down on them for a change, thirty feet down to the river.

William hears the compressed sound waves of an eighteen-wheeler approaching. He feels the energy as the truck roars by, at seventy miles an hour and only eight feet away. The ground shakes, and the wind tosses his hair. He smells diesel, a manufactured, oily fuel smell. As the smell drifts away, it is replaced with the natural smell of burning pine from the campfire below.

~~~~~~~~~~~~~~~~~~~~~~

Once, I took my daughters to the river and the Shamburger Lakes to show them how much fun it could be. The gate key changes frequently, and the key I had would not fit this lock. We parked the red Rodeo, climbed the fence, and proceeded to walk the half mile down the blacktop road. We were wearing our swimsuits and carrying our towels. My swimsuit was a pair of cutoff jeans, with a margarita wine cooler in each front pocket. We walked by the Little Lake and the place where my son and I had once seen a large alligator.

It was near the spot where my fly-fishing days came to an end.

As a child, I remembered Cousin Carl Shamburger majestically smoking his pipe and fly-fishing on the lake. In the early morning, with a low, foggy mist upon the lake, he would sit or stand in the boat, flexing and swaying the long rod, feeding the fiber out, making a super-large S above his head. Then he would gracefully lay the filament down to that intimate spot where, he hoped, a hungry bass would be waiting. Attached to the heaver fiber line would be a light nylon fishing line, and delicately attached to that, a fly. Hidden in the fly was a hook.

"I decided I would carry on this tradition," I told the girls, as we walked down the tree covered roadway. As I spoke, we could hear a droning sound in the river bottom, like a chain saw in the distance.

"After three hours of cracking the fly-fishing whip and no fish, I was getting bored. The metal fish-stringer with its spring clips, designed to hold ten largemouth bass, was lying empty on the floor of the little flat-bottom boat. Right there on the bank," I said, pointing, "a large cottonmouth water moccasin was enjoying the sun. He paid no attention to me; after all, he had all the venom. I wondered if he would eat a fly."

I paused for dramatic effect. "I worked my rod, and then lay that fly an inch from the nose of the serpent. There was no movement, except a large, black-forked tongue began to shoot in and out. He was ignoring me! I decided to teach him a lesson. I drew the line back and up, like a whip, then snapped it and popped him in the head. This got his attention, and he coiled. The secret to popping a whip is throwing out and pulling back at the right time with the right force.

"A smart snake would have run," I continued. "This was a big, poisonous dummy, and I popped him again, harder, and all he did was look around. Pop, pop, pop. I was hitting him fast, one right after the other.

"'You will feel this one!' I said, as I put an extra tug in at just the right time. The hook set in the middle of the snake. When I tugged, the snake flew, wagging four feet above the water. I fully understood the namesake of the snake as he hyper-extended his mouth by unhinging his jaws, revealing white fangs and a puffy white throat. All this as I saw the cottonmouth flying through the air and into the boat. The fishing line was flopping and looping, giving me no control of the flight of the snake. I thought about jumping out of the boat. I wondered if that snake had kinfolk beneath the surface. I managed to move away from him as he landed right in the middle of the twelve-foot flat-bottom boat.

"The hook was still set in the middle of his back. I looked for my pistol but really did not want to shoot holes in the bottom of the boat. The snake lay between me and my .32 automatic pistol anyway. At least I had sense enough to keep holding on to the rod. I quickly drew in the line. The long, flexible rod kept the excited, wiggling snake a safe distance away.

"Now, if the hook would hold, I could pick the monster up and put him back into the water. A fly rod is flexible, which means it bends. As I began to lift, the rod began to bend. The weight of the snake and the flexing of the rod made the snake get closer and closer.

"Finally, the snake saw the water. We both agreed it was time to end the game. He slithered over the side of the boat. I shook the rod a few times, which freed the hook,-which freed Mr. Cottonmouth Water Moccasin."

~~~~~~~~~~~~~~~~~~~~~~~~~

A mosquito bites William's ankle, one of the many bites he receives that night that he does not feel. The mosquitoes feast on him without his knowledge.

The wheelchair pulls up to the sign marking the border of Smith County. This sign is ten feet before the next one, identifying the Sabine River, where the two-lane bridge begins and the shoulder of the road disappears. With no cars in sight, William rolls onto the bridge. The concrete curb is a foot tall, and the rail some fifteen inches beyond. William's plan is to get out on the bridge, collapse the wheelchair, and climb onto the curb, holding onto the railing. Then, he can swing his legs over the side and sit, almost normal, looking down on his friends. After a while, he can yell at them and maybe even get someone to throw a beer up to him.

When he is almost to his destination, he sees a pair of headlights approaching. He thinks, looks at the curb and then back at the car. He realizes it is not a car but an eighteen-wheeler crossing Pump Station Lake and coming fast. He spins his wheelchair around to race the oncoming truck, struggling to get out of the traffic lane. He makes it to the end of the bridge, but not far enough. He fully expects that his life will very shortly come to an end. His head hurts from a loud sound suddenly blaring in his ears. The trucker blasts him with his air horn and swerves the twenty tons of big rig in an attempt to miss the traveler. Big trucks are not made to share the road with wheelchairs.

William sees red and amber running lights along the side of the truck, then miraculously sees the taillights. He is still alive. Before he has a chance to rejoice, he is caught in the air turbulence of the truck and spins out of control. His hands are useless as he tumbles, and the chair bounces away, landing next to the sign for the river.

He finds himself lying centered in the southbound lane, his useless legs pointing north and his aching head pointing south. He lies there, breathing, thinking, trying to regroup.

~~~~~~~~~~~~~~~~~~~~~~~~~~

"No way are we going swimming with alligators and snakes!" the girls said.

"Don't worry," I answer. "We are going to the Big Lake, where people have been swimming for years." I tried to reassure them and noticed that I was speaking louder than before.

The drone sound was loud and became a buzzing, sounding something like standing on an airstrip with ten planes grinding their propellers against the air. I was bitten by a mosquito, then another. We walked faster, and the buzzing was all around us. I brushed layers of mosquitoes off the kids with a towel as we ran to the swimming hole. When we arrived, no questions were asked and no protests given. We all went into the water, hoping the mosquitoes were not deep-sea divers and not thinking about where mosquitoes come from. Only by going underwater in one place and coming up in another could any of us get relief, and then only for a short while.

When the inside of your nose is tickled by mosquitoes, it is time to go! We had had all the fun we could stand. The two wine coolers from my pockets turned into mosquito repellant; I poured them over the kids. Maybe, what little alcohol they contained would offer some protection. We turned tail and ran back down the road.

In my many years of going to the river, I have never seen or heard mosquitoes like that. My memories of the lakes will be different from those of my daughters.

Now, family members venture to the Shamburger Lakes on weekends and holidays. At night, men stand around campfires and change the color of the flames.

Except when someone brings out a machine gun or a new rapid-fire 12 gauge shotgun for a demonstration, it is quite calm around the lakes. It is especially calm when the campfires have turned to ashes.

~~~~~~~~~~~~~~~~~~~~~~~~~~~

Misty notices the sound change to the gentle whine of asphalt as the Pump Station Lake bridge ends. Then, in less than three breaths, she again hears th-thump, th-thump, th-thump. She is now on the Sabine River Bridge.

Th-thump, th-thump, th-thump. Her headlights show something in the road, at the end of the bridge. It is not anything big. "Maybe a jacket," she says to herself as she slows down, straining to see.

William sits up, facing her. His eyes meet hers, and time is frozen for a split second. She screams and jerks the steering wheel, putting the car on two wheels, sliding onto the wrong side of the road. She regains control of her car, but not control of her senses. All she wants to do is run, run, run.

~~~~~~~~~~~~~~~~~~~~~~~~~~~

Today, she would quickly dial 911 on her cell phone and report the emergency. Or she would be in the middle of a text message and wonder what the extra th-thump was.

Tonight, however, she drives into Winona and pulls up to a pay phone. Zero is all her shaking hand can dial in pre-911 days.

"OPERATOR!" she screams into the phone. "There is a man sitting in the road! He was lying there, and just before I got to him, he sat up and looked right into my eyes. Oh, God, he looked right into my eyes!"

"The number to the Sheriff's Department is 593-53—"

"I'm on a pay phone! There's a man in the road!"

"Let me connect you to the Sheriff's Department."

"Smith County Sheriff's Office."

"There is a man sitting in the road! He's was lying there, and just before I got to him, he sat up and looked right into my eyes."

"What is your location?"

"I'm at a little gas station in Winona."

"Is the man lying in the road in Winona?"

"No! It was on a bridge outside of town, maybe a couple of miles."

"In what direction?"

"Direction! He looked right into my eyes!"

"Were you on 155 or FM 16?"

"155!" Misty says, shaking her head.

"That will be the Department of Public Safety," says the dispatcher. "I will connect you."

"Highway Patrol," said a new voice.

"There is someone in the road. He sat up and looked at me. I think I may have hit him."

"Are you on Highway 155?"

"Yes," she answered.

"It has been reported. An officer is en route."

A few more questions and answers and Misty hangs up the phone. She walks out of the phone booth and sits on an old wooden bench. She does not know eight years later a football player will burn up in his Mercedes ten feet from where she is sitting.

~~~~~~~~~~~~~~~~~~~~~~~~~~~~

Two major differences between a human and all the other animals that get run over by automobiles and trucks are the size of the victim and the thickness of the skin. Neither is an advantage to the human race. Human skin is rather frail in comparison to most hides and is easily torn apart as a body twists, turns, and rolls under a motor vehicle. As for size, a cow or horse usually gets knocked aside or over the top of a car, whereas a human fits nicely under most front bumpers. Dogs and cats, being fairly small, get most of their damage from tires. Many dogs and cats can be seen in the rearview mirror after rolling under a car, surviving and virtually unscathed. Some learn, and the ones that don't will suffer tire damage someday.

People do not fare as well under a car. We have long bones that snap like toothpicks under a two-thousand-pound auto-press. These sharp, jagged, broken bones become entangled with flesh as the body is rolled and crushed. The result is a crumpled pile of what used to be human.

~~~~~~~~~~~~~~~~~~~~~~~~~~~

Th-thump, th-thump, th-thump, came the car behind Misty. That one did not swerve. It did not miss William. Th-thump.

I am not sure if Misty hit William or not. I do know she and the driver of the next car will forever see the nightmare of a lump of clothing lying on a dark road turn into a living being, sitting up, eyes glowing in the headlights and looking at them eye to eye.

Accident or suicide? We will never know for sure. I ruled accident.

Chapter 9

Cinco de Mayo Party Time

Inquests #1250 and #640

The United States of America is considered the melting pot of the world, its residents coming from many different cultures, races, religions, and backgrounds. Some cultures melt and blend easier than do others.

I have always thought of the melting pot as a cooking utensil used in the making of a mulligan or stew, not a container for melting and mixing metals! I always thought about the large pots down on the river, hanging over an open flame, with anything and everything from squirrel to squash in them. I never cared much for stew and always wondered what the big deal was in using that analogy to describe America. I assumed the analogy suggested that Americans all come together to create a special flavor, the melting pot/stew pot giving off the sweet, spicy aroma of roasting chili peppers, spices, vegetables, and roast beef, or whatever unfortunate animal ended up in the pot. I could see some giant with a wooden paddle stirring the pot of American humanity — kind of cannibalistic.

The various cultures and people add spice to the stewpot. Many of those who venture into the "New World" expect to enjoy the benefits and privileges of American society while holding on to their own history and culture. Others come to America with the attitude the U.S.A. is in need of what they have to offer. Most are searching for a better life for themselves and their children. As immigrant generations take on the red, white, and blue, conflicts develop between the old and the new. While writing this book, I learned about another kind of "melting pot," as in a steel foundry. We are melting together to create a better metal/people rather than a better meal.

In some cultures, if the wife causes a problem, the solution is simply to beat the hell out of her. It is amazing to see the puzzled expression on the faces of some foreigners in jail when I say, "We don't do that here in America." Some Far East cultures brought with them a type of lottery. You play, you pay, or you suffer the price, which may mean a beating should you decide not to play. Then there is the drug culture, which has its own set of rules, by which laughter and feeling good can quickly turn to tears and death.

Texas is more like a salad: lettuce, tomatoes, onions — things plucked from gardens all over the world, then tossed together. Driving around Texas is like driving around the world. German, Asian, French, English, Czechoslovakian, African, Hispanic — you name it, we got it. The Gulf Coast, mountains, plains, the big thicket, swamps, deserts, pine forest, rolling hills and flatlands, all mingled with industry, farming, ranching, mining, and retirement centers; then add crude oil, and you have a recipe for Texas living. From Houston, the fourth largest city in the United States, to Winona, with a single blinking traffic light, there is a place for everyone. You can travel to "world locations" of Moscow, Paris, New London, Sudan, China, Germany, and Turkey; you can even go to Whitehouse (where I am the municipal judge) and never leave the state of Texas.

When you enter the Lone Star State, you are greeted with six flags: French, Spanish, Mexican, Texas, Confederate, and that of the United States. Each flag represents a nation that once claimed Texas. The Lone Star flag of the Texas Republic is now the only state flag that legally can fly at the same height as the Stars and Stripes. If the flags of the Indian Nations were added to "the six flags," there would be a hundred more. Most Native Texans will say their great-great-great grandmother was a full-blooded Cherokee/Caddo/Apache/Navaho or some other tribe of

Indian. It is seldom a great-great-grandfather; it always seems to be a mother of the past. If all the "great-greats" are accurate, we are really an Indian nation.

Throughout the year, many cultures celebrate their uniqueness. March 2 is Texas Independence Day. Some Texans give more reverence to this day than July 4, remembering the Alamo. Fall wakes up Oktoberfest. A large German immigration settled around Fredericksburg, like the Czechoslovakians settled around the city of West. German beer shipped all the way from Shiner, Texas, is consumed in mass quantities that rival the Oktoberfest celebrated in Europe. "Juneteenth," or Emancipation Day, originated in Galveston, Texas, and for more than a century, the state of Texas was the primary home of Juneteenth celebrations.

Cinco de Mayo (May 5) celebrations honor our neighbor to the south, Mexico, with a strong jalapeño flavor. Many people believe, incorrectly, that Cinco de Mayo is Mexico's Independence Day. Originally, it was a celebration of the day Mexican soldiers won a battle against French invaders. Now, it is a celebration of Hispanic pride and culture. Since the mid-1500s, with the founding of missions in such locations as Nacogdoches and San Antonio, the Spanish/Mexican influence has been cultivated in Texas. Cinco de Mayo has become a celebration of this influence. As during Oktoberfest, many are under the influence of *cerveza* (beer).

Inquest #1250

"Judge, we need you," the city police department dispatcher telephones to tell me. "1600 Guadalupe Street; looks like a suicide." It is eleven o'clock at night.

"I'm on my way," I reply.

Cinco de Mayo celebrations are happening all over the county. Hundreds of homes are cooking and eating tamales, enchiladas, chicken mole, chili, red sauce, and green sauce, and grilling everything you could imagine. Hispanic people like to eat, sing, dance, and shoot their guns during celebrations, especially Cinco de Mayo. The old-timers remember the days when there were no fireworks. Celebrating means taking your firearm, pointing it toward the sky, and firing away. Rifles, shotguns, pistols—the bigger the bang, the better.

At the house on Guadalupe Street, the celebration has stopped. I arrive to see brightly colored piñatas pregnant with candy, dangling from tree limbs. The piñatas wait to be batted around by blindfolded children, then explode with sweet rewards when one of the kids hits it just right. They gently sway with a light breeze, and all is quiet. The breeze brings aromas of various spices to my nose, reminding me of the many Hispanic weddings I have officiated.

~~~~~~~~~~~~~~~~~~~~~~~~~~

At Hispanic weddings, the magistrate or official is treated royally, often seated at the head of the table and served while others get in line for the Mexican feast. I am not sure if this is an expression of honor or if party-goers want me to finish and leave so they can do some serious drinking. I have officiated at several weddings where "I no speaky Spanish" and they "No hablan ingles." but when the ceremony is complete they are husband and wife, and the food is always wonderful. It is hard to come home and pretend to be hungry when Fae has a hot meal waiting.

~~~~~~~~~~~~~~~~~~~~~~~~~~

In the back yard on Guadalupe Street stands a small mountain of recently emptied beer cans. Many aren't quite empty and present the thick aroma of fermented hops. Alcohol and guns do not mix.

~~~~~~~~~~~~~~~~~~~~~~~~~~

Many arguments have been initiated by a drunk and ended with a gunshot. Then, realizing what happened and desperately regretting it, the drunk calls or goes to the police, with head in hands, tears in his eyes, "I killed him/her/them. I just wasn't thinking." (So much for the right to remain silent.) "Wasn't thinking" is exactly the result of too much alcohol.

~~~~~~~~~~~~~~~~~~~~~~~

Tonight, an old Mexican señor lies on his back in the grass with a blank stare; his eyes look to the dark, star-speckled sky above. His arms are stretched away from his body, at perpendiculars, forming a cross. One hand holds a beer can, the other, an old .32 revolver. A pool of blood forms a maroon halo on the ground beneath his head. There are no other notable injuries.

There is the possibility of a cover-up, a death made to look like a suicide. Somebody may have lost control. Someone was jealous, or a bet was lost or won, or someone owed money, or someone did not keep their word. Maybe someone lied, or lay with the wrong girl, or someone stole somebody's beer or dope. All of these are common motives to kill, especially if they are drinking and not thinking.

The exit wound, the size of a quarter, is in the top back of the man's head. The entrance wound is in the roof of his mouth. Entrance and exit wounds are very important in an investigation. Witnesses tell you what they think happened and what they think they saw. Wounds give you angles and possibilities, and they can verify or discredit what witnesses say.

~~~~~~~~~~~~~~~~~~~~~~~

A contact gunshot wound (GSW) leaves the markings of the barrel with a small amount of powder burn around the entry. As the distance from the barrel to the skin is increased, so is the diameter of the powder burn, until the distance is such that it would no longer be considered a contact GSW. Small-caliber pistols have less gunpowder, and thus less explosive gas. The bullet does the damage. In larger-caliber weapons, the explosive release of gases produced by ignition of the gunpowder can do more damage than the projectile in a contact GSW. A firecracker going off in your hand is painful, but not because of the impact of the paper compressed around the gunpowder. It hurts because the hand catches the resulting rapid expansion of the gases. A contact gunshot to the head with a large-caliber weapon is like a huge firecracker going off, except the skull and skin take the place of the paper.

Ten years ago, the general rule was men would shoot themselves in the head and women would go for the heart. This was because of vanity: Women were more concerned about the leftovers than men. More recently, men have become vain enough to shoot themselves in the chest. And women tend to shoot the men!

~~~~~~~~~~~~~~~~~~~~~~~~

This Cinco de Mayo celebration turns into a going-away party. There are many witnesses. The stories are the same, some in broken English and some in Spanish. Some party-goers are crying, and some are still in a daze.

"The party was going on and on," one of the victim's sons tells me. "Papa was laughin' and drinkin' and singin' and dancin'. He had much to drink and started having a problem standing up. Papa gets funny when he drinks too much. We took him to bed so he could lie down. Then, later, he stagger back outside and took a beer from that cooler over there. He pops the top on the beer and pulled a pistola. The pistola was stuck in his pants. It musta got hung on that old belt or something 'cause he had to fight to get it out. I thought he was going to shoot his . . . uh . . . uh. . . . I thought he was going to shoot himself. Then out it came! He's waving it in the air."

The son pauses, then completes his grim tale. "'EEEYYYAAAA!,' he yelled, and shot the gun in the air. Everybody all got quiet."

Inquest #640

It is strange how a party can change gears when someone comes out with a gun. On another inquest, young people are mixing with older people in a place in the woods. The place is known for parties, drugs, and the age mixture. Everyone is laughing, drinking, smoking, and enjoying the music. The priority at this party is to mix it up and have fun.

Billy, a twenty-year-old, walks out the sliding doors and onto the large wooden deck. In his hand is a small pistol, and he proceeds to point it indiscriminately from one person to another. A few people run, but most freeze, in total surprise. How fast things can change. Priories change when you do not know how long you are going to live.

"Are you scared?" he asks as he points the pistol between the eyes of each potential victim.

"Are you scared to die?" he says, grimacing as he sees the faces melt in fear before him.

"I'm not!" he says, pointing the gun to his head and pulling the trigger, leaving friends and family with scars that will never go away. His mother never accepted that her son could do such a thing. A friend was so moved that he got a tattoo, "In memory of Billy" across his shoulder. I read it a few months later when I did his inquest. He joined Billy with a shotgun blast to his own head down on the Sabine River.

On the other hand, some say was it all a cover-up and the "friend" was the shooter in both cases? Maybe Mom is right.

~~~~~~~~~~~~~~~~~~~~~~~~

"'EEEYYYAAAA!' echoed down Guadalupe Street as Papa yelled. Then he takes a drink of beer and rocks back on his heels, holding the pistola, high over his head, and BANG, like he was shootin' the moon or somp'n. Den he take another drink of beer and another bang. Each time he rock back and forth a little more on his heels. We all just look at him."

The man pauses, then continues the story. "As the can of beer got lower and lower, he had to lean his head farther and farther back. He also rocked farther and farther back with each shot (both drink and gun). We yelled, 'Papa! You can't do that here. We are in the city.' But he don't listen. He keeps on drinkin' and shootin.'

"Then he stops. He looks at the beer, and then he looks at the gun. He looked confused. He looked at the gun then looked at the beer.'EEEYYYAAAA!,' he yelled."

He raises his beer can, pointing it to the sky, the moon, the stars, and all the Comancheros who have gone before him. He places the gun in his mouth and turns it up, possibly thinking he is sucking down the last sip of his alcoholic beverage. Then, bang. It is his eternal Cinco de Mayo.

After listening to the witnesses and viewing the evidence, my ruling: "Gun Shot Wound to the head; accidental."

Chapter 10

I Wish

Inquest #936

Question: what does a nylon rope or belt; towel; swing rope; extension cord; quarter-inch steel cable; quarter-inch plastic-coated steel cable; clothes line; bed sheet; exercise machine cable; glittering red, white, and blue metallic fringe pennant streamer; telephone cord, parachute cord; USB computer cable; pair of pants; shoestring; and terry cloth robe belt all have in common?

~~~~~~~~~~~~~~~~~~~~~~~

Summer camp is the closest thing to an adventure many kids will ever have. It is a time for them to venture away from home and share excitement and misery with other kids. It is living outside their familiar room, house, and bed. While at summer camp many find out where and how they will fit into society. Some will be leaders, some followers, and some will be wallflowers or onlookers.

Lakeview Methodist Camp was my annual summer pilgrimage, grades six through eleven, except that one summer at the Baptist Camp. The differences between the Methodists and the Baptists are told in a million jokes. Both summer camps were good, but the Methodist camp had one thing the Baptist camp did not—GIRLS! With two older sisters, I knew about girls and had even had a girlfriend (or two or three), but summer camp awakened the knowledge of the difference between the two sexes. For two summers, my camp love was with Marilee Thomas. She was a seventh and eighth grader's dream, a blonde beauty who gave new dimensions to swimming pool time ($36 \times 24 \times 36$ divide by 2). As we walked around the lake, we practiced electrified hand holding and then, that first meaningful kiss. I had played doctor and even explored a little with the opposite sex, but this was different; just being with Marilee felt good.

We wrote love letters during our times apart. We picked our star in the sky, knowing that although we were separated by distance, we were joined together as we gazed upon that star. Every night, if I was not watching TV or doing something else, our very souls would be tied together by that solitary star, our star. But the distance from my house to her house may as well have been measured in light-years. Letters became fewer and fewer. Young love's light flickered, and then went out, to be replaced by another.

Inquest #936

"Never swim alone" — the twelve-year-old boy can hear it in his head. But the swimming hole is sitting there, empty, as the sun rises in the cloudy eastern sky. Johnny stands outside the camp cabins on a hill, with not another soul in sight. Everyone else is getting ready for breakfast. He can see across Lake Tyler, or at least the jagged finger of the lake before him. Jet skis, party barges, and water skiers all have plenty of room. At this hour, only a few bass fishermen are on the water.

The campground swimming area is a very small part of the lake. There is no sand beach leading to the water, and a large gray wooden pier goes out into the lake, providing a place for sunning and swimming. Much of the shoreline is green grass and ancient giant oaks. Most of the bank is steep, with a five-foot drop-off to the water. In one tall tree, a rope is tied to a limb thirty feet up. The inch-thick rough hemp rope dangles over the water, with a large knot at the bottom. The boy watches the knot sway back and forth in the breeze, like a watch on a chain, hypnotizing.

He has seen the other kids take the leap. They swing out over the water and drop. Some will hold their arms tightly by their sides, pointing their toes down to pierce the water smoothly and leave only a ripple. Others will finesse themselves into a headfirst dive, while others flip, flop, and fling arms and legs; they all will plunge into the wet coolness below. Some will jump high enough to catch the knot between their legs. Crossing their legs and locking their feet into place, they will sit and swing until those waiting in line yell, "Come on, it's our turn!"

Twice he had stood in line, wanting to make the jump. Twice he stood on the bank looking across the water and measuring the distance to the rope. Twice the other kids called him "Chicken!" as he turned and walked away.

~~~~~~~~~~~~~~~~~~~~~~~~~~

As I approached age thirty, I pumped gas during the summer and went to college the rest of the year. While I worked at the service station one day, a sleek red Mercedes pulled up to the pumps. I walked up to the darkly tinted window. (Note to younger readers: Not too long ago, most gas stations provided an attendant who would put gas in the car, check the oil, wash the windshield, and even check your tires, all at no extra charge! The transition to a "pump it yourself" or "self service" has cost many a high school job and not reduced gas prices a bit.)

The window tint made the glass a mirror. I could see my reflection as I looked at the driver's side window. A long, curly beard and wavy hair thrown over my shoulders looked back. Hair that had been cut off during my Army years had been allowed to grow — with a vengeance. I was a hippie, dressed in a greasy Texaco uniform. "You can trust your car to the man who wears the star" — and who carries Herman in his pocket.

Herman was my albino pet mouse. One time, he poked his little head out of my beard and caused a lady to drive off without getting her gas. My sister's cat put an end to Herman's life. He lived with me for only two weeks. Politically, he will live with me the rest of my life. (Every election someone will say, "He had rats in his hair." My answer? "Now I have neither rats nor hair.")

My image disappeared as the window motored down, and a young lady came into view. At least she looked younger than I was.

"Can I help you?" I said.

"Do you have unleaded?" she asked. (Note to younger readers: Have you ever wondered why we do not have just "gas" instead of "unleaded" or "lead-free" gas? The world once put lead into gas to make cars run better. There was gas that did not have lead; it was called drip gas and was cheap but made your motor clatter and clang, and sometimes keeps running after you turned it off. It was good for cook stoves and heaters. Environmentalists probably looked at gas station attendees and felt they were breathing too much lead. Gas companies learned that by not adding lead, they could charge more for a gallon of gas. Auto companies learned they could build a whole new fleet of unleaded or lead-free cars! There was also petrol we called "Ethel," but that is another story.)

"Yes, ma'am, we have regular unleaded and super unleaded. The super unleaded has an additive, probably gold."

People, like cars, come in many different makes and models. Some catch your eye and cause you to look twice and evaluate just what you are seeing. This sophisticated blonde definitely required a second look, and she also took a second look at me.

"Fill it up with super," she said.

I found the gas cap under the license plate, removed it, stuck the nozzle in, and wondered what I would see if given the opportunity to wash her windshield.

The door opened, and a pair of black spiked patent-leather high heels connected to a pair of shapely legs reached for the asphalt pavement. The legs seemed to go on forever as they oozed from the car. The woman soon stood before me, sun at her back, creating a bright halo around her. My eyes squinted at the vision of a shapely, five foot eight dream that could have come from one of the *Playboy* magazines I would get (and quickly hide) on my teenage birthdays. The little black miniskirt worked its way down to cover the tops of her thighs. I was "filling 'er up" (the car with gas, that is).

The spiked heels clicked on the pavement as she walked toward me. She looked out of place in Winona on this hot summer day. The Mercedes made slight "tink, tink" noises as it cooled, and the gas flowed. Twenty years later, another Mercedes would take out this gas pump in a ball of fire.

"Do you know a Shamburger who lives here in Winona?" she asked. I instantly recognized that voice and the deep blue eyes. It was Marilee, and I began to melt. It was hot, and now would be a good time to go swimming! I could drive off and swim forever in those deep blue eyes.

"Yes," I said. "I am a Shamburger."

"Really?" she asked. "His name is Mitch. Do you have a son about my age?"

I smiled. "Nooooo," I said slowly, thinking. A son about my age? If she was kidding, I was not laughing. If she was serious, had I aged or slipped into some other world of which she had no knowledge. Was I beyond the recognition of my youth?

"But I do know Mitch," I continued. "He has been traveling all over the world and just got out of the military. He is doing fine, going to college. He's been married about eight years now and has a daughter named Marilee." All this was all true except the part about the daughter; I had a son named Noah Mitchell.

She placed the tip of her index finger on her lips, painted deep red, and her thumb rested under her chin in the thinking position.

"R-e-a-l-l-l-l-y," she said, stretching the r-e-a-l and putting too many l's in the word. She turned and went back to the coolness of her car. The door closed and the window slid up, to hold in the cool air, and I wondered if I had put one over on her, or she had put one over on me.

The transaction necessitated her signing the credit card receipt, and I stood by, waiting. She lowered the window and looked up, with a wondering sort of smile. Her eyes said the jig was up. She signed and handed back the receipt.

"Tell him an old camp friend stopped by to say hello, should you ever see him. My name is Marilee. I have a son named Mitch."

The transaction was completed. We both moved on.

I went back inside the station and walked into the dingy restroom. I looked into the faded mirror hanging over a porcelain sink stained with rust from its water. I saw a twenty-six-year-old hippie. Then Herman climbed out of my pocket and onto my shoulder. He turned around and sat down, and his beady red eyes looked into the mirror too.

Harry Chapin sings a song about a taxi driver picking up an old girlfriend. I know how he felt.

~~~~~~~~~~~~~~~~~~~~~~~~~~

Johnny looks at the empty pier, knowing it will later be full of kids laughing, swimming, and playing. Some will take turns leaping off the bank and catching the thick rope in their hands.

But swimming comes later, and for a twelve-year–old, it is an eternal three hours away. Here and now, this morning, there is no line. "I could swing as long as I want," Jimmy thinks. There is even the possibility of swinging and dropping back on the earth without even getting wet! No one would even have to know about it.

~~~~~~~~~~~~~~~~~~~~~~~~~~

When I was in my school-aged but pre-teen years, some of my best times were spent in the woods. Alone, I would venture into the Winona wilderness with Mom's butcher knife and slay dragons, save princesses, or explore the deep, dark jungle. If a friend, or two or three, would join in, we would fight Germans and/or the imaginary invaders of our territory.

Often I would return home wet and muddy. Once I returned without Mom's long butcher knife. There is something about trees, vines, creeks, mud, water, and woods that draw kids and adults into them. Maybe we have a primal instinct to get back to Mother Nature.

Large vines hung from the treetops. We cut the vines for two reasons. The first was to allow us to swing like Tarzan, screaming the bloodcurdling, animal-summoning Tarzan yell. Cutting the vine meant killing the vine. A good vine would last a week or more before it came loose from the branches above to drop you into the water and muck below. The second reason for cutting the vines was that someone told us you could smoke a grapevine.

Every tree in my yard had a tree house in it at one time or another, and each was equipped with a rope for climbing and swinging.

~~~~~~~~~~~~~~~~~~~~~~~~~~~~~

Johnny walks down to the swimming area and looks around. A few people are stirring, but no one pays any attention to him. The rope looks farther out than he remembered. Yesterday kids were jumping out on the rope, some smaller than he. He thought it would be easier to swing with no one around, but in truth, challenging activities often seem harder when you are alone. The goal is to catch the rope as high as possible, straddle it, and then slide down into the knot saddle. The plan is to get a running start, then leap at the very edge of the bank, jump high, reach high, and grab hold.

~~~~~~~~~~~~~~~~~~~~~~~~~~~~~

Life is a risk-taking adventure, to some more than to others. As we grow older we become more aware of the consequences of the risks we are taking. On the ledge of a cliff in the Rocky Mountains, I remember how my heart throbbed when my ten-year-old daughter, Lena, wearing flip-flops, hopped three feet out to stand on a rock. The surface area where she landed was only a square foot. The space around her was a sheer drop and certain death. Her fond memories of this event are matched by ones that were frightening to me; even though I could not count the many times I have faced the real possibility of my own death.

Could we or should we avoid the experiences of life that may cause pain? Physically and emotionally, we take risks all the time. "Risk taking" for no other reason than to have that experience is a uniquely human concept.

We may want to raise our children in cocoons, protected until we turn them loose to fly away, but children do not learn to walk without falling down. The value of a friend is not realized until "a friend in need is a friend indeed." Love without pain is cheap. One cannot experience standing on top of the world without the battle, and risk, of climbing to the mountaintop.

~~~~~~~~~~~~~~~~~~~~~~~~

Johnny runs as fast as he can. He jumps as high as he can and reaches as far as he can. His hands grasp the rope, and he feels the rope glide perfectly between his outstretched legs. He grips hard but is not strong enough to hold himself. He begins to slide down the rope. His rear begins to pucker, and he crosses his legs. The knot takes hold as it meets his rear, and he sits on it. He is locked onto the rope. The wind stirs his hair as he quietly glides through the air. He leans back confidently, pulling the rope with his hands to make the pendulum swing higher and higher. Back and forth he flies, feeling those brief moments of weightlessness, reaching pinnacle after pinnacle. Higher and higher he goes. In all the days of camp he has seen no one reach the heights he now enjoys. He is kicking and pulling back when the ringing of the breakfast bell invades his adventure.

"Maybe I won't get in trouble if I can get to the mess hall in time," he says aloud. No one can hear him, but maybe by saying and hearing it, he can make it true.

He stops rocking and pulling to let the swing slow. He

looks down while over the water and sees fish. He knew of the "nibble screams" kids—especially girls—made as they made contact with fish. Now, looking into the undisturbed waters of the swimming hole, he realizes that he had no idea there are so many fish there, or how big they are. This vision moves below him in slow motion. Then he sees the green grass below; he is back over land. He spreads his legs and lets go of the rope. He tries to adjust his body to land feet first, but the effort only causes him to look like a wiggle worm flying through the air, blindly trying get somewhere. Ker-plunk! He hits the ground, nearly feet first, but at an angle that leaves him flat on his back. He lies there for a few seconds that feels like several minutes. "I am OK," he thinks, then springs to his feet and begins running to the mess hall. He slows to a walk as he approaches his cabin mates and slips into the chow line.

"Where have you been?" It is the low voice of the adult counselor.

"Nowhere," he says, trying to control his heavy breathing.

"Well, let's don't go 'nowhere' again." The counselor smiles and puts his hand on Johnny's shoulder. Johnny feels the strong grip of the calloused hand that next week might be hammering nails or driving a tractor. Johnny feels a little older, like they are both men.

"This has got to be the best day of my life!" the twelve-year-old boy thinks.

~~~~~~~~~~~~~~~~~~~~~~~~~

Returning from overseas and leaving the military, I found myself again at Lakeview summer camp. The Reverend Bert Bagley persuaded Fae and me into assisting as counselors for seventh grade camp. The older Methodist preacher, "Big John," was serving his last year as camp director. He was grooming Brother Bert into the position. After that year we were hooked. For several years Fae and I made the pilgrimage. In later years, Fae stayed home, to raise our own kids, while I continued for one week each summer, playing guitar and working with the kids at camp. It is amazing how much one can learn when immersed in a pool of seventh grade boys and girls.

Politics and obligations, mandatory schooling, and other activities eventually took the place of Lakeview summer camps. I will always treasure those moments as a camper and as a counselor. I can still see the white cross planted on an island out in the lake, the foggy morning mist on the glassy water surrounding it. The Reverend Bert Bagley is now the senior pastor at Moody Memorial United Methodist Church in Galveston.

How I Wish

"The parables Jesus told were true stories!" Mom says, during a heated discussion about that Sunday's sermon. "The preacher is wrong to say they are just illustrations and may not have actually happened!"

"Mom, the preacher said there is truth in the parables."

"But he did not say the parables were true stories. There is a difference. Jesus would be a liar if the stories were not true," she adamantly continued.

Then Dad, who did not even go to church that day, spoke up.

"Time has no relevance to Jesus. He sees the past, present, and future. He told of a seed falling on fertile soil, and a woman searching for a lost coin. The actual events He spoke of in the parables may have happened in the past or in the future, or they may be happening right now."

Like the parables of Jesus, I am sure that somewhere, during some time, this story is true. A full life is made of such experiences. I hope kids and counselors will return to the real world from camps, trips, and adventures with wonderful memories of times spent together and with renewed hopes for the future and things to come. I hope somewhere in the world, every night, at least two people are gazing at the same star. I wish all stories had a happy ending.

~~~~~~~~~~~~~~~~~~~~~~~~~~~~

Johnny runs as fast as he can. He jumps as high as he can and reaches as far as he can. He grasps the rope high enough to allow plenty of slack, but the knot flings outward, like a whip, flipping around. He twists his body, trying to wriggle free, and the rope responds by making a loop that slips over his head, the knot dangling down his back. It takes both hands to hold on as he swings back and forth. He does not know what to do. His arms ache, and he feels the rope slip through his fingers. He lets go of the rope, hoping to soon feel the water or earth beneath him. He falls three feet before the rope snaps tight around his neck.

And so, what do a nylon rope or belt; towel; extension cord; quarter-inch steel cable; quarter-inch plastic-coated steel cable; clothes line; bed sheet; exercise machine cable; glittering red, white, and blue metallic fringe pennant streamer; telephone cord; parachute cord; USB computer cable; pair of pants, shoestring, and terry cloth robe belt — and a swing rope over the water at Lake Tyler — all have in common?

I have seen every one of them hold up a lifeless body.

Chapter 11

Down a Well

Inquest #320

Calvin, a big black guy with the mind of a child, has gone missing. He is often seen walking the country roads, day or night, but has not been seen for more than two weeks. He has a history of wandering around, but he never wanders off too far. His cousin said of him that "You might look up and see him at a window or in the doorway, just standin' and a-grinnin.'" But he was Calvin, and everyone knew he was harmless, at least everyone in the neighborhood.

~~~~~~~~~~~~~~~~~~~~~~~~~~~~

In my neck of the woods, it is not uncommon for Mama and Papa to give a spot of land next door to daughter and son-in-law to put in a mobile home, thus helping to continue raising their twenty-year-old kids. After all, their son built that nice house on the front of the property next to Granny's house. Sometimes you think you are way out in the woods, in the middle of nowhere, and then you find yourself in the middle of a family community. Instead of relying on wills and probate courts, families just build houses on the "old home place."

~~~~~~~~~~~~~~~~~~~~~~~~~~~~

A manhunt with dogs and a volunteer posse searches

for Calvin. The Smith County Sheriff is proud of the horses, dogs, and manpower ready for search-and-rescue missions or to find the occasional criminal who might take off on foot. Drug dogs, cadaver dogs, tracking dogs, even pet dogs—the sheriffs had them all. Once, while tracking a criminal, they found the hound dogs tied to a tree. The fleeing criminal had been an inmate in the jail, and as a trustee he had cared for and helped train the dogs. They must have been happy to see him and probably were confused as he walked away, leaving them tied to a tree.

Calvin is now a footnote at the shift change in the Sheriff's Department. The family hopes he will just mosey in and sit down for supper one night, like nothing has happened. "Pass the taters," he would say. But that was not to be.

~~~~~~~~~~~~~~~~~~~~~~~~

"Judge, I think they found that guy that has been missing," says Gilyn, the court clerk.

It is a hot summer day, and a fresh, dry shirt is soaking wet in the time it takes to tie your shoes. Shirts get wet because the water, or sweat, has nowhere to go. The air is heavy with moisture even though it had not rained in weeks. Some places keep tally of the days when temperatures are above 100 degrees. This is just another week of triple-digit temperatures. Yankees don't even know what hot is! Heat and humidity are really not good for a dead body.

~~~~~~~~~~~~~~~~~~~~~~~~

I walk up to the scene, and Deputy Ramsey is interviewing Papa.

"We noticed the water started tasting funny a few days ago, and now we can't even drink it," Papa says. "I figured somethin' musta died in the well, and when I saw that slab o' concrete pushed over to the side . . . well, that concrete is heavy. Ain't no little varmint gonna move it and fall in! It would take two strong men, or someone like Calvin. You know, he wasn't strong in the head, but he was a strong kid. Good Lord a' mercy! Good Lord, have mercy!"

Five big red fire trucks are lined up, bumper to bumper, on a dirt drive at the top of the hill, creating a semicircle. The red clay bank of the hill matches the trucks. Like an amphitheater, at the bottom of the hill, center stage, is the well. A concrete cylinder about three feet tall and four feet across sticks out of the ground, with the top laid to the side. Fire and police personal take turns looking into the abyss and quickly step back. Soon, it's my turn to look. A deputy uses a long flashlight, which sometimes doubles as a baton, to shoot a beam of light thirty feet to the bottom. I can see the top of a head, broad shoulders, and a man's chest. There is just enough room for Calvin to bob up and down in the water. It does not take long to observe the scene and take in the details, so I quickly step away from the well and the smell.

~~~~~~~~~~~~~~~~~~~~~~~~~

Science teaches that smell is the strongest of the five senses. It also connects powerfully to memories. When I smell bacon cooking, memories of my mother's breakfasts immediately come to mind. Other smells stir the olfactory nerves and can conjure strong reactions. The odor of decomposing man or beast burns into the brain. Riding my motorcycle, I can catch a whiff of decay and know that something that used to be no longer is.

My first experience with the aroma of human death came early in my career as a new justice of the peace. I was still on the Winona Independent School Board and had received a new black jacket with "Winona Wildcats" written in gold letters on the back. During a football game, I was called to do an inquest. The death was due to natural causes, and the body had been there a while. The man was found in a little travel trailer off a county road, where he had been waiting, with dogs and cats, for three or four days for someone to find him. The animals and the body combined made a putrid atmosphere. I put on my tough show and snickered at the officers who couldn't go in. On my way home, I noticed that my jacket had absorbed the smell. I took it off when I got back to the game. I noticed my mustache had absorbed the smell. It is hard not to smell your own mustache. When I got home, I took a shower. I had the jacket cleaned several times; it was never the same.

The memory has returned time and time again as the familiar odor floats in the air. Some judges light up a cigar to cover the odor. Old Judge Cashion probably used his for just this purpose.

~~~~~~~~~~~~~~~~~~~~~~~~~~

The stench in the well is one of the worst I have ever encountered; the odor has nowhere to go but up. The stagnant air at the bottom of the well makes it worse. Water can aid in the process of decomposition, unless the water is cold, and this water was not cold. The men take turns trying to get a rope around the body or otherwise rig something to pull Calvin's body out of the well. Chief Johnny Beddingfield of the Smith County Sheriff's Department is in charge assisting Ralph East, of the Texas Parks and Wildlife. Because it is a drowning the game warden, technically, they are in charge.

"You might want to think about the rope," I tell Chief Beddingfield. "He has been down there a while, and if you get the rope only around his neck—well, I don't think his neck will hold him. Anyway, it's been a long time since there has been a lynching around here, and we really don't need one now!" I sweep my hand toward the crowd gathering in the amphitheater.

"Hold up!" Chief Beddingfield calls out to the firemen. He explains the situation to the Allen Adams, the fire chief.

Next, they try to grapple the body using ropes and hooks, poles with hooks, and whatever else they can come up with that might grab hold of clothing. The shirt he is been wearing is no match for the heavy body it covers. It rips into shreds, and Calvin just bobbed in the water at the bottom of the well.

The big firemen usually get the big jobs—carrying equipment, working the wrecking bar, lifting hoses full of water, and carrying victims. This time, however, it is a little guy who draws the short straw.

Allen gathers his firemen around and explains, "We need someone to put on an air pack. We will tie his feet to a rope, and the rope will be connected to the winch line." He points to a wrecker-hoist combination that stands ready, with an A-frame over the center of the well.

"The wrecker will let you down headfirst. Hopefully, the winch will stop in the proper position and you can slip a rope around the body."

The "tunnel rat" (as they were called in Vietnam) is to do this without the air pack falling off (they are not made to wear upside down) and with the mask staying in place, although the worker will have to use both hands over his head, working upside down.

"Any volunteers?" the chief asks as his eyes peruse the fifteen firemen standing by, listening—and smelling.

~~~~~~~~~~~~~~~~~~~~~~~~~~

I will state here and now that I have the utmost respect for professional fire fighters. They are paid to do a dangerous job and perform where most of us do not want to go. Even before the falling of the World Trade Center, which starkly dramatized the lives of these heroes, those who have been pulled from flames, water, or other life-and-death situations have long attested the value of the fire fighter.

I admire volunteer fire fighters even more, though that is barely possible. They are the "Minute Men" of today. Many years ago, the Winona Volunteer Fire Department was called to the Winona School for a grass fire. Children watched as the one-fireman operation proudly displayed his fire-killing ability putting out the grass fire around him—as the fire truck went up in flames! Today our volunteer fire department is made up of men and women who are well trained. They have expensive equipment and communication technology. They are as dedicated as their paid counterparts and are required to obtain much of the same training. Most pay out of their own pockets for the privilege of serving others. Some pay even more by adding stress to a marriage and being on call twenty-four/seven. Too many pay with their lives. Whatever their motivations, I have never asked a fireman to do something and been refused.

~~~~~~~~~~~~~~~~~~~~~~

"It's my case," says Game Warden Ralph East stepping forward as he speaks. What is his motive? Maybe he wants to show the others how brave he is. Maybe he is volunteering so one of them will not have to go. Maybe he simply sees a need and is ready to fill it. "Duty calls."

As he is suiting up for the descent, I think about the story of the "big truck stuck under the bridge." Engineers and members of the highway department were ready to get a big crane or use a bulldozer to rip a truck out from under the bridge, hoping the damage would not be severe. A little boy suggested, "Why don't you just let the air out of the tires?" Sometimes, there just has to be a better way of doing things, and sometimes it takes an outsider to see it.

"Chief," I say, "I am not looking to be a hero here, but I was just thinking. He is bobbing up and down, which means he is floating. Water seeps into a well. If we can put water in the well faster than it seeps out, we can fill it up and float him out."

"That is the craziest damned thing I have ever heard!" The chief shakes his head and then yells, "Get those fire trucks down here!"

Four fire hoses go down the circular well. The concrete casing narrows as the well goes deeper. It is a close fit, and difficult working the nozzles beside and below the body from the top of the well. One hose remains up top. The fire trucks rumble as their pumps began to do their work. Bubbles mix with turbulence at the bottom of the well, and then the water settles down, with the nozzles below the water line. One fireman holds a nozzle, shooting a strong jet stream down the well and against the concrete casing of the well. The goal is to pour as much water as quickly as possible to raise the water level. The body begins to rise. It takes effort and strong arms to control a fire hose shooting out somewhere between 50 and 150 gallons of water per minute. The fireman moves the nozzle changing the stream to another direction.. The stream of water shoots straight down the well. Getting hit by a jet stream of water at high pressure is not good for a healthy body, and it is *really* not good for a corpse that has been decomposing for a few days.

"Hold it!" Immediate cries come from several people peering into the top of the well. The hoses are shut off. Flashlights point downward. Streams of light replace the stream of water. Something white is shining where Calvin's hair used to be. He is just fifteen feet from the top now, halfway up from where he started.

"Easy now!" the fire chief says, and the filling resumes, this time a little more carefully.

When the body is less than a foot from the top, one of the fire fighters wraps a rope around the body, under the arms. The winch truck becomes useful after all. With a click of a switch, the motor whirs, and the remains of Calvin rise out of the well, ripe and swollen, swinging and swaying, but still intact. A cheer erupts from those standing around the well.

"I was real glad to see your plan work," said Officer East. "I was dreading the decent to the bottom of that well."

Calvin's body is laid in a black plastic body bag, which is zipped tight and taken to the forensic center.

~~~~~~~~~~~~~~~~~~~~~~~~~~

Water will last for a long time. Water is one of the main reasons we have life on this earth. More than 70 percents of the human body consists of water. No living thing — plant, animal, or whatever else science may call life — is totally devoid of water. It takes electricity or some chemical reaction to change a molecule of water into its elements of hydrogen and oxygen or combine it with other elements to form another substance. When water evaporates into the air, it leaves behind impurities to become clean again, but the molecule of water remains the same.

It may join with other molecules of like kind and return as a drop of rain or join 100,000,000,000,000,000,000 water molecules that make up a typical snowflake. Water is filtered by soaking its way through sands or running along streams. Contaminants may be picked up along the way, but these are cleaned out when nature recycles the water again and again.

The water you drink may contain the same H_2O molecule that once quenched the thirst of a dinosaur. It may have traveled over Niagara Falls and around the world several times before joining the ice cube in your glass of tea. It may be the same water Jesus was baptized with, or the water that passed through His lips as he drank the water offered by the woman at the well almost 2,000 years ago. It may once have rested, with Calvin, in the bottom of East Texas water well.

~~~~~~~~~~~~~~~~~~~~~~~~~~~~~

The man hunt for Calvin is over. He and his family now can rest in peace.

Chapter 12

Ray Jones

Inquest #848

Note: I performed inquests and signed the Certificates of Death for my father, my brother-in-law, my niece, my friends, and other family members. I do it because I know I can do the job. This story may seem sad, but actually it reflects the joy and support within my family.

When my children were experiencing dating and driving, I could not help but think of their safety, especially when my phone would ring and the kids were not at home. This was brought "close to home" when one of my mentors and my friend, Judge Mary Guthrie, was called to an inquest at the hospital. A drunk illegal alien had run over a motorcycle. The cyclist lasted long enough to get to the emergency room, but the effort to maintain his life was futile. Judge Guthrie walked up to the Medical Center Emergency Room counter. The receptionist handed her a billfold she recognized. It was her son who lay dead in the emergency room.

Brother-in-Law Ray Jones

Evie Leola McClenny Shamburger, known fondly as LoLo, was correctly accused of having another baby when the last one started school. In those days, seven was the age to start public school, and six or seven years separate my sisters Perry Jo, the oldest, from Gerry Sue, and her from the late-life baby, Thomas Mitchell.

I am the youngest and the only son. As I rode the bus to the first grade, Perry Jo had already graduated from high school. Suzie was in junior high. We all attended Winona schools, from beginning to the end. With three kids, Mom had at least one child attending the Winona schools for twenty-seven consecutive years, beating my own household by four years.

Perry and Suzie married, moved, and had babies.

Perry Jo (named after her grandfather) left Winona with the last name Jackson and came back with a new husband, Marvin Miller, and with two boys and a girl: Arden, Jeff, and Deadra (DeDe). Soon came baby Marlee, and life was sweet. Later came another husband, Ray Jones, and a final baby with him, daughter Morgan. Perry is a two-time widow.

Perry Jo is about as close to a chain smoker as one can get without lighting one from another. She has come a long way from being the teenage daughter who cried and pleaded to her mother, "Those cigarettes are going to kill you!"

Mom has not smoked in close to sixty years and has given up trying to convince Perry Jo to stop, but she still manages to complain. Perry Jo now works with Marlee, owner of the Back Porch Restaurant in Winona. When she is not helping out, she spends a lot of time watching the sun rise on the Texas Gulf Coast at Rollover Pass.

Sister Suzie has outlasted two husbands (who are still alive) and is working on a third. She lives on the West Coast and visits her three kids Jerome, Connie, Anntoinette (Twan) and grandkids scattered from Arizona to California.

As for me, I have been married only once and, if figured in dog years, I have been married longer than I have been alive.

~~~~~~~~~~~~~~~~~~~~~~~~~~~

The new millennium began with celebration and hype. First there was the question, "Did the new millennium, the twenty-first century, start in 2000, or did it begin in 2001?"

Logic said 2000 and mathematics said 2001; the majority decided the celebration would be New Year's Eve at the end of 1999. Predictions of mass confusion, computer crashes, power grid failures, and the end of the world fortunately did not come to pass. Many people were disappointed when Monday came and they all had to go back to work. The biggest problem was that a gazillion written forms had blanks ready to be filled in, with 19___ already in place. Many forms were changed to read 2____, so these forms will be good for the entire millennium. For once, people were smarter than computers: *People* can tell the difference between a one-year-old baby and someone a 101 years old. A government computer tried to tell me I would not be born until 2052. I responded, "Fine; that's when I will start paying taxes."

For me, Y2K was a record year for inquests. The first two months were filled with departing souls, many of whom survived by sheer willpower long enough to live into the new era. For my sister, Perry Jo, the months of June and July made the year 2000 one that will live in infamy.

~~~~~~~~~~~~~~~~~~~~~~~~~~~~

"Get over here quick! It's Ray, and he's not breathing!" It is Perry Jo. Her deep grainy voice, from years of smoking, comes out slowly, one word at a time. She is trying to control her emotions, but the shaking voice of distress reveals her panic. She has already called 911. I am next on her emergency call list.

"I'm twelve minutes away," I reply. Winona volunteers are already en route to her home.

~~~~~~~~~~~~~~~~~~~~~~~~~~~~

Running through the screen porch and into the open-space house, I see members of the Volunteer Fire Department performing CPR (cardiopulmonary resuscitation). Perry Jo is sitting at the dining table on a white wicker chair. She buries her face in a towel. She sobs in anger and desperation, "Not again!"

The fire fighters focus on Ray, lying on the concrete floor. A fireman is kneeling by his side. The heel of his right hand is on Ray's sternum, or breast bone; the other hand is stacked on top, and both are pumping.

"One, two, three, four, five," the pumper counts under his breath, but loudly enough that the team works in rhythm. You can hear the effort in his voice as he pushes and counts at the same time. "Twenty-eight, twenty-nine, thirty."

Another fire fighter, a woman, tilts Ray's head back with one hand, to hyperextend the neck. The other hand pinches his nose closed. Then face-to-face, mouth-to-mouth, the rescue worker makes an airtight seal, breathing for Ray and forcing his chest to rise, twice. Then her hand goes from the nose to the carotid artery, feeling for the faint throb of the compressions and hoping for a natural pulse. Between breaths and during compressions, she listens, waiting for a gasp or cough from Ray. She watches his skin color and for any pupil reaction—any sign of life.

~~~~~~~~~~~~~~~~~~~~~~~~~

The American Heart Association provides the guidelines for teaching CPR. The lay rescuer should open the airway and check for normal breathing. If no normal breathing is detected, the rescuer should give two rescue breaths. Immediately after delivery of the rescue breaths, the rescuer should begin cycles of thirty chest compressions and two ventilations and use an A.E.D. (automated external defibrillator) as soon as one is available.

~~~~~~~~~~~~~~~~~~~~~~~

The room is spacious. The kitchen, the dining area, the television along with two couches and a recliner, a computer hutch, and another table with additional seating are all in the open area. Ray designed the exterior walls, which are completely made of glass panels. The house is surrounded by trees and hills. The open view to the outside, the trees, bird feeders, vines, and flowers, makes standing in the room like standing in the middle of nature itself. Ray is lying by a circular fireplace in the center of the room.

I work my way through the fire fighters to take my turn at CPR. A white plastic pharyngeal airway parts blue lips. Ray is cool to the touch, and his pupils are fixed and dilated. None of these signs is good. He may be gone, but we are not ready for him to go and not ready to give up.

~~~~~~~~~~~~~~~~~~~~~~~

When doing emergency CPR, you meet the patient skin to skin, breath to breath. You blow life-giving oxygen from your lungs into the patient's. Even with the best technique, some air will go into the stomach. Chest compressions often break ribs, and it is common for the patient to vomit during the process. If you're lucky, it is between breaths. One of the duties of the airway performer is to keep the airway clear. Some who do CPR vow they will never do it again. Because of AIDS and other communicable diseases, precautions are taken and equipment is available to lessen exposure. Most fire fighters, without a thought for themselves, will instinctively and immediately rush to provide cardiopulmonary resuscitation to save a life, even a dog's life.

~~~~~~~~~~~~~~~~~~~~~~~

We work on Ray until the ambulance arrives with a defibrillator and monitor.

"Make way!" someone says as the emergency medical technicians (EMTs) move in.

I step back. I go to the table beside my sister, put my arm around her, and look out the window. Down the dusty driveway, a bit more than 100 yards, I see an older brick house, where Perry and Marv (her second husband) once lived.

My mind flashes back nineteen years and to that house, where I had done CPR on Marvin Miller. Marv and Perry met while skydiving. (I am not the only one in the family to jump out of airplanes.) Marv was the first in my immediate family to jump into politics, as a Winona School Board member. We served together on the school board for two years, until his death. Marv was younger than his wife, a marathon runner with a stringent running schedule and a perfect weight for his height and age. At forty years of age, he ended up lying in the floor just like Ray, and with friends and neighbors trying to keep him alive.

We wondered if Perry would ever marry again after Marv's death. She showed little interest in having any kind of lasting relationship — and with four kids, who would have time. Then Ray Jones stepped into her life. He was a rustic, easygoing counterbalance to Perry Jo. Ray was a hunter, nature lover, "one-day-at-a-time" kind of guy.

I married them. I forgot Ray's first name during the wedding ceremony, falling back on the awkward "Mr. Jones, will you take Perry Jo to be your lawfully wedded wife?" For Perry, life began again: two years later, at age forty-five, she was expecting. Two weeks after Morgan Taylor Jones was born, my youngest, Amy, came into the world. Morgan's nearest sibling, Marley, turned 20 the year she was born. Now, at 13, Morgan's dad lies dying on the living room floor.

"ALL CLEAR!" The green glowing line across the monitor screen jumps as the EMT applies electric voltage to stimulate the heart back into a rhythm. The chest and back muscles contract during defibrillation and relax when the shock is gone. The horizontal line goes flat.

"ALL CLEAR." Ray's muscle contractions are less and less forceful with each shock.

All eyes are on the monitor as a bright dot travels in a

straight line across the screen. Ray has flat-lined. Finally, it is over. Shoulders slump as tension, expectations, and hope leave the room.

"I can handle it," I say, changing hats and putting myself into inquest mode. I have faced this scenario many times. The evidence and testimony, and his lifestyle, line up with a massive myocardial infarction, or heart attack.

Medical equipment is gathered, returned, and prepared to meet the next life-and-death situation.

In June, 2000, Perry Jo is again a widow, facing life as a single parent with a child in junior high.

By 2010, she was enjoying life and doing whatever she wanted to do.

Her 70th birthday was celebrated at the Back Porch. Our ninety-one-year-old mom drove in, a little late for the celebration. The younger waitresses who worked with Perry Jo were embarrassed to discover her age — embarrassed because she works circles around them.

Chapter 13

DeDe

Inquest #860

Does England Have a Fourth of July?

Funerals and holidays provide opportunities for family and friends, and friends who have become extended family, to travel across the country to come together. Holidays are remembered as wonderful times when families get together to share food and love. With all the traveling and activity, however, a holiday can quickly change from a fond memory to a tragic day. For many, a Christmas or a Thanksgiving celebration carries with it the memory of the loss of a loved one: a child, parent, husband, wife, brother, or sister.

On Independence Day my family would gather together at Mom and Dad's ranch and eat watermelon and barbecued chicken. July is a hot month, and the celebration requires various liquids, including ice tea (sweet and non-sweet), cold soft drinks, cold beer, and wine.

My dad's barbecue sauce was so good that all it needed was a slice of bread. The tang of lemon, the bite of peppers, and spices with a touch of a yeast smell (beer) made your palate jump for joy as the aroma permeated the house. T.J. could barbecue twenty chickens at a time in the ancient, enormous homemade stone grill in our backyard — made from stones that looked suspiciously similar to those used throughout Texas by the New Deal era Civilian Conservation Corps in the 1930s. Each bite would melt in your mouth, leaving the taste of smoke, tomato, spices, and a little bite, like a touch of vinegar. "Tastes like chicken" has a different meaning after eating *Dad's* chicken. When you chose your piece of chicken, it was half a chicken. I have been known to eat several "pieces." Occasionally a newcomer would wear a white shirt and attempt to eat the chicken with a fork. There should be a law against eating barbecued chicken with a fork. You ate Dad's chicken with your fingers and many napkins or paper towels. My saliva glands ache just thinking about it.

Everyone visits to catch up on the lives of everyone else. Every year was different. Nephew Arden brought his horses one year, and we sometimes had the rumble of a motorcycle: Marv's (Perry's second husband), Jeff's, or mine. Fireworks occasionally would go off during the day. Kids would learn the dangers of fireworks as they blew up anthills or set off a stream of Black Cats by lighting an intricate woven mass of fuses attached to little black paper cylinders stuffed with gunpowder. The night would end with the grand finale lighting up the sky and exploding in what sounded like World War III.

After Dad's death, we began to meet at Perry Jo's house or the home of one of her kids. The oldest to youngest are Arden, Jeff, DeDe, and Marlee (all Millers), and then the youngest, Morgan Jones. In 2000, three weeks after Ray's death, we are celebrating Independence Day at Jeff's house.

~~~~~~~~~~~~~~~~~~~~~~~~~

Perry Jo is proud of her son's new brick/metal home. Earlier that year, we had a housewarming for Jeff (another skydiver) and Rose. Out in the country, at the end of a long, sandy driveway, the high, vaulted bronze metal roof gleams as the sun finds its way to the west. A long, narrow porch goes from one end of the house to the other. The shade is comforting in the hot July heat. Ceiling fans stir the air and cool us as we rock back and forth in rocking chairs on the porch. Tricycles and toys are scattered on the concrete floor among the adults.

"Where is DeDe?" someone asked.

"She is at the Miner's house," another answers. Scott Miner was marriage number three for DeDe.

Then, like the cartoon character Tasmanian Devil, coming down the driveway, there is a little red sports car, leaving a sand and dust trail rising like a tornado behind it. It storms its way up to the house and stops. Windows stay up, waiting for the dust to settle. When the dust clears, all the tinted windows are lowered electrically, simultaneously, four inches each, and then the driver's door opens. Two short, fashionable legs topped with red short shorts reach for the ground. DeDe appears as classy as the car she drives. She has "arrived."

"This in-law thing is wearing me out!" she announces as her excuse for being late. Her in-laws also have a family tradition, one that her husband would like to keep. They live four miles down Estrada Lane, a winding blacktop county road.

DeDe lives life in the fast lane, literally. Her car is known by every Department of Public Safety trooper in two counties, and most of the sheriff's deputies know her by name. I often heard "I stopped your niece the other day" from visitors to my office.

"DeDe, you better slow down," I would say.

"Uncle Mitch," she would answer, "I am careful, and I always wear my seatbelt."

With makeup just so, hair fixed just right, all clothes recently purchased, and wearing one pair of the twenty thousand shoes she has stored in their original boxes, she can impress anyone. Between husbands (and when she is not spoiling her little sister), she drives the guys crazy. She can get a job whenever and wherever she likes, preferring secretarial work. Standing almost five feet tall, she looks like a cute, innocent little girl, until she smiles. When she smiles and her eyebrows go up, all bets are off. If that smile does not win you over, get ready for the assault. Her demeanor can change faster than the car she drives.

Jeff's son, Tommy, is following in Granddad and Dad's

footsteps; the twelve-year-old spins out on his little mini-dirt bike, stirring up more dust. We hear the motorcycle buzz as he shoots down the wooded trails and then makes his way back home.

"Want to ride?" he asks. "Or can you?" he challenges.

"I can handle it," I say reaching over and twisting the throttle, revving the engine. The automatic transmission makes the cycle jump, and it takes a couple of quick steps for me to jump on. My butt fills the little seat, and I am off. Two hundred pounds on a cycle built for less than half that weight means the springs and shocks do little good, and the bumps are hard. The little engine is not deterred by the weight, however, and the bike quickly accelerates to as fast as I want to go. Free riding in the woods is like running through the forest and feeling the breeze without getting tired and out of breath. It is like skiing without the cold or the waiting, standing in the ski lift lines. Twenty minutes of twist and turns with humps and bumps, and this forty-six-year-old is ready to go back to the front porch rocking chair.

"Look at you, old man!" says DeDe as I unfold from the cramped position of riding the mini-bike. I stretch my vertebrae, compressed by the humps and bumps of the ride.

"Older than some, but apparently I feel younger than others," I respond, throwing out the challenge and offering the handlebars to her. She takes them like a pro and throws her leg across the bike. With a twist of the throttle, she takes off around the house and into the woods.

"Check the chicken," someone tells me before I can take my seat.

~~~~~~~~~~~~~~~~~~~~~~~~~~~~

I inherited some of Dad's cooking skills, mostly that of leaving the kitchen in a mess. To cook T.J.'s barbecue sauce requires hours of gathering ingredients, mixing, tasting, cooking—and drinking beer. It cannot be done in a few minutes. As the only son, I am called upon to view the chicken. The chicken is piled alongside weenies and hamburger patties on a gas grill one tenth the size of Dad's barbeque pit. The sauce comes from a bottle, and although it is pretty good, it won't ride a piece of bread like my daddy's.

~~~~~~~~~~~~~~~~~~~~~~~

"DeDe is riding the motorcycle!" says Perry Jo. "She can't even ride a bicycle!"

"She can ride a horse!" I say. DeDe loved and grew up riding horses. As a little girl, she could take control of a huge horse, and Lord have mercy on the beast that did not obey!

We can hear the engine buzzing in the woods. Then it stops. We wait.

"I told you," Perry says.

"Maybe we better go look for her," Jeff says. He yells, "Tommy, all y'all come on, we have to go look for DeDe. She is probably lost or something."

"Somebody come get this damn thing." The voice comes from the wilderness, as DeDe pushes the little motorcycle back to the house.

"I am not driving through all that dust and dirt," DeDe proclaims, stepping off and letting the bike go. Tommy catches it before it hits the ground. She continues, "Well, it fell over and died. Then it refused to start. I don't know what is wrong with it! It wasn't easy, but here I am!" Her smile is bright, and you can tell she is proud of having conquered this disaster. She is back with the family, enjoying life.

Later, I notice that Perry Jo and DeDe are walking and talking, away from the group, a mother-daughter conversation. DeDe loved Marv and Ray.

"Dying is part of life. It is not your fault. We have to move on," Perry Jo says.

DeDe had a hard time accepting Marv's death, and now, still in the shadow of Ray's death, her mother is concerned.

"I know, Mom. Today, I am at peace with the world." She smiles and looks into her mother's face and says, "Life is good."

"This chicken looks good to me," I say with approval. I signal, "It's time to eat."

In our family tradition, we gather together to pray. We give thanks for the food, but even more, we give thanks for each other.

"Let's hold hands," Mom says, and we create a circle that looks more like a glob. LoLo is the uncontested matriarch of our family. From the youngest to the oldest and even the great-great-grandchildren, who live over a thousand miles away, LoLo can have the final say if she wants it.

Our meal prayers are not long. Mom usually designates someone to say a prayer, or occasionally we will each give thanks one after another in the unbroken circle. This time Mom takes over.

"Lord," she says, "we come before you thanking you for this food and all the blessings that you have given us." This takes care of all the requirements for a meal prayer.

"Thank you for our family and friends, those who are here and those who are far away. Bless them, guide them, and protect them." This covers the family portion of the prayer.

"Lord, sometimes we don't understand why things happen, especially when one of us is taken away. We know T.J., Marv, Ray, and others are with you. And heaven must be a pretty nice place, if they would rather be there than here. The tears we shed are for us, we miss them all. But you are the same God who has seen us through troubled times. You promised you would not allow more troubles than we could bear. We believe and trust in you, that all things will work together and we will understand it all, by and by." All is quiet for a minute.

"Forgive us for our sins." Mom always includes this in her prayers.

"Amen," we echo, and we commence to dispense. We prepare plates as we circulate around the kitchen, piling on Rose's German potato salad, Perry's deviled eggs, and Mom's salad. The final stop is at the grill, where four chickens are dismembered and lying among pork weenies and beef hamburgers. Jalapeno sausage is an added treat. It is a good evening meal, capped off with a relaxing drink—then back to the front porch.

"Where is DeDe?" someone asks.

"She had to go back to the Miners. Isn't this about the third trip?" It is tough to try to make everybody happy. The advantage of having relatives living nearby is you get to see them all. The disadvantage is you have to see them all. Christmas and Thanksgiving can result in running back and forth and having three fantastic meals within three hours.

We quietly watch the sky turn bright red, orange, and purple with a majestic sunset. The small fireworks have been popped, fizzled, and turned to broken, burnt leftovers.

An electric motor whines, creating homemade vanilla ice cream, while the older kids whine because they have to turn the crank on another ice cream freezer, creating homemade peach ice cream. When all the whining is over, the sweet coolness of the ice cream will relieve the heat of this July day.

"Can we do the big fireworks?" the kids beg. For many, the tradition of fireworks has changed with city and county ordinances. Many make a pilgrimage to the local "hot spot" where they can sit in or on their automobiles and watch from a distance as city fathers or private enterprises shoot off mortar rounds of explosives in a calculated rhythm to match the simulcast of "God Bless America" playing over a certain radio station. Along many coastal shores, people gather for the celebration, and on High Island fireworks go for miles and miles.

"Wait a little longer. It needs to be dark," say the parents with an excuse to extend the quiet moment.

"But look!" the kids say, pointing to the horizon and an umbrella of sparkling colors floating back to the earth. It is Lindale's fireworks display ten miles away.

"Light 'em up!" someone yells, and the big kids and parents, who act just like big kids, fire up the show. The smaller kids light sparklers, one to another, and write their names in the air, staring at the bright glow and leaving the writings on their retinas.

"Shhhhhhhhhhwhew." Bottle rockets stream to the sky, some to explode in an orgasm of colors and sparkles, others to just pop and fizzle. Little fan-shaped metal disks spin and take off into the air, powered by a spray of sparks. Where they go is unpredictable and, like the chasers, everybody cautiously looks when they hear their distinctive sounds.

"Pa-pow, pow, pow!" (times one hundred), and the last of the Black Cats are done. The sulfur smell of gunpowder floats in the air, and the paper and plastic remains of fireworks lie on the sandy driveway.

The adults make a halfhearted attempt to get the kids to pick up the litter. Most are ready to call it a night.

"Load 'em up." The cars line up and exit on the dusty drive. Some turn east, some turn west, all going back to our respective homes and our respective beds.

"That was nice," I tell Fae, shucking off my blue jean shorts and stepping on the toe of a sock. "Jeff and Rose have a nice place, and everyone seemed to enjoy themselves." I pull my foot out and repeat the sock removal process, leaving the crumpled white and sandy brown socks on the floor. Then, flopping back on the waterbed, which sloshes Fae side to side, I say, "Life is good." There are days in our lives when we lie back in our beds and think such thoughts. Sometimes it is a day when all went right, goals were accomplished. Sometimes it is a day when problems were few. Sometimes it is a celebration of family and/or friends who come together, providing the feeling that you are not alone and even the troubles of the world cannot take that joy from you. "Life is good." The phone rings.

"Shamburger," I answer.

"We have an inquest out on County Road 315."

"Where is County Road 315?" I ask, trying to focus. It is thirty minutes before midnight.

"It is just off Sand Flat Road. County Road 315 is also called Estrada Lane."

"I was just there," I say, looking at the clock and

rubbing my eyes, "thirty minutes ago." A sickening feeling comes over me. "Do you have a name?"

"The trooper said she may be kin to you." The dispatcher hesitates, letting it sink in. I recognize the technique.

"Go ahead."

"The car is registered to a Deadra Glen Miller. Would you like for me to call another judge?"

"I'll handle it," I say, thinking it was just like DeDe: three marriages and never changed her driver's licenses.

I drive past the place where less than an hour ago we were celebrating the Fourth of July. A mile further is a red sports car. It is angled on an embankment next to a small tree. The driver's window is open, and DeDe is halfway out of the car.

Had a pig, deer, dog, or other animal run out in front of her? Or was she just going her usual (too fast) speed down the county road? She strongly believed in seatbelts and always insisted that anyone riding with her be buckled up. Yet here she is, half in and half out of the car. Maybe she was trying to get out, or maybe she was in a hurry to get back to family and just did not buckle up this one time. Maybe . . .

Chapter 14

What a Pileup!

Inquests #1280 and #1281

A sign in my office says, "When I die I want to go peacefully like my grandfather, in his sleep, and not like all the other people who were yelling and screaming in the car."

Construction on Interstate 20 is never completed. Engineers are always coming up with new ways to "save lives" and spend money. Take culverts, for instance. The highway department has replaced the original round, blunt, flat culverts with more *crash friendly* culverts. Road signs are now made with breakaway posts. Every now and then you can see one that has been tested, with its broken leg angled back, looking like a scarecrow sign, and leaning to one side. The immovable concrete bridge pylons that used to kill on contact are now protected by a technology of barrels filled with water or sand, collapsible guardrails, and concrete walls. If your car wanders too far to the right, grooves cut in the road shoulders are designed to wake you up and scare the be-jeebers out of you and your passengers.

New kinds of asphalt, concrete, or mixtures of asphalt and concrete, and new methods of construction results in roads that will always be worked on but never completed. Huge machines now crawl down one lane and chew up the old pavement, while other giants lay down the new. Meanwhile, traffic is backed up for miles.

On the interstate, traffic often is divided by a median of twenty or thirty feet of grassy earth. Unfortunately, that distance is not enough to keep an out-of-control vehicle from crossing over into head-on traffic.

When two vehicles collide head–on, a tremendous amount of energy is released. Metal crunches and at times snaps like a pretzel; safety glass splinters into pieces, leaving thousands of little prisms reflecting the colors of flashing emergency lights; plastics crunch and rip like tissue paper. The air carries the remaining scent of acid, electricity, and sulfur after such an explosion. This happens within seconds, so fast that it is over before a fire can get started. The human body is more frail than metal. Strange things happen when such accidents occur.

Someone said, "It's not the speed that kills you, it's the sudden stop!"

An example of a "sudden stop" happened late one night on a two-lane highway. An automobile hit an eighteen-wheeler almost head-on; the driver's side of the car hit the driver's side of the truck. The two auto victims were instantly killed. Both were thrown through the windshield. Airbags and seatbelts lose their effectiveness when fourteen thousand pounds of tractor trailer collide with four thousand pounds of car at a combined speed of 150 miles an hour. The occupants of the auto were outside the vehicle, lying on the pavement. Their "insides" were on the outside, chest and belly deflated, as though someone had reached down each throat, grabbed intestines, and jerked them wrong-side out. This left a mess of blood and guts, and the pair of twisted mangled bodies lying on the side of the road. The bodies matched the twisted and mangled 1998 Chevy Malibu. Cars do not fare well in collision contests with trains or big trucks!

Something else was lying in the middle of the road about fifty feet from the two bodies. It was far enough from the debris that it looked out of place. I did my usual snooping-around inspection, and curiosity led me to the mystery down the road. As I approached, using what little light the emergency vehicles gave, I could see what it was. It was a man's heart, dark deep red with purple arteries. My science classes in middle school, high school, college, and nursing all had anatomical pictures of the heart. This looked like a picture out of a science book, or something from a horror movie, where a madman rips the beating heart from his victim and holds it high for the world to see. The strobing colored lights of the emergency vehicles made the heart look as though it was still beating, pulsing red and blue, red and blue. I had heard of explosions that would send a man's heart through his mouth, but until this, I did not really believe it. I wondered if it continued to thump as it left the body and flew through the air. Did it stop beating after it bounced and rolled like a tennis ball? It had stopped rolling, and it lay there between the double yellow stripes on Highway 31. I took a picture of it with my cell phone.

~~~~~~~~~~~~~~~~~~~~~~~~~

If there had been a wall, instead of painted stripes between the eastbound and westbound traffic lanes, I would have had a peaceful night's sleep. The newest engineering technological feat in East Texas extends for miles and miles down the middle of the interstate, making the divided highway even more of a divided highway.

Interstate 20 crosses Texas, east to west, 635 miles from the Louisiana border to intersect with Interstate 10 around Pecos, another 193 miles to El Paso, and then across into New Mexico. Interstate 20 also transects Smith County.

From Shreveport west toward Longview, about fifty miles of Interstate 20 is divided by steel one-inch cables stretched taut, from post to post. Each replaceable post is secured with a concrete footing. The setup is supposed to work like a net snagging a fish, capturing straying vehicles and preventing them from going into the oncoming traffic. Quite a few autos and trucks have challenged the fence; there are often sections of the road where the cables have been jarred loose and hang like limp spaghetti for a half a mile or more.

From Longview and continuing west a hundred miles, a concrete wall 42 inches tall goes from hill to hill. If you look at a cross section of the wall, it appears as an inverted or upside-down Y with the triangle filled in. The wider base is designed to lift a vehicle's wheel and correct the direction of travel when the vehicle makes contact. The "Jersey barrier" was first implemented in 1959. Now, fifty years later, it stretches its way across Texas.

"What do you call this thing?" I ask a trooper at a fatal accident, pointing at the concrete structure.

"I don't know," he says. "I never thought about it."

At the scene, a truck driver writes a statement that I read later. "Truckers call it a median wall." That sounds good to me.

My first contact with a median wall of the Jersey barrier variety was on the "raceway" in Houston. Most people call it Loop 635. With a mixture of high-speed motorcycles, cars, pickup trucks and big rig trucks, and up to twelve lanes of traffic, the "Jersey barrier" seems to be all that keeps people going in the right direction.

I was thinking the lane inside, next to the wall, was a safe lane in which to travel. My daughter's little Mazda managed traffic well. As I poked along at seventy miles an hour; trucks and cars passed me like I was standing still. A Houstonian race car driver was working his way through traffic as though heading for the checkered flag. At times he would fall back to jump across to a faster lane.

Then he challenged me, and the race was on. An eighteen-wheeler was ahead in his lane. The little Mazda was no match for the Mercedes as he pulled half a car length ahead. With less than fifty yards to go, he made his move and began to wedge his car into my lane. I slowed, but not quickly enough, and he squeezed me into the wall. Blump, scrape, blam, and I was back in my lane, shooting straight down the road. I drove on, looking at the taillights of the Mercedes, dreading the sight of the damage I had done to the side of my daughter's car. The scraping sound was awful. I could see in my mind's eye what the concrete had done along the entire length of the driver's side of the car. The only thing to do was to keep going.

When I finally came in for a landing, I climbed out of the car. To my surprise, there were little scratches on the rims of the driver's side wheels, and that was all. There was almost no damage! The Jersey wall had done its job.

It may be common in big cities to feel like you are getting squashed between a big truck on your right and a concrete wall on your left. Now, we can get that same feeling while traveling out in the country, down the interstate. The safety factor of hitting a concrete wall as opposed to slipping and sliding and rolling in a grassy median does not sound too appealing. Still, a high percentage of deaths on the interstate are from head-on collisions; almost as high as those from not wearing seatbelts. When two vehicles meet head-on at 70 miles an hour, it is worse than hitting a brick wall going 140 miles an hour. A brick wall will crumble. With a head-on collision, each vehicle will absorb the impact, with the larger heaver vehicle winning the shoving contest.

At first, I thought the Jersey barrier was just another way the government could find to spend money, another semi-useless project. Governments spend money, and they also taketh away.

Texas does not have an income tax, so the state government depends on a sales tax, property tax, and other sources of income. One income source for the state is called court costs, but only because the court collects the money. Most of the money actually goes to the state capitol in Austin. Texas governors and legislatures over the years must agree that "court costs" is a grand source of income. Court costs have gone from $6.50 to $110.10 dollars per case during my tenure. What does this have to do with a Jersey barrier?

This type of median wall hurt my ticket business. Cops can no longer work traffic in both directions anywhere on the interstate. Before the Jersey barrier, they could get you coming or going. Now, with fewer turnaround opportunities, fewer citations are written. Fewer tickets mean less revenue. However, raising money is not the purpose of the court. At one time, many judges were paid according to the number of convictions and fines paid. This was long before my time and, rightfully, this practice was ended. Now it is against Texas law for governing bodies, or those in authority, to even suggest quotas to peace officers or judges. Our goal is to get people to comply with the law and to make the road safer for all.

The wall causes a problem: getting from one side of the road to the other. Firemen, law enforcement, and I, the coroner, find ourselves driving by accident scenes and going for miles looking for a place to cross over.

And what about the armadillos, rabbits, turtles, pigs, wolves, coyotes, skunks, raccoons, rabbits, dogs, and pedestrians that cross the road? They once ran freely, in and out of traffic, from one side of the road to the other. Unlike deer, they, and we, cannot easily jump over such a barrier.

The problem of crossovers was addressed by spending more money. Placing the wall alternately on one side or the other of the grassy median creates breaks between sections that allow crossovers for authorized personnel and for animals. However, one man's cure is another man's poison.

Most Jersey barriers are tagged with black writing in the form of tread marks. The many markings indicate the times someone has marched up and down the wall, leaving spiraling and swirling tire graffiti on it. Each mark is a testament to how well the wall works. Each marking indicates the potential of a head-on collision. The wall makes the road safer.

Eighteen Wheels and a Dozen Roses

An eighteen-wheeler consists of a tractor, commonly called a cab, and a trailer or trailers. These trucks are big and powerful, and they carry virtually everything that will ever need to be carried. The men and women who trace the nation's highways and live "on the road" are of a special breed. Frequently they visit with other truckers on CB radios so powerful that a trucker in Pluto could answer a trucker in Venus (both cities in Texas): "Ten–four, good buddy!" Mostly, though, truckers spend hours and hours driving, thinking, listening, thinking, talking to themselves, and thinking some more. All of this thinking can cause problems. Just because you "think it" does not mean that "it is"!

Truckers come in two basic varieties: short haulers and long haulers. The long haulers practically live on the road and do a whole lot of thinking. They seldom see their families. Their kids grow up while they are thinking. The spouse, usually the wife, lives in a dream created by miles and miles of asphalt. Family life becomes a fantasy. The telephone becomes their lifeline, and when the signal is dead or the phone rings and rings, and there is no answer, the mind fills the void. The little time spent at home is intense, trying to compress a "normal" family life into a few hours or days before the driver goes back on the road. It is no wonder that there is conflict when a trucker comes home to rest and rejuvenate, only to find kids to raise, bills to pay, and a yard that needs mowing.

My dad, Thomas Jefferson "T.J." Shamburger, grew roses before I was born. The city of Tyler is known for its roses, and the Tyler Municipal Rose Garden is visited by travelers from around the world. The Rose Garden is beautiful, but the real East Texas beauty lies in the rose fields scattered throughout the area. The sweet fragrance of roses in full bloom is heavy in the breeze. It takes three years of hands-on care to prepare a rosebush to sell. The Shamburger coat of arms displays several roses, hinting of my roots in the German soil. When I was seven, T.J. bought a truck to transport his Gumwood Nursery Roses from coast to coast. He soon began carrying roses from several rose growers to distant markets. The return trip was compensated with a load of freight. Sometimes, the freight would need to go out of the way in order to get another load that would bring him home. Eventually, the roses grew fewer and fewer, the freight loads became more and more frequent and larger, and the trips became longer and longer. Finally, he was another long-haul trucker spending a few nights a month at home. In the summertime, I would load and go with him.

"Are we still in Texas?" I would ask from the sleeper, a

mattress in the boxlike compartment behind the driver. There is no better rest than lying in the sleeper and feeling the rocking massage and powerful thrust of an eighteen-wheeler. Before I was twelve I had traveled through all the continental United States as well as some of Canada and Mexico. I did not go to Alaska, but many Texans still do not recognize Alaska as a state! The engine whining and gears grinding, I would look down on the little cars below. I would bundle up in a blanket and hide from the ICC (Interstate Commerce Commission) as we would go through the weigh stations. I was a stowaway as far as the law was concerned.

"Are we still in Texas?" Mom says I would ask that question over and over until the answer was no, and then I would climb out from the compartment behind the driver to see the world go by. As a child, I guess I didn't see much sense in getting up and looking around if we were still in Texas. I had seen Texas; I was ready to see the rest of the world.

In Chicago I climbed over the saddle tanks and dismounted the truck dressed in shorts and cowboy boots. The boots echoed as I ran to catch up with Mom and Dad. I heard a little boy tell his friend, "That boy is from Wyoming, Texas!" I was one proud kid, although I knew the legally required six-inch letters on the truck door said "Winona, Texas."

After Dad decided to settle down and bought the gas station, the fire engine–red Big Mack tractor truck stayed at the house in Winona, then later moved with us to the Starrville ranch. For twelve years T.J. would get a couple of twelve-volt batteries and jumper cables to boost the old truck off. Black smoke would bellow out the exhaust stacks, smoke signals marking its annual start-up. One day several men made the pilgrimage to our house. Again the big diesel shook and shuddered and came back to life. A stranger drove the monster around the pasture. A negotiation, a handshake, an exchange of money and title, and Big Mack was going to join the highway again, this time without T.J. I could see the pain in Dad's face as this part of his life jerked and rumbled away.

Dad would tell stories about driving with one eye

open, the other eye asleep leaning over the steering wheel guided only by the white dashes of stripes zipping one after another down the middle of the road. He sometimes slept and even dreamed while still ticking off the miles. As Dad grew old, and as dementia crept in, we would reminisce about the days of the highway, sometimes all night long.

They say that once trucking gets into your blood, you can never be still again; the call of the road will always be there. The smell of diesel still reminds me of those days and the adventures on the roads across the U.S.A.

What a Pileup!
Inquests #1280 and #1281

Thirty minutes before midnight, an eighteen-wheeler is rolling eastbound down Interstate 20. Driver Two is in the sleeper. He had done his time behind the wheel, and now it is time for him to sleep. Truck drivers keep a logbook showing when, where, and how long they have driven and rested that day. Driver One is now in control. He has driven this stretch of road before, and millions of miles just like it. How long has he been driving tonight? Only Driver One knows if the logbook really reflects actual miles and times. Drivers and the officials who enforce the regulations often refer to a logbook as "The Book of Lies."

~~~~~~~~~~~~~~~~~~~~~~~~~~~

The methodical rumble of the big diesel engine, the floating bucket seat, and the music or voices on talk radio all has a hypnotizing effect on Driver One. Cars and trucks around him notice as he begins to weave. They back off. The truck slowly veers to the left. Where is the Jersey barrier? He should hit it, leaving nothing but black tread marks on the concrete. The wall should straighten and awaken, leaving only his black tire graffiti as a mark of what could have been. The wall is across the grassy median, on the westbound side of the road. A turnaround is ahead, and the wall will then be on his side of the road, without the grassy median between him and the barrier. If he can hold on for only thirty yards more, the wall will be in the correct place. The wall, the inverted Y, is protected by a guardrail.

~~~~~~~~~~~~~~~~~~~~~~~~~~~~~

If you have ever looked closely at a steel guardrail, you realize just how thick and heavy they are. They start out like a playground slide twisted to the ground, contoured and made to lift and direct. The rails are galvanized steel, three-eighths of an inch thick. Most have wooden weather-treated posts, six to eight inches in diameter. The posts are set four to six feet apart, with the first few posts made to break away by having holes drilled through them close to the ground to weaken them. This allows the rail to bend and conform partly to the vehicle's path, rather than causing an abrupt stop, like hitting the end of a Jersey barrier. The remaining guardrail, like the wall, should direct a vehicle back to the road or at least stop it. The idea works well for autos but not for heavy trucks.

~~~~~~~~~~~~~~~~~~~~~~~~~~~~~

Driver One wakes from his stupor when the truck crashes into the guardrail. The guardrail is all that stands between him and the beginning of the Jersey barrier. The galvanized steel railing crumples as each of the thirteen posts snaps like a toothpick. Thirteen times, the posts splinter against the force of the big rig as the momentum carries the truck to the Jersey barrier. A mile-long wall made for protecting and directing becomes a concrete post a mile thick.

The heavy, thick steel front bumper of the eighteen-wheeler hits the end of the wall dead center and folds like a stick of chewing gum. Driver Two is tossed around in the sleeper and wakes up to the rig shooting straight up in the air, as the Jersey barrier rips right down the underside of the tractor. The trailer goes to the barrier's right side, and like a baseball bat shoots out into the road. The cab slides along the top of the barrier, dragging the trailer behind, and the trailer slams back against the wall. The tires try to climb the wall, skipping and jumping up and down, leaving the coal-black etchings that say "Something happened here."

As the cab loses momentum, the weight of the trailer takes over, pushing the cab along before it jackknifes across the eastbound traffic lanes. When it folds, the saddle tank on the right side ruptures, spraying diesel fuel and coating both the truck and the wall. The truck has gone two hundred feet down the top of the wall when the cab stops; the trailer tips heavily to the right until finally it falls on its side, blocking both lanes of the eastbound side. An explosion rips the night, much louder even than the sound of metal against concrete, and flames shoot out from the ruptured tanks and the undercarriage. Soot and diesel flame drape the wall. The noise of the crash gives way to the screeching of brakes and the sound of tires trying to hold the road as approaching traffic responds. Finally, all seems quiet.

Amazingly, traffic traveling at seventy miles per hour comes to a standstill in a matter of seconds. It is not an orderly stop of two lanes of traffic. Trucks and cars are arrayed across the eastbound side of the interstate like a child's "pick-up sticks" strewn across a table, at different angles, having slid or stopped wherever they could without hitting the surrounding vehicles. The two traffic lanes, shoulders, and grassy median have as many as four cars packed side by side. The light of the fire spreads to the trailer and sends an eerie red glow pulsing across the scene.

Driver Three sits in another big rig. From the height of the cab, he has a clear view of the fire and flames and the mixture of parked autos and trucks zigzagged and packed in front of him. "Wow!," he says to Driver Four, who is crawling down from the sleeper, "We're lucky to be alive!" Their cab and trailer form a forty-five degree angle, still hooked together. Behind them, a little red sports car is stopped, holding Joe and Joseph.

Roommates Big Joe and Little Joe, as they are known by friends and family, are on their way back from a Dallas shopping spree. Dallas is their stomping ground. Ticket stubs from the World Wrestling Federation and rock concerts litter the car. Although they are not rich, probably not even middle class, they enjoy outings and enjoy each other's company. Both have long hair and are overweight. One works in a video store.

"What's going on?" Big Joe asks.

"I think there's a wreck or something up ahead. Looks like a fire," Little Joe responds. All he can see is an aluminum silver outline of a box trailer in front of their car. They are stopped with room to spare.

"Great. Now we're just sitting here. If we had left five minutes earlier, when I wanted to leave, we would still be 'runnin' down the road try'n' to loosen our load!'" Big Joe sings in his best Eagles imitation, and then they both laugh.

"Life is too short to let things like this bother you," Little Joe says.

An eighteen-wheeler approaches the accident. The speed limit at night is sixty for trucks; he is doing all of that and more. The glow of the fire and the taillights of stopped cars for some reason do not prompt him to slow the truck. Maybe someone on the other side of the road had flashed bright lights, trying to warn of the hazard ahead. Surely someone had put the warning out on the CB radio. His mental filter however blocks his vision. Cars are not *supposed* to be stopped in the middle of the road in the middle of the night, especially on the open interstate and in front of a trucker — so he doesn't see them. Or maybe he is just sleepy and inattentive.

Big Joe's hand rests on the shifter next to him. Little Joe reaches over and rests his hand on Big Joe's. They look at each other as the inside of the car becomes bright with white light. The truck zooms closer, and the light gets brighter. The last thing the roommates will see is each other. The truck never even slows down. The cab centers itself over the little red car, then goes right over it, tearing and crushing it. The truck's cab rolls right over the top of the little red car, centered on it, five of its wheels on each side. The heavy metal undercarriage of the cab rips away any protection the Joes have. The twisted metal of what so recently was their car emerges from under the cab and goes under the trailer, in the time it takes to blink an eye.

Underneath the trailer is the dolly. The dolly is a jacking mechanism with a crank to raise and lower the trailer so that when the rig is parked, the trailer can be freestanding. It is made of heavy tubular steel with a cross-member to stabilize it so the tractor can disengage.

Tonight the dolly's cross-member snares the roof of the little red car, peeling it back like the top from a can of sardines. The topless wreck of the car is jettisoned to the side of the road from beneath the trailer, and the assaulting truck hits the trailer of the rig holding Drivers Three and Four, starting a chain reaction from back to front. Now there is more smoke and another fire.

Someone calls 911. All agencies are called out, and the eastbound side of the interstate is closed.

~~~~~~~~~~~~~~~~~~~~~~~~~

"Call the judge," says the volunteer fireman, examining what's left of the little red car. "These two are gone."

I take the call, roll out of bed, and hit the road. The stars are out on this warm summer night so I take my motorcycle. Westbound on the interstate, I pass the accident on the eastbound side. Because of the Jersey barrier between us, I have to ride on ahead. Heavy traffic extends for miles. I finally find a crossover. Working my way back to the accident, I drive carefully around stopped vehicles. Along the way a motorist jeers and complains.

"Who do you think you are!" shouts a trucker. "There's an accident up ahead!" No doubt he thinks an inconsiderate motorcyclist is jumping ahead of everyone else. Little does he know that the traffic won't be going anywhere until I have performed my duty, the inquest.

I drive on, then park where they can all see my motorcycle when traffic starts to move again. Chances are they will be long gone before I am through. Every now and then I think about getting a Kojak light, a small red or blue light in a plastic bubble that you can throw on the dash or stick on the roof with a magnet. I could stick it on the gas tank of my motorcycle.

The two Joes and what is left of their little red car are surrounded by activity. Both front seats are broken and in a reclining position, as though they had pulled to the side of the road and leaned back to take a nap. The newly converted convertible is opened to the sky. Stars glisten between clouds of black smoke. Big Joe and Little Joe seem at peace as they gaze up at the sky.

"Call the funeral home and advise them there are two, and they will need bags," I say to Fire Chief Wilson as we go through the Joes' personal papers looking for indications of insurance, address, or names among the ticket stubs from past good times.

There is a problem locating next of kin. One of the Joes had an old cell phone, and I use it to chase the numbers. Friends and co-workers answer. All are shocked. I can tell each had friendly thoughts and warm feelings toward both Big and Little Joe. Finally, Little Joe's dad is on the other end of the line. He lives in Ohio.

"They were happy. Where you would find one, you would find the other," Dad says. "They enjoyed life and they enjoyed each other. They were gay." He paused. "Big Joe is HIV positive." An HIV–positive status means that special precautions must be taken for those who come into contact with the victims. Although the virus cannot survive long outside the body, it is still considered a danger to fire and medical personnel and anyone else who might make contact with body fluids.

It is a miracle that no one else was seriously injured. The "body wagon" from John Harmon Undertakers arrives. Because criminal charges will be filed, I order autopsies.

"Take them to the forensic center," I say.

The next day Little Joe's dad calls. He is worried about cost. Transportation for the body and arrangements could be tough for someone on a fixed income. Little Joe's niece lives close by and will coordinate things.

"Don't worry about cost," I say. "A trucking company or their insurance will be glad to pay any expenses. There is no rush to do anything. Take your time."

~~~~~~~~~~~~~~~~~~~~~~~~~~~~~~

Death is life's ultimate way of telling you to slow down. It is important in this time of crises to slow down, to think about what you have to do, what you intend to do, and the lasting results. Not everyone needs a five-thousand-dollar casket (or one of the many that cost even more).

It's important to have a plan for your funeral and tell it to someone, or better, write it down. If you're the responsible survivor, think about what the deceased would have wanted and make it fit into your budget. Remember, funerals are more for the living than the dead.

Most of us plan on being alive tomorrow. We also expect that most of our friends and loved ones also will be alive. When our plans and expectations prove wrong, the mental crisis affects the way we think. Often people spend money they do not have on elaborate funerals and on shipping bodies and ashes all over the world. They try to spend their way into creating some kind of closure or reconciliation. The fact is, no matter what they do, it will not undo the tragedy. "Until death do you part" is a vow in the wedding ceremonies I perform. I can't guess how many graves lie unclaimed because the "loving wife" or "loving husband" inscribed upon the tombstone has gone on to another loving wife or husband. At the time of grief, the desire is that one day the two will be rejoined in eternal bliss. At many inquests, I find that the victim's spouse had died within the past year. Sometimes life deals us a new set of cards and life goes on. Most of us who are left to live, are left to *live*. Some, however, are left to shrivel up and die on the vine.

~~~~~~~~~~~~~~~~~~~~~~~~~~~~~~

As for bodies of Joe and Joseph, one went to Ohio and the other to Athens, Texas. I don't know where they will spend eternity. That call is far outside my jurisdiction.

Chapter 15

A Pit-i-full Story

Inquests #839 and #1235

I have always loved dogs and cats, and they have always loved me. When I was a child, the backs of my hands and arms were masses of scratches because of the way that I trained my cats to be playful. They would attack when least expected and lock on with front paws while scratching and kicking with their back legs and claws. I had a rabbit that would do the same.

An old story goes like this: The dog thinks, "He cares for me, feeds me, and shelters me; he must be God." The cat thinks, "He cares for me, feeds me, and shelters me; I must be God."

~~~~~~~~~~~~~~~~~~~~~~~~~~~~

I grew up with collies that showed little or no aggressive behavior. Whitey, pronounced White-e, was an albino collie and my childhood protector. Occasionally, Mom would find five-year-old me walking down the street, Whitey by my side, shielding me from traffic and keeping me next to the curb.

One of Mom's many favorite childhood stories involved Whitey and the puppies born under our little white framed house. She could produce no milk, so the babies were doomed from the start. As each one died, Whitey would remove it from the litter and bury it somewhere in the backyard.

It was summertime, and Mom was sewing, sitting by an open window at the back of the house. I was six years old and playing outside when I made the discovery. Lying on the ground, underneath a window, was a dead puppy.

"Mama!" I exclaimed through the window, "Here is a puppy and it is not moving." I prodded it with a stick.

"It is dead," Mom answered. "Do you know what that means?"

"Yeah," I said slowly, prodding the body again. "It's not alive."

"Come inside. We'll find a shoebox and have a funeral. Then we will bury him." This was not a new operation. Living next to a busy highway meant that we had several pet funerals over the years. They were not only for dogs and cats; we had also buried turtles, an alligator, a hamster, lizards, and a rabbit or two. I went inside, and we gathered the necessary implements.

Whitey had already dug a grave. She returned and picked up her dead baby to perform her own funeral. While I was inside preparing, she was outside burying.

With the shoebox casket in hand, I went back outside to get the body. It was gone!

"Mama! Mama!" I yelled. She hurried to where I was standing. I turned and looked up to her, my big brown cow eyes gleaming. I was excited about seeing this miracle and exclaimed in a high voice, "Heaven done come down and swooped him up!"

~~~~~~~~~~~~~~~~~~~~~~

While in junior high school, I drove my first new motorcycle to our new country home in Starrville. From my birth to my marriage, I lived in three houses, all within five miles of each other. When I would putter down the drive way to the garage Tramp would run beside me.

Tramp was a large collie mixed breed, brown with a long white tail that constantly wagged. Living on the ranch, he had the benefit and range of country living. He was also a hunter, occasionally dragging up a dead mouse or rabbit.

One night as I drove down our winding driveway, I noticed Tramp was distracted.

"What you got there?" I asked him, wheeling my motorcycle around to shine the headlamp in his direction. He proudly held his head up to display his catch for the night.

A pair of reflective eyes looked at me. Tramp had caught a little black kitten. He held it excitedly in his mouth and trotted over to me. His eyes sparkled as he held the cat in his mouth, with just enough pressure to prevent escape but not enough pressure to hurt it. The cat was meowing, begging to be set free.

"Hold it!" I commanded Tramp.

When I said, "Hold it," what I meant was "Stop." What Tramp heard was "HOLD it and do not let go!" The exclamation excited Tramp, and the kitten even more. The cat struggled and began to twist and wiggle. Tramp continued to hold on tighter, until I heard the crunch. Tramp stood there, tail waving from side to side, thinking he was doing exactly what I told him.

"Put him down!" He must have sensed my disapproval because he dropped the kitten to the ground. The poor kitten took off like a bullet ricocheting in a concrete room, zigzagging and running into a big elm tree, zigzagging again and then hitting the chain link fence. His back legs did not coordinate with his front legs, and I think one back leg did not work at all. Zigzag and zip, he shot across the cattle guard, then across the road and into the woods.

Years later, I awoke in darkness to what I thought was a child crying in my room.

"Ohhhhhhhhh," I heard the cry. "Ohhhhhhh, owwwwwwww."

"It's OK," I said, dazed by sleep and trying to comfort the howling child. I found my way to the light switch. The light revealed a wild, black tomcat. He had climbed into my room through an open window. His fur was tattered and worn, and much of one ear was missing, but he was big and healthy and probably as confused as I. He might have been that same cat. I wondered if Tramp had taken one of his nine lives.

~~~~~~~~~~~~~~~~~~~~~~~~~~

Back in the big city (Winona, population 580) and raising my own kids, we had Whistle, a black and white border collie. Border collies tend to be smart — sometimes too smart for their own good — and Whistle was something of an escape artist. No pen built could hold Whistle for long. He would be at the house when I left for the Justice Court Center and waiting for me when I arrived at the office. He was there for Noah's and Lena's childhoods and out-survived several other dogs that spent shortened lifetimes with our family. I am thankful for those dogs, like Laddie, that came and went. They taught my children that running out in front of a car could be fatal.

Occasionally someone would complain about Whistle, sometimes a neighbor, but usually another good citizen who kept his dogs contained. To the neighbors, I would advise, "If he is causing you any trouble, go ahead and shoot him and don't tell me about it."

This may seem harsh to some, and I guess the times are changing, even in Texas. There was a time people took care of their own problems. The warning was courtesy. I did not want the neighbors to shoot Whistle, and I did not want Whistle to bother the neighbors. People have the right to protect themselves and their property, which is the only legal reason to shoot a dog or a cat. I could have tied Whistle to a tree or put him in a small kennel restricting his life to food and water. If I were a dog, I would rather be shot.

The city adopted a leash law.

"What about the judge's dog?" came the complaints. Every black and white dog seen was identified as Whistle, Judge Shamburger's dog. Whistle did have his supporters in town. He would visit, and they would feed him and tell me about how much they liked him. To the complainers I said,

"He is really not my dog. I donated that dog to the city of Winona. He is the town dog. Therefore, he is protected by a grandfather clause, like the mockingbird, the state bird of Texas."

Attempts to keep Whistle in the yard were futile. As soon as he was tall enough, he learned to unlock the gate of the chain link fence. As an adolescent, he learned to dig under the gate.

Electricity was the answer. I ran a "hot" wire around the bottom of the fence. The electric charger was made for keeping horses in and was plenty strong to hold a dog. Whistle yelped with pain the first time his investigative nose met the spark of that wire. A few weeks later, however, Whistle was waiting for me at work again. I searched the fence. The chain link was intact, much of it six feet high. The electric horse shocker made its distinct clicking sound, sending megavoltage with each click: The wire was alive. To make sure, I took a blade of grass and held it next to the wire. It wilted with each click. I would have to catch the dog in the act of escaping.

I spied on him from the kitchen window. I could see him pacing, his long, black and white hair shaking with each bouncy step. He began to run back and forth in front of the big double-wide gate. With each pass, he exhibited more and more anxiety: He wanted out. Finally, he made a big circle, and three feet away from the gate, he lay on his stomach with his front paws extended toward the gate. He then laid his head flat between his front legs, with his tail flattened to the ground. His hind legs folded up and tucked in next to his body. He held this position for a minute and then began rocking side to side and edging inch by inch toward the gate. I had patched the soil from his previous gate diggings, but then I noticed a five-inch dip in one area. Whistle was not a huge dog. He was just tall enough to sniff your butt while standing on all fours.

As I watched his rocking, I noticed it was in rhythm to the clicking of the electric fence: left, right, left, right. Click, click—and he is off. He jammed his nose under the wire and gate and thrust his head through the dip.

Click, and he jerked. Click, and he jerked again. Each time, the electricity caused his muscles to contract, but each time he worked his way farther under the gate. Six clicks and he was on the outside, wagging his tail.

"Whistle!" I yelled, stepping out the back door. "Get back in this yard!"

He waited for me at the gate, tail still wagging. I opened it and he jogged in, awaiting his reward of petting and admiration.

I closed the gap again, with concrete blocks this time, and it was a couple of months before I found Whistle waiting for me at the office. Again, at the kitchen window, we waited and watched. His new escape plan was simple.

First, he looked around to see if anyone was watching. Then he went to the outdoor staircase of our two-story garage. The blue metal stairs went up to the shop, twelve feet above the ground. The garage was old and had a gap at the bottom of the entry door in the upper room. Whistle made his way inside, through the gap. Out popped Whistle's head, from a broken window on the second floor; his body soon followed. Stepping on a little roof ledge, made to shed water, and like a cat on a fence, he made the ledge a walkway. The walkway ended next to a tin-roofed lean-to, attached to the end of the garage. He jumped three feet around the corner to the tin roof, walked down the sloping roof to the edge, five feet above the ground, and jumped over the fence to freedom. Wagging his tail, he trotted down the street. I decided the city of Winona had a pretty smart dog.

During the winter that he was fourteen years old, Whistle disappeared. With the spring thaw came a strong odor, and we discovered that he had died under the house. With black plastic bags, rubber gloves, and perfumed rags over my mouth and nose, I crawled into the narrow space under the house. I worked the decaying body into one of the bags. That probably was the most disgusting thing I have ever done—and remember, I deal with dead human bodies as part of my job. That is not what I try to remember when I think about Whistle.

~~~~~~~~~~~~~~~~~~~~~~~~~~~~~~

With our youngest daughter, Amy, came Domino, named for the Dalmatian spots that covered him. Domino was one of only two dogs we ever had to get rid of. (The other, Katie, was Lena's German Shepherd, which bit Constable Wilson on the ass.) Domino felt the need to "spread his spots" in a real bad way and was reported miles away from home, out spreading his seed.

One day I received a certified letter at the office putting me on written notice. The return address indicated the neighbor who lives catty-corner from my house. The justice court gets certified letters frequently, but the clerk was not sure how to handle this one.

"Judge, you need to read this one," said Gilyn.

I read it. "Your dog impregnated our valuable dog. We keep her contained at all times. We did not want her to get pregnant. She is half malamute and half wolf. There are four spotted puppies and you are responsible. They will be weaned in three weeks at which time you will pick them up, find them a good home, or keep them yourself. We are considering monetary damages."

The allegedly sexually violated dog was a graceful, and beautiful, Alaskan Malamute. A Malamute is light gray with black markings. An impressive black "V" goes down her forehead. (It reminds me of Michael Landon in *I Was a Teenage Werewolf*.) Her size and distinct markings left no doubt of her pedigree. Her long black and light gray hair would bounce as she played with the goat (bought for her pleasure) in the yard beside the brick house. The secured yard was two thirds contained with an eight-foot-tall wooden privacy fence. The remainder of the yard had a five-foot-tall chain link fence with sharp barbs pointing to the sky. I wondered if the alleged victim got out or my dog got in, or even if my dog in fact was the father. I went for a visit.

"How do you know it was Domino?" I asked in

defense. "Do we need to do a paternity test?" Besides the tell-tale spots, there was no evidence.

"There is a witness!" the neighbor said. "Eddie saw the whole thing." She pointed to the house next door. There was Eddie, in overalls, arms and elbows working back and forth, hoeing in the flowerbed.

Now I was detective Shamburger, investigating *The Mystery of the Doggy Style Rape*.

I walked over to the old white frame house with its tall pyramid roof.

"Hey, Eddie, how's it going?"

"Fine, 'cept the grass grows faster than I can mow it."

"Yeah, I know what you mean," I said, looking over to my jungle yard. "My dog is being charged with rape. I hear you saw something."

"Yep," he said, standing up, one hand resting on the hoe, the other on his hip. "Damnedest thing I ever saw. Domino" (he knew him by name) "was standing there on his back legs leaning up against the fence, his front legs spread-eagle, hanging on to that chain link fence." Eddie paused and the hoe moved, pointing to the scene of the crime. "And that wolf dog was backed up to him. They was gettin' it on, right through that chain link fence!" He leaned back and laughed. "I don't know how you can call it rape. You can't rape the willing."

I took the puppies: add four more to the dogs I had to get rid of.

~~~~~~~~~~~~~~~~~~~~~~~~~~~~

Pongo, an Australian Heeler, took Domino's place for eight years. Amy, my youngest, brought her home as a puppy from my sister Perry Jo. She was smart and arrogant—Pongo, that is. I had never had a dog that thought it was more intelligent than its owner. For six of those eight years she would often look at me with the expression of "You poor, ignorant human." She got it from Honey Bee, her mother, who was just as "highbrow." Pongo disappeared, and a week later buzzards circled in the meadow behind our house. A month later I found her remains, mostly bones. From fire ants and bleached by the sun, her skull was a sparkling white, with an impressive set of teeth. I buried all but the skull.

Now I am stuck with Charles, Amy's black pug, son of Golly (short for Golgotha), also my daughter's dog. Much bigger than his father, Charles is full of energy and excitement, the epitome of man's best pest. He can fetch. He can sit. And he can chew, pee, shit, run off, and bug the hell out of you. Charles is who I think of when someone says, "Lock your wife and your dog in the trunk of your car. An hour later see who loves you when you open it."

~~~~~~~~~~~~~~~~~~~~~~~~~~~~~

Some dogs can be as mean as they are friendly, and some are unpredictable. I have seen the damage not-so-friendly dogs can do, leaving physical and mental scars that can remain throughout a lifetime. The victims usually are kids, and sometimes the wounds are fatal.

Inquest #839

I performed an inquest involving the body of a two-year-old who was scratched from head to foot. A helicopter brought the child to the trauma center from out of the county. The parents claimed they found the boy in the midst of a pack of dogs and tangled in a barbed-wire fence. The scratches did not line up with the stories; the wounds did not look like an animal attack. An autopsy confirmed the scratches matched a toothed curling iron found at the little boy's house. The investigation revealed that many strange things went on at that house, including devil worship. Charges were filed against the parents, whose defense was that a pack of dogs inflicted the injuries. The dogs got them off.

~~~~~~~~~~~~~~~~~~~~~~~~~~~~~

T.J. Shamburger could cow a dog with his voice. That same voice was all that was needed to discipline me. Mom said he spanked me once, but I don't remember it. He once drew his hand back as if he was going to slap me and said something in that same "dog cowing" voice. I thought I was dead. It is no wonder that an animal or human would scurry away for its life on a command issued in that voice.

"Get out of here," he would command in his gruff voice. The animal — dog, cat, bull, or cow — usually would make haste to leave the area.

I have been known to use that voice successfully in the courtroom.

~~~~~~~~~~~~~~~~~~~~~~~~~~~~~

"Go ahead," said Constable Wilson, "go put my card on the screen door."

Today the constable is answering a complaint about a Rottweiler and a Doberman pinscher running free in Pine Springs. The old community has the largest concentration of Shamburgers in the New World.

A white, wooden-framed house sat twenty feet from the pickup, with a welcoming front porch and a screened front door.

I was told early on, "When you get into the car with Wilson, you better have a flashlight and a change of clothes. There is no telling when you will get back."

This was true. Once I found myself spending a few days in Garrison, Texas, looking for a drug crew that murdered Constable Daryl Lunsford, a good friend of mine. Today was no exception. A trip that was supposed to be "to the County Courthouse and back to the Justice Court Center" became "an animal control call."

A blast from the horn brought no one to the door. Two large beasts stood thirty yards away, looking at us as though deciding to ignore us or perhaps make us their next meal.

"No problem," I answered back to the constable's request, taking his card and pulling the handle on the pickup's door. I took the request as a dare. Bouncing out of the pickup, I decide not to close the door all the way. With confidence, I walk to the front bumper. The Doberman's ears perked up, then both dogs trotted toward me and stopped about twenty yards away. The Rottweiler stopped and crouched down, assuming the position, with his head on the ground and his butt in the air. I took another step and he bounced twice, closing the gap to fifteen yards. The Doberman pranced up beside him. He stood tall while the Rottweiler crouched like a lion, waiting to pounce.

"GET OUT OF HERE!" I shouted, using my best "T.J. dog-cowing voice."

The Rottweiler dog breed originated in the town of Rottweil, Germany, many years ago. Almost extinct, the breed made a comeback during World War I. Because the dogs were big and aggressive and took orders well, the Germans utilized them as soldiers. The "Rottie" at this particular house did not speak English or still held a grudge against Americans, or he was trained that "Get out of here" means "KILL!"

Midway through his next bounce, I was running back to the pickup. I grabbed the door handle and swung myself into the seat, the "centrifical" force almost closing the door behind me. (Note: For most of my life, I thought there was a "centrifical" force, one that keeps water in a bucket when you swing it around you and keeps a yo-yo spinning and a gyroscope gyrating. The Internet says there is no such word. The word "centrifical" is not even in the dictionary! "Centrifugal" *is* in the dictionary but is foreign to me.) The "force" did not close the door all the way. WHAM! The Rottweiler hit the door with his head, closing the issue and putting a dent in Smith County equipment.

"Here," I said, handing the card back to the constable. "I changed my mind."

Two things can end a political career: Don't mess with people's kids, and don't mess with their pets. Constable Wilson took on animal control in the north end of Smith County; the next election, he was defeated.

~~~~~~~~~~~~~~~~~~~~~~~~~~

People have Pit Bull Terriers for two reasons: They make great pets, and they are great fighters. The ancestors of the American Pit Bull were put into an arena, or pit, with a bull. Their mission was to take the bull down, usually by getting a grip on the bull's nose, neck, or head with strong jaws and teeth and then shaking violently.

Inquest #1235

On the old Kilgore Highway, out in the country, is a strange-looking pen about ten feet long and ten feet wide. It has tapered corners, so it is not a circle and not a square. It is made of ragged old wood boards of various heights, most between three and four feet, standing upright. The earthen floor is natural sand, light brown next to the fence and darker in the center. It is a pit, made for Pit Bulls. It is used for fighting and training dogs.

Fighting dogs and roosters is against the law in Texas. I guess if people did not break laws, I would be out of a job. Like most laws, this one gets broken. There is money to be made in the Pit Bull trade: gambling, prize winnings, drugs and fighting accessories, swapping dogs, and selling puppies.

Next to the ragged fighting pit is a ragged tan mobile home, a "single wide." The brown metal skirt around the bottom of the house has wide rusted-out gaps. After standing in the same place for so many years, the mobile home is not mobile anymore; it would not stand the rigors of moving. Sparse clumps of tall grass stand uncut around the house. A few bright plastic toys litter the bare sand spots, indicating that a child lives there.

Mom has a crack cocaine problem, and she is tired. "Go play outside," she tells her five-year-old son, then lies down on the couch, seeking to drift into a state of tranquility. She thinks, "When my eyes are closed and my mind is at peace, nothing else matters."

Little Byron goes out the door, not to play with the plastic toys in the yard but to play with the twelve new puppies that run loose around the house. He has played with them before, and they are fun. All are soft and cuddly and lick him as he rolls and plays with them in the yard. The puppies do not have names: Names are "reserved" for the masters, who will own and name them later. When the pups get bigger, they will go away, like so many other puppies before. Dad sells them so Byron can have toys and the family can eat and have a place to live. Dad says, "Lucille is one fine bitch."

Lucille is the mother Pit Bull in the backyard. She is chained with a large logging chain, one end locked around her neck and the other locked around a large pine tree. Lucille is locked with padlocks because she is a champion fighter and the mother of champions. She is a valuable animal with valuable children. Lucille can't run free and play with her puppies because someone would snatch her up in a heartbeat if they could. That is why there are two padlocks on the logging chain.

Byron has played with Lucille before. She is OK but not as much fun as the puppies. They climb on Byron, and he flings them off, one after another. They just keep coming back for more. This fun lasts until it is puppy supper time. Lucille gives the bark. One pup responds with the feeding whimper, and then all the pups cease playing. They leave Byron, traveling as one. The twelve herd together, running, tripping, and bumping each other as they all go to their mother. Byron stands and watches as the pups dive in, each one finding a teat and a meal.

But Byron has not finished playing.

~~~~~~~~~~~~~~~~~~~~~~~~~~~~

"Judge, we have a body on the Old Kilgore Highway."

I arrive at the scene, where police and animal control vehicles fill the yard. Several sheriffs' deputies, along with Constable Wilson and his animal control officer are chasing little puppies, scurrying about the yard and going under the house. As the puppies are caught, they are put in wire cages in the back of the animal control pickup.

"I don't know how many there are," Wilson says, wiping the sweat from his brow. "We have eight, and more are under the house."

Detective Whitham, from the Sheriff's office, meets me out front.

"It is a mess, Judge," Whitham says. "The mother says she was taking a nap and when she got up, the kid was gone. Then she found him out back. She said that the dog had never even barked at the kid before and the kid played with the dog, Lucille, all the time."

"Let's see what we have," I say. The detective leads the way to the backyard.

Around the corner is a pile of old rusted stuff: a washing machine lying on its side, a lawnmower, angle iron pieces, and a rusting barbed-wire fence with rotting fence posts. All this "mess" is at the bottom of a tall, majestic pine forest. Looking up, you can see the peaceful swaying of the limbs, limbs laced with pine needles letting in tiny sparkles of light. The coolness of the shade is a break from the burning heat of the sun. A cool breeze feels good and looking up seems to place me in another world. A familiar aroma brings me back to earth and the job at hand; it is the thick, sweet smell of blood.

Lying on the ground in a large pool of blood is a dog.

She is a Pit Bull and probably the mother of all these puppies. The head of the dog lies open. She is the victim of a shotgun blast, fired from far enough away that the shot pattern removed her face and much of her skull. Dad had killed this "one fine bitch." A huge chain is wrapped around her neck and around a big pine. It is not a long chain. The ground around the body, worn smooth, shows that she had about six feet of roaming room. Beside her is a white ceramic bowl, dirty with crusted dog food. A red clay bowl holding a little water sits three feet away, and between the bowls and lying by Lucille is a five-year-old child.

With a few facial cuts and a disfigured head, Byron

looks as though he is sleeping, even cuddling, next to Lucille. Nobody knows what actually happened. Little Bryon probably jumped right in with the rest of the puppies. Lucille may have grabbed him with her wide jaws, taking in most of his head and then sling him around and shake violently back and forth. This is what her ancestors would do, what they were bred and trained to do. Maybe if there had been no puppies, or if Mom had not laid down on the couch, or if Dad had been home — and for sure, if there had been no Lucille — there would still be a Byron.

Closer inspection shows that the boy lost two fingers and a piece of ear. These were recovered with Lucille's autopsy.

"We got ten of them," Constable Wilson says. "The dad said that was all. I think some hit the woods."

"What are you going to do with them?" I ask.

"Put them down, all of them," he answers. "Would you believe the daddy got pissed when I told him we were taking them?! He started raising hell. I told him it would save him a trip to jail if he would shut up and sign the release. He signed."

Both parents were charged with child endangerment. Mom did prison time, and Dad's charges were dismissed.

~~~~~~~~~~~~~~~~~~~~~~~~~

It is strange how most of us react to the tragic plights of animals. Are animals inferior to humans? They rely on us to be treated well. Animal rights groups and strict cruelty to animal laws are witness of the desire to assist those lower down on the food chain. In the movie *Patton*, I remember the scene where a mule was on a bridge; hooked to a wagon blocking the road, it would not move. General Patton walked up to the animal. Bam, we hear, and the next scene shows the animal dropping off the bridge. Splash, and the convoy moves on. None of the battle scenes where humans were killed, mauled, and mangled made such an impression on me.

One evening my teenage daughters were crying. "Those poor abandoned puppies. They are living underneath the road, in a culvert. It is cold and wet, and they are lonely!"

They had seen the puppies, if six months old is still puppy age. "How can people do such a thing?" they asked, and the tears continued. "Can we go get them?"

Ironically, I had done an inquest that same day. A three-year-old child had wandered into the backyard and fallen into a hole dug for a septic tank. The tank was half full of stagnant water. They found the little child floating face down in the cold, dark, mucky water. I told the story to my girls, hoping to get the message across that there are worse things in life than starving, abandoned dogs. They were undaunted and unaffected by the tragic death. The dogs were real to them. They could see the dogs and feel the cold. My inquest was just another story.

"You can shed tears over a couple of dogs and not be fazed over the death of a child?" I asked, shaking my head. This is one of the many mysteries of teenagers and women I will never understand.

We ended up with three deformed dogs. One died before we could give it a name. Culvert, named whence he came, lived long enough to introduce the parvovirus to my backyard, a virus that later killed several other dogs. Laddie was the final survivor. His bent bones and deformed feet were the results of malnourishment in puppyhood and surviving parvo. He looked a miserable mess. I thought it best to put him out of his misery. I took the .25 automatic pistol to the backyard. Laddie looked at me with those sad eyes, tail wagging. I shot him, aiming for his heart. He stumbled back, then looked at me quizzically and continued to wag his tail. I could not shoot him again. Laddie lived a happy life with us for several more years, until the auto accident.

~~~~~~~~~~~~~~~~~~~~~~~~~~

Some will read "Pit Bull" and feel pity for Lucille; she was just protecting her pups. Some will have pity for the puppies; all they did was get born. Some will pity Dad; he lost dogs, son, and wife. Everyone will feel pity for Byron, dead at the age of five. Some may even have pity on Mom, living in a hellhole of a house with a monkey on her back (slang for "drug problem"). Hey, some even may pity me; I had to go look at all this mess. Yep, this is one Pit-i-full story.

Chapter 16

Noah, Amber, and Max

Dog Inquest #15

Red fire trucks fill the narrow street and position themselves to fight the blaze at the suburban two-story dwelling. The gold lettering on the red trucks indicates that volunteers come from several surrounding communities, called in by the smoke signals, seen for miles. The ordinarily quiet street, with manicured yards bordered by curbs and sidewalks, is now full of activity as firemen, equipped with air tanks, run in and out of the burning house, taking what they can to awaiting hands, which take the items to greater safety. First come the smaller pieces of furniture, then the wedding china, then pictures from the mantel. The items get smaller and smaller as the firefighters' air packs run out. One fireman runs back into the house. "Max!" he yells, but the call is muffled through the breathing mask he wears. The flame goes higher, and the shuffling line of items being saved reduces to a trickle, then stops. Finally, there is nothing left to do but water the hot spots and watch a life's work go up in flames.

The difference between a burning house and a burning home is felt when it is yours, especially when you see memories go up in smoke. Pictures, mementos, and other special things can never be replaced. Even things that are replaced will never be the same; the substitutes will always be "like the one I had before the fire." If there are survivors, their feelings of relief are replaced quickly by feelings of loss, as they see so much of what they have worked for drift up to the sky, creating a black cloud with no silver lining. It especially hurts when somewhere in the flame and ash is a pet.

"Dad, I am standing here watching my house burn." This is my son, Noah, a NASA engineer, calling on his cell phone. "There are fire trucks everywhere, and they are doing what they can, but when they come out for air, the flames and smoke . . . We can't find Max . . ." His voice drifts off. Max, a black and white border collie, has been with Noah and Amber since their college days, before they were married. He is fourteen years old.

This is, or was, the third house they had moved into while living in the Houston area and their first house since Amber became "OB/GYN" Doctor Shamburger. The house itself was a good purchase, selected with much time and patience, meeting all the requirements they had set.

Noah had told me how realtors gave them a ho-hum response as they investigated nice houses in nice neighborhoods. They assumed the young couple was reaching for more than they could afford. When "Dr. Shamburger" appeared on the applications, the realtors quickly changed their attitude to "Let me show you what we have!"

The media room Noah had personally built was his pride and joy. Reclining theater seats sat among surround sound speakers, and the humongous digital screen was capable of receiving anything a cable, computer, satellite, video recorder, or video game could direct its way.

From the second-floor balcony, which looked out over the Jacuzzi and pool, they could see a beautiful green golf course. After Hurricane Ike, the balcony developed a leak.

A construction crew had been working on the balcony, using a torch to melt in tarpaper. They left one day, and thirty minutes later Noah was called at work. His house was on fire. Fifteen minutes later, he is on the phone with me.

Houston is three hundred miles from Winona. It is Friday.

"We can come down Sunday or Monday," I say, looking at my calendar filled with appointments. The weekend is booked up with a music gig, a large Rose Garden wedding, and church.

"You don't need to come," Noah says. "Here comes Amber. Talk to you later."

By the end of the day Fae and I have cleared our calendar. On Saturday morning Mom and Dad are on our way to Houston. By noon we are there. Judy, Amber's mom, had already made the trip.

Like the picture Noah sent by text message, the brick house sticks out like a burned thumb among the many tall brick and rock houses in the subdivision. The remaining brick of their house stands like a skeleton holding up bones of charred lumber. The burned portions of the roof accent the absence of the remaining roof. Most of the back wall is broken into chunks of brick lying in jagged angles on the ground. A dangling metal flashing is all that is left of the balcony. It hangs over strands of rebar and a frame where Noah's next project, an outdoor patio with a full kitchen, was going to be.

The flames and smoke are gone, but the smell of a burned house remains. The weather is hot, and the air is heavy with the added humidity of leftover firefighting. Noah and his engineer friends have on hard hats. With their safety logic, they are muddling through water-soaked ashes, clothing, bedding, and rubble, finding a vase here, a clump of melted jewelry there, and a twisted pipe that used to be a shotgun somewhere else. Somehow the refrigerator survived, and the beer is cool. We share a few.

"I wonder what wine tastes likes after five or six hundred degrees," says one searcher, holding up a charred but intact bottle from what was an extensive wine collection.

On the minds of all the searchers is Max.

The firemen had valiantly looked for Max during the fire. Other people had looked throughout the day. I was concerned about how Max would look: Was he a "crispy critter"? I thought it best not to find him, but the search continued.

After loading a few boxes of salvaged smoke-covered items into the pickup, we were through for the day. With handshakes and hugs, friends and helpers went home. Noah and I began cleaning up, washing soot and ash off with a water hose — the only utility left working.

"I would just like to know about Max," Amber says. "I would feel better if I knew."

Amber, her mom, and Fae go to the neighbor's house where they are staying. Everyone on the street is ready to do whatever they can. It is strange how a simple "Hello" every now and then, or the wave of a hand in passing, can develop meaning when spread over a year's time. One neighbor walked up to Noah with a roll of money; holding it out, he said, "Take what you need." Noah refused the kind offer. When most of your earthly possessions can be put in a few boxes, you have no idea what you need.

Noah is rinsing off his shoes. "Noah," I say, "are you ready to find Max? We may not find anything but a skull, but if you want to find him, we will." I think about a lady I had seen the week before: Her house had burned and blown up. Her exposed skull and charred remains reminded me that there is always something remaining, even with a hot house fire.

"We need to find him," Noah says. The cleanup ceased.

We put on the bright yellow hard hats and climb back onto the crumbling brick. Fae walks up. "We are going back in to find Max," I say, and then Noah stops and turns to us.

"It seemed like Max knew it was going to happen," he says. "Usually, when you did not want to play with Max you could just tell him to go away and he would go away, but for the last few days he insisted . . ." He is trying to hold back tears. Fae isn't, nor am I. We stand a moment, quiet, with only sniffles.

"Let's go get him," I say. We climb in, Noah with a shovel and me with a hoe.

We look around in places where the firefighters may have overlooked. Thousands of gallons of water saturated the house. Everything is covered with black ash and wet muck. Sweat pours onto my glasses and into my eyes, making it difficult to see. We look under fallen sheetrock, beside a bed; we go to a place where Noah thought he may have smelled something.

Finally, it is time to really go to work. Off comes my T-shirt and hardhat. With a few twist and ties, my already damp T-shirt becomes a headband. I am determined.

"If Max is here," I tell Noah, "we will find him if it takes all night. Where do you think he went?" I ask, getting back to the basics.

"When he was scared, he would go into our bedroom closet." The bedroom was gone. Charcoal two-by-fours outline where the closet was. "The firemen looked in there."

"Well, let's look again."

It looks more dangerous than it really is. Charcoal boards are not as heavy as their unburned originals, and I am not afraid of those dangling above us. I work my way to the closet, and Noah follows. I pull away burned layers of ash debris and come to wet clothing. Short of breath, I step away and Noah takes over. With the hoe, he pulls back more layers of clothing. Each layer is dryer as we work our way down.

"Amber hated these!" Noah says, holding up a pair of baggy faded blue pajamas, undamaged. "I guess fate has decided what would and would not stay." Then he goes back to work.

"Look, these clothes . . ." He stops and sighs. "There he is," he says, exposing the familiar long black and white hair of the Border collie. He steps back, feeling first the relief of knowing, then the sadness of knowing.

"Go get a couple of trash bags," I instruct Noah, hoping the mission will give him time to settle down and me time to inspect the damage. While he is gone, I uncover Max. He is not burned at all and is still intact, a good thing. Max had gone into the closet, his refuge, his place to hide, his safe place. He breathed the air that held no oxygen, went to sleep, and was gone before all hell broke loose.

"This is bad," I say, as we place Max in the makeshift body bag, "but do you remember Whistle?"

"Oh, yes. He died under our house. That was a mess," Noah says in remembrance. We talk about other dogs we had growing up.

We carry Max's body over the rubble to the backyard and lay him on a surviving bed sheet. Noah goes back inside and finds some of Max's things: knotted ropes, Frisbees, balls, and chew toys. We place them alongside Max and fold the sheet over, covering him. I think of the many human bodies I have seen wrapped in such fashion.

Noah calls Amber on the cell phone to tell her that we found Max. She and her mom come quickly. With a sigh of relief, "Dr. Shamburger" diagnoses that Max did not suffer from the heat. In another role, "pet mom Amber" cries.

As the sun goes down and darkness settles around us, Noah, Amber, Judy, Fae, and I stand around Max. We talk about the friend that saw the kids through college, a wedding, and life. Max was always there when they needed him, and he was there even when they did not need him. He seemed to listen when you talked to him, and his answer to the most complex problem was, "Let's play."

We call the veterinarian for ideas of what to do with the body. We place him in Noah's Toyota pickup truck, which also survived the fire. Fae, Judy, and I always claimed Max as our grand-dog. We stand in silence as Noah and Amber, pet mom and dad, take their loved one to be cremated.

~~~~~~~~~~~~~~~~~~~~~~~

Aftermath: Two years later the insurance settled with Noah and Amber.

The firefighters managed to save and salvage several things, including the grandfather clock LoLo gave them and an old chester drawers. (If I called it chest of drawers I would lose my Native Texan status.) When they had a new home, they moved in the smoke-damaged items. Painful memories were attached to each item, reminding them of the things that did not make it through the fire.

"The chester drawers will be lighter if we remove the drawers," said my son the engineer.

As each drawer was removed, a renewed hope came. These things survived the fire, and so would Amber and

Noah. The bottom and final drawer was pulled open. To their delight, it was full of photos and mementos, undamaged.

The new house is in a nice subdivision in Friendswood, just outside of Houston. Noah continues to work on the International Space Station for NASA, and Amber has opened her own practice, Friendswood Women. They have adopted Tom and Huck, who are brothers of mixed breed. The young dogs run around the pool and tussle for play toys and attention. They are as big as Max but not nearly as smart. After all, they are only children.

Chapter 17

The Gunslingers

Inquests #3282, #328, #329, #1236, and #878

Thirty years ago, one of every four people seriously considered suicide. That includes your neighbors and yourself. That is what my college research paper said. A national survey found that more than eight million adults in the United States seriously considered suicide in 2008, with younger adults the most likely to contemplate taking their own lives.

In addition to nearly 8.3 million who thought about committing suicide, 2.3 million made a plan to do so, and 1.1 million actually attempted it.

It's Over . . . Well, Maybe Not

"It's over," my steady girlfriend told me. Love goes deep into the heart and mind of the adolescent.

Tears streaming across my face, I rode my little Honda motorcycle toward the cliff of Pricket Hill. OK, so it is only a hill, but it is the closest thing we have to a cliff around here. My intent was to make straight that curve in the road, fly off that cliff, and never come back. As I approached what would have been at least a broken arm, I realized that some of the best things in life can be painful. If I had a choice between never knowing and caring or loving her versus the pain of parting ways, I would choose the experience. My motorcycle turned. I zoomed down the hill. The wind dried my tears, and

I grew up a little that day. I wonder how many people wake up the next morning to see a suicide note they had written the night before, or how many souls wished that they could take it back.

The first suicide victim I encountered was a Sunday school student of mine. A student in church on Sunday, two days later he was a body found alone, sitting in a chair in the middle of his living room, a bullet in his head. He graduated from high school with honors and was a straight-A college student until he had made a C on a test. That grade appeared to have pushed him over the edge.

Inquest #3282:
Accidents Happen

She is a Christian lady, a singer and songwriter. At the age of sixty-eight, she feels that she is at the pinnacle of her career. Because of her weakness, it is difficult for her to climb on stage. Before taking the spotlight, she removes two little green tubes from her nasal passage that connect to a larger green plastic tube, which in turn connects to a machine that provides a constant flow of oxygen. Then she will sing her award-winning songs. Afterward, she will take her bows, make her modest smiles of appreciation to her audience, and get back to the oxygen. Usually the performance is in a church; sometimes she is at a festival or a fund-raiser.

Golden trophies and plaques fill shelves that cover a living room wall—trophies and awards she had won in contest after contest. The shelves were built by her husband explicitly for the purpose of displaying these marks of her vocal achievements.

"Don't you think it was an accident?" she asks. "It is just not like him to do such a thing. He was going back for another cancer treatment the day after tomorrow. He was on medication, and I think suicide is a side effect of one of those medications. Then, there is this million-dollar accidental insurance policy."

A few days and several phone calls later, I politely listened to Mrs. Accident for twenty minutes, occasionally interjecting something that would go against the grain of her line of thought. You can tell when a mind is "made up" and someone is determined to believe what they want to believe. I dance around, trying to insert some logic here and there. She refuses to understand why I would not rule her husband's death as an accident. There are side effects of several drugs that can lead to suicide. Certain diet pills and other medications can push an already depressed person over the edge. In this case, I even listed the medication as a possible contributing factor on the death certificate.

"Well," I finally say, exhausted, "I would have to say he accidentally waited until no one was around and accidentally found the deer rifle that had been put away for years. He then accidentally dumped the ammunition on the bed and accidentally picked out the bullets he wanted to use. Then he accidentally loaded the gun. Accidentally, he took all this out to the storage shed, where he accidentally shut the door. He then accidentally pulled off his right boot and accidentally put the gun in his mouth and then accidentally, using his great toe, accidentally pulled the trigger. I am sorry, but that is just too many accidents."

~~~~~~~~~~~~~~~~~~~~~~~~

The idea that someone would take his or her own life is difficult to grasp, especially when that someone is close to you. Most suicides leave a trail of signs, including veiled threats, multiple light attempts, giving away their possessions, and even telling people good-bye. Still, we often remain oblivious until it is all over.

"The last few days he/she was in a good mood. He/she was joking around the other day as if everything was great." Everything was great because the decision had been made, and there was no more pressure. Nothing can harm or upset the walking dead.

When they plan their departures, some suicides want to be alone, and some want to make a point. Some want to take others with them. Those who suffer depression feel alone in their misery and want to be alone when they exit this world. They think the world will be a better place without them, and they would rather be dead (or gone) than face another day.

Guns

Some type of firearm is the tool of choice for many suicides. After all, most of us have seen thousands of lives ended by the hands of others on television and in the movies. Sometimes actors squirm and suffer a theatrical death, but for the most part they simply fall over dead, without any apparent pain or suffering. Only the stars in the show develop into "real" people, gaining our empathy and sympathy when tragedy happens. Most of the victims on television simply die. To our knowledge, they die without family, friends, or real lives. Their acting part is simply to be the one in front of the make-believe bullet for the "hero" or the "villain" to eliminate.

Some of the gunslingers who inflict harm upon themselves get creative. You might think it simple and quick to put a gun to your head and pull the trigger; this does happen. Usually, there is some preparation and planning. The planning is focused on self and is irrational. Suicide notes say things like these:

"I am doing this because I love her/him so much."

"I can't afford to live."

"I would do anything to make it better."

"I'm sorry. It is all your fault. I can't help it."

Suicide preparation can take days or months. When the plan is finalized, sometimes with a dress rehearsal, not much can change it.

"He has attempted this before. He just wanted attention." I have heard this many times.

"Now he has it!" I have said, in response, at an inquest.

It is a falsehood that if someone attempts and fails at

suicide, they will not attempt it again. Just like a reformed alcoholic may go back to drinking, the alternative to life remains for those who have attempted to take their own.

Some things are often NOT taken into consideration. Who will find me? Who will clean up the blood and brain matter splattered all over the place? When will I be found? Will maggots infest my body? Will I be decaying, and will the odor be strong enough to make ambulance, firemen, law enforcement officers, and Judge Shamburger gag?

Some discover that planning requires more effort than the act. You have to know about weapons in order to make them effective. Many a suicide has been thwarted because an arm was not long enough to reach the trigger on a rifle or shotgun. To offset short arms, victims use coat hangers, sticks, and strings tied to the trigger and pulled by various means, including a doorknob, like they were pulling a tooth. Then there is the classic one shoe on and one shoe off. I wonder how many people have been killed with their big toe pulling the trigger.

Hundreds of people are still alive today after placing a gun to their head, closing their eyes, and slowly squeezing the trigger . . . harder and harder . . . expecting all their troubles to be over in a flash, and nothing happens. The safety would not allow them to pull the trigger. There is no explosion; their eyes open, giving them a little more time to think, and they live another day.

Most guns have a safety feature that disables the weapon until it is deactivated by pressing a button or flipping a lever with the thumb. Some pistols now have the "safety" in the trigger itself. This means that when you place your finger on the trigger, the gun is ready to fire. This enables the shooter—we can hope that it is a peace officer or me—to quickly engage the target, which we can hope is a piece of paper, an empty can or other harmless target, or some person who truly needs to be shot. This type of trigger safety completely defeats the many other purposes of having a "safety" on the weapon, primarily that of not shooting someone with a supposedly empty gun. The need to release a safety is an added step that stops little fingers from pulling triggers and stops big fingers when a person is not thinking straight.

Inquests #328 and #329:
Size Doesn't Matter

Big guns make big holes, little guns make little holes, and both guns leave you dead.

A .22-caliber pistol's bullet tends to ricochet or bounce around in the body, and especially in the skull. A .45 tends to rip through at a speed that allows it to gather tissue and bone, to make the exit wound bigger than the entrance. Big guns require more gunpowder and therefore produce more gasses to propel the bullet. The gases have to go somewhere, and with a contact gunshot wound, they will proceed and follow the bullet into the wound, causing a buildup of pressure. This can cause an exploding headache.

~~~~~~~~~~~~~~~~~~~~~~~~~

Javier is Mexican, he is angry, and he is drunk. Rufus, an old black man, had been messing with Javier's woman. She also happened to be the old black man's wife.

Javier parks his old pickup truck across the street, halfway blocking the traffic lane. He does not care where his truck is parked: It is get-even time! He is a man with a mission, and he is going to put an end to Rufus. His .357 Magnum revolver is loaded with six large shells, each over an inch and a half long and 0.357 inches in diameter. Fully loaded, the gun weighs 2 pounds and 14 ounces.

Javier steps up to the front screen door and finds it locked. He knocks.

"Ven aquí," he yells, now beating on the door. Old man Rufus opens the wooden door. The Mexican has not come to talk. He points the big revolver, with its six-inch barrel. BOOM, BOOM, BOOM, and BOOM: four shots point blank, right through the screen door. He would have emptied the gun, but the old man stumbles back inside and out of sight. Satisfied, Javier sticks the pistol into his pants and high-steps down the porch steps to strut back to his truck.

Rufus falls back into his house. He is thinking, "Damned screen door may keep out flies, but it doesn't slow down bullets. Wasn't that my wife's friend? What the hell has she gotten me into?" His shirt feels wet and sticky. He looks down and realizes, "That son of a bitch shot me!"

He reaches into a table drawer next to the old padded sofa and pulls out his little .25 automatic. His hand covers most of the pistol that he keeps there for protection. It is loaded with six little bullets less than an inch long and 0.25 inches in diameter. Fully loaded, it weighs 14 ounces.

He stumbles his way back to the door and sees Javier swaggering back to his pickup. Leaning against the door, he manages to unlock the screen and steps out onto the little front porch. He points the two-and-a-half-inch barrel toward the truck, twenty yards away, and pulls the trigger. One shot fires, and it is the last sound either of them ever heard.

When I arrive, Javier is dead in the street, his feet on the ground and his body crumpled on the pickup's floorboard. The half-opened door holds him in place. On the porch lies Rufus. A big gun and a little gun both did "the job"; both men are dead.

Mrs. Rufus now lives in the old house, drawing a widow's Social Security, and with a new boyfriend.

Home Protection

Tony, a friend of mine, told me he awoke hearing something or someone in the house. His wife was also alarmed, and he retrieved his pistol to go after the intruder.

"It was dark," he said. "I was afraid if I turned on the lights, he would shoot me first. I couldn't just hide and do nothing, my kids and my wife's safety comes first. I held that .357 as steady as I could. Silently, I made my way down the dark hallway to the living room. I could tell someone was there. I decided to guard the hall and kill anyone who crossed the line. The noise stopped. I waited, standing my ground at the hallway entrance. The light came on, and I quickly tracked my gun to the light switch, my finger on the trigger."

The .357 Magnum's rear sight is notched; at the end of the long, shiny barrel is the bead or front sight. When these line up, a sight picture is created.

"The sight picture scared the shit out of me," said Tony. "It was my little girl, still standing on her tiptoes, barely reaching the light switch. She was dead in my sights."

This kind of happened to me once, during a thunderstorm. Fae and I had just bought the old house where we now live, thirty years ago. We learned quickly that old houses creak and groan at night when the winds blow, but tonight there was a new sound mixed with those of thunder and rain. I got my little .25-caliber automatic pistol. I went down the dark hallway, the one we call the bowling alley because of the long oak wooden floor. Originally, it was the breezeway or dogtrot, which was closed in long before my time. The end of the hallway is what used to be the back door that led to what used to be the back porch. When indoor plumbing became a part of the house, a bathroom was added next to the porch. Later, the porch was expanded and enclosed. The original door, with its large glass window, separates the hall from the den. Eleven years later, daughter Lena flew down that "bowling alley" on Christmas roller skates and cut her arm as she rammed it through the single large pane of glass. To this day, it is a door without glass.

I could hear the soft, irregular thud of something happening in the den. I took the safety off. Constable Bill Grady, who furnished me with the little pistol, warned me, "You probably won't kill anyone with this, but it will leave a mark on whoever killed you and make it easier for us to find 'im."

"Hold it right there," I said in my best command voice, like I was talking to a dog. "Stay where you are." I stood behind what I thought was cover. I have learned since then that bullets from most guns will travel easily through walls and sheetrock. It was quiet.

Then THUMP—a flash of light and a bang. I could have shot, but at what? I had practiced with the little .25 automatic, and it had a history of jamming. There was a strong possibility I would have only one shot. I would be left standing with nothing but a useless jammed threat, unable to defend myself and family. I wanted that single shot to count.

I quickly realized there was no shooting; it was lightning and thunder. The lightning continued, and I peered through the spooky shades of black, white and gray. There was no target. Then I thought, "Who the hell would be robbing me in this weather?" I reached in and turned on the light.

Some ceiling tiles are made of a cardboard fiber. Each individual square foot is stapled either to a wooden lath or the old ceiling; each one is locked into the next by way of a groove. This type of ceiling will last forever or until it gets wet. When the ceiling tiles get wet, they absorb water, swell, and turn to mush. The staples stay in place, while the tiles began to disintegrate around them. The locking grooves hold groups of the ceiling tiles together as they warp and sag until that last staple gives way. Then the group falls, leaving the survivors hanging until they too grow heavy with moisture. I had found my intruder.

The next day, the room looked like a battle had taken place. Ceiling tiles lay in globs all over the room. Pink bat insulation hung in spots. The soaked carpet gave off a musty smell. The battle of living in an old house began.

Loaded vs. Unloaded

When someone puts a gun to their head, there is a problem. Whether the gun is loaded or unloaded, there has to be some kind of death wish. Few deaths of this type are accidents, but accidents do happen.

"Do I need to go get my gun?" I asked the deputy sitting at his desk. He could tell by the tone of my voice and the way my eyebrows were pointing up that I was not kidding.

He was showing his pistol to some other policemen and nonchalantly displaying it, indiscriminately pointing it at everything and everyone, including me.

"If you are going to point that gun at me, then I am going to get my gun and point it at you," I said.

"It's not loaded," he said.

"YOU think it is not loaded. I know mine is," I respond. "My dad always said most people are killed with an *unloaded* gun, and I was taught never to point a gun, loaded or unloaded, at anything I do not want to kill." These are two good pieces of advice for anyone around guns. Law enforcement people are trained with safety in mind, but sometimes familiarity breeds the wrong kind of complacency. Because their weapon becomes a part of their being, they often become too familiar with it, and like the fable of the beautiful snake that needed help, its bite can be fatal . . . or not.

~~~~~~~~~~~~~~~~~~~~~~~

It is amazing that someone can miss a target less than an inch away, themselves being the target. Many "would-be" suicides are left lying in a hospital bed in their own mental hell because they missed. When I was a nurse, I had a patient who missed.

"Wait a minute," I said. We were playing chess in a military hospital. He was a victim of a self-inflected gunshot wound to the head. He had placed the gun under his chin, pointed it straight up, and given himself a tongue piercing and injured the frontal part of his brain. I was told he would never be able to think or communicate, but he showed interest in a chess set I was carrying to another patient. I sat him up on the side of his bed, and we set up the chessboard. Let the games begin. "It is my turn. You have to wait until I move."

Speechless, he would reach out, pick a chess piece, and move it, thinking ahead much faster than I. He won the first game. This meant that he still had cognitive ability, or it meant

I could not win a chess game playing someone with half a brain. Later, he learned to talk in a slow cadence and progressed his way out of the hospital.

In psychotherapy days of old, an ice pick was inserted beside the eye and into the brain. Later, the instrument became an orbitoclast or leucotome; it was used to scramble the frontal tissues of the brain. This type of frontal lobotomy removed all the violent tendencies of the patient, including that toward suicide. My patient had done his lobotomy with a nine-millimeter pistol.

Inquest #1236:
Unhappy Birthday

"I bought him the shotgun for his birthday. I told him not to play with it. It was not a toy," exclaims an emotional wife, sitting on the couch and crying her eyes out. He had done this before.

"Don't worry," he would say, pointing the gun to his head and pulling the trigger. "It's not loaded."

The last time, it was.

Inquest #878:
Just Like the Movies

"I'm not afraid to die," the teenager says, pointing the little pistol to his head and pulling the trigger. He is acting, imitating and quoting a scene in a recent popular movie. Unlike the actor in the movie, this child's days of play are over.

~~~~~~~~~~~~~~~~~~~~~~~~~

Where is the "line" between suicide and accident? Suicide is the act of deliberately killing yourself. Science says it is a uniquely human act. I wonder about beached whales and lemmings. If someone is mentally ill or drugged out of their mind and jumps off a building and dies in the act, can we say they deliberately killed themselves? Is anyone who takes their own life, or the life of another, absent from some form mental distress?

Is Russian roulette a form of suicide? Suppose the person playing does not want to lose? Do we all tempt death in one way or another? Jumping out of an airplane, smoking, and even speeding down the road may be a test of our mortality.

In some religions, a self-inflicted death is an unpardonable sin. In other religions, it can be the road to eternal bliss or the only honorable course of action.

Many family trees have stumped limbs, cut off by a gun. Accidentally or intentionally, the members are just as dead. For those of us left behind, the question will linger: "Did they really mean to do it?" Regardless of any official rulings, we all draw our own "lines."

Chapter 18

Kids and Guns

Inquests #41, #3699, and #632

Inquest #41:
Out of Sight, Out of Mind

The pistol always sits upon the gun cabinet. The father has taught his daughter the dangers of the weapon. It is for home security, so it needs to be accessible. What good is a locked-up gun in the event of a house invasion? Having it on top of the gun cabinet makes it available to Dad and not available to his little girl; at least was not available until she grows up.

Now Cathy is fifteen years old, and she has a visitor. The young man is impressed with the locked gun cabinet. Rifles and shotguns are lined up side by side and visible through beveled hardened glass.

"You could start a war with all these guns," Tom says, pulling the brass handle. "It's locked."

"Dad keeps it locked," Cathy answers.

"He doesn't trust you? Suppose somebody broke in the house and was going to rape you or something? What if we needed to shoot somebody? You would be dead meat. What good is a locked-up gun?" Tom clearly is taunting Cathy.

"Well," Cathy hesitates, "I'm not exactly defenseless. Dad has a gun hidden."

"Yeah, sure," Tom says with a doubtful drawl.

"I'm not supposed to mess with it. Come on, let's go

watch TV."

"Where is it?" Tom responds as she turns to go in the den. "You're bullshitting; there ain't no gun."

"Yes there is, on top of the cabinet." Before the words reach his ears, Cathy knows she has made a mistake.

"Let's check it out," Tom says, reaching up for the treasure. He is just tall enough to touch the top, but he cannot reach over and feel the gun.

"No way! Tom! Leave it alone. It's loaded!" Cathy knows Tom, and she knows there is no turning back. He pulls a chair from the dining room and places it near the arsenal.

Standing on the chair, he is able to reach over and feel for the gun. He lays his hand on it, feeling the cold steel. He has played with plastic toy guns, and this gun was much heavier than he had imagined. He has shot his friend's BB gun. His mom would not allow any guns in their house.

This is a real gun. He brings it down, holding it with both hands, marveling over the prize he has found. In his hands, he holds life and death. As a young teen, he has not yet really experienced life; as a young teen, he is too young to die.

"Put it back!" Cathy says, and then screams when he points it at her. "Don't point that thing at me, and don't put your finger on the trigger!"

"Like this?" Tom asks, then draws down on her while he is still standing on the chair.

"I'm out of here," Cathy says, turning away and quickly stepping toward the doorway.

~~~~~~~~~~~~~~~~~~~~~~~~~

Gun triggers require various amounts of pressure to set the hammer in motion. An automatic pistol that is cocked and ready requires less than two pounds of pressure on the trigger, which will release the hammer and put the firing pin in motion. The firing pin hits and dents the soft metal cap, causing the primer to pop inside the casing.

This sets off a larger explosion of the gunpowder within the shell casing, creating compressed gases that cause the lead projectile to travel the length of the barrel. At this point, all the sound and energy is contained within the confines of the weapon. Then the projectile, usually lead, is freed from the barrel to fly, spin, and/or tumble to its destination. With the release of the projectile, the gases blast forth, some still glowing, and a bang results. If you are shooting outside or in the woods, it is loud; inside a room or car, it is deafening.

~~~~~~~~~~~~~~~~~~~~~~~~

"BANG!" goes the gun. Cathy does not see the gun go off. She hears and feels the concussion. Quiet follows.

"Am I dead?" she thinks. "It is so quiet. I am still standing. I do not feel shot."

Then she cries out, "What do you think you are doing!" Even though her mouth is moving and she can feel the air being forced through her throat — she can even feel the vibrations of her scream — she can hear no words. A second seems like an eternity as she stands frozen. Then a ringing sound takes over the silence.

She turns to see that her visitor is no longer standing in the chair. He lies crumpled on the floor. She runs to the phone and dials 911.

"I should never have told him where the gun was," Cathy cries to the dispatcher.

Some feel Cathy's father was at fault and should be prosecuted for not securing the weapon. Some feel the boy should have learned about guns at home. I can see future laws requiring trigger locks and securing weapons. I would be surprised if a lawsuit was not filed because of this incident.

Ruling: GSW (gunshot wound) to the head; accidental.

Inquest #3699:
The Empty Gun

"Judge, we have a gunshot wound to the head," the

nurse says. She is calling from Mother Frances Hospital. "He arrived here three days ago, and the doctors have determined he is not going to recover. The family decided not to prolong the suffering, and life support has been withdrawn."

"What happened?" I ask, finishing up my breakfast and getting ready for the paperwork.

"The twenty-one-year-old white male named Robert Rhine was at the shooting range with his girlfriend. He was shooting a .38 pistol, and she wanted to shoot it, so he gave it to her. She shot him in the forehead, right between the eyes. He thought he had emptied the gun. It was an accident."

"When did all this happen?"

"Three days ago. Let's see. . . . He was flown here by helicopter and arrived at zero eight thirty."

"Where was the shooting range?" I ask.

"Don't know."

"What agency is investigating?"

"Don't know."

"What county did it happen in?"

"Don't know."

"Where did the helicopter land?"

"Willowmuck."

"Is there any family here?"

"No, but the mother is on her way."

"Do not pull any tubes; I will get back to you."

There are several flags on this one. A .38 is a revolver. When you empty most revolvers, the cylinder is cleared by ejecting the shells, and the cylinder is easily inspected with the classic spin. Some add a flick of the wrist to snap the cylinder back into place. Next, revolvers are single action or double action. This means the hammer has to be cocked manually or is cocked by pulling the trigger. Either way requires an extra effort and not just a bump on the trigger. Finally, what twenty-one-year-old gets up before eight in the morning on a Saturday and goes to a firing range to shoot his pistol with his girlfriend?

I start calling the county dispatchers.

"Sorry, Judge, there is no record of any shooting in

Smith County."

"Sorry, Judge, there is no record of any shooting in Gregg County."

"Sorry, Judge, we do not show anything in Wood County."

"Sorry to hear he didn't make it," says the dispatcher in Zulu County. "The family is pretty torn up about it."

"I need to speak to whoever is working the case," I say.

"That would be Lieutenant Harrington," the dispatcher answers. "I will have him call you as soon as I can find him."

"Thank you. I need to talk to him soon. I need to know if you want an autopsy."

"I'll page him," the dispatcher says, and the waiting game begins.

Fifteen minutes later, I answer the phone.

"Shamburger."

"Judge, this is Lieutenant Harrington from the Zulu County Sheriff's Office. I understand that Mr. Rhine has died. It is a dang shame."

"I hope your story is better than the one I have been hearing," I answer. "What happened?"

"The victim was in the backyard shooting a .380."

This changes things. A .380 is an automatic. The bullets are contained in a clip rather than a cylinder. The clip slides into the pistol grip.

~~~~~~~~~~~~~~~~~~~~~~~~~

Clearing an automatic takes three simple steps. 1. Remove the clip. 2. Slide and eject any round in the chamber. 3. Look into the empty chamber. Always put the weapon on safety.

~~~~~~~~~~~~~~~~~~~~~~~~~

"Come on back to bed," Robert Rhine says, begging Vickie, his nineteen-year-old girlfriend. "Hell, it's not even eight o'clock in the morning."

She pulls up her loose-fitting black jeans. Her short, coal-back hair glistens as it falls across a white face that sees little sun. "I've got to get ready for the garage sale," she says as she buttons up her long-sleeved black blouse, prissing out a hip. "Come on." She looks at him seductively over her shoulder, tilts her head, and slaps her butt, making a popping sound. "You promised you would help."

He gazes at her standing there with her hand on her small waist. She views him through bangs that shadow her huge dark eyes. Her eyes appear larger than life because of eyeliner left over from the night before.

They have been boyfriend and girlfriend long enough. He is seriously thinking about living with her the rest of his life. (I guess he did.) She is into Goth culture: white skin and black clothing, dark shades, and avoiding the sun. He went along just to be with her. She acts seriously about everything, and he needs some seriousness in his twenty-one-year-old life. Maybe it is time for him to settle down. (I guess he did that too.)

He rolls out of bed and slips into the dark clothes he had worn the day before. It is Saturday, and he did say he would help with the garage sale, but there is something else he wants to do first. Under the seat of his pick up is his new pistol. What would it hurt to take a little time out before the garage sale?

~~~~~~~~~~~~~~~~~~~~~~~~~~~

Garage sales are common around East Texas. They are called garage sales even if the sellers do not have a garage. You can tell when a Yankee is having a garage sale because the signs will say "Yard Sale" or "Moving Sale," which is fine, because they usually have good stuff they need to get rid of. Most garage sales are full of items bought from other garage sales.

~~~~~~~~~~~~~~~~~~~~~~~~~~~

Vickie follows Robert, walking to his pickup. He takes out the pistol, and she hops in the on the driver side, then fires up a heavy metal CD. The truck shakes with the music, which echoes in the early morning.

Vickie's house is in the country, which makes the backyard a good place for playing loud music and shooting, whether it's a shotgun, a rifle, or, today a .380 automatic pistol. The wooded area provides the targets. In the little pond behind the house, a portion of an old green wooden boat sticks above the water. Holes in the boat show it has been shot many times before.

"First, I think I will fire off a few rounds," Robert says. He slips bullet after bullet into the clip. He then takes the gun from the zippered leather pouch, points it away and to the ground, and inserts the clip into the pistol grip with a click. Robert is safety conscious with his weapon. "You stay here," he says, knowing that people should not be running around people who are shooting guns.

The .380 is not a large pistol and fits nicely into Robert's hand. With the grip in his right hand, he grasps the slide on top. Pulling it back cocks the hammer; letting it go springs the slide back, slipping the bullet into and closing the chamber. This action is the "chucking" noise you hear on television when there is going to be a gunfight. The pistol is ready to fire—just point and pull. It is a natural feeling for gun enthusiasts.

~~~~~~~~~~~~~~~~~~~~~~~~~~

Early in life, humans learn to follow the imaginary line drawn from the index finger to wherever it points. This line could be an inch long, or it could extend for light-years. The ability to point and visually follow that line is a feat few (if any) other animals can accomplish. Some cultures point with two fingers, or all the fingers; some point with only one finger.

The pistol is an extension of the ability to point; it also adds the ability to destroy whatever you are pointing at. The power to look, point, and penetrate is held in the palm of your hand. This makes the little petite lady gun as dangerous and powerful as the burly giant. No matter your age, sex, race, sexual orientation, religion, or socioeconomic class, the weapon makes you equal as long as you can point and pull.

~~~~~~~~~~~~~~~~~~~~~~~~

"It doesn't get better than this!" Robert says, stepping away from the pickup and looking for an imaginary enemy lurking in the woods. Which one will he take down?

The tree! Bang, bang, bang. Three quick shots eliminate, or at least disable, that threat. The brass from the third shot lands ten feet away, ejected to his left. He holds the gun with an extended right arm, bracing it with his left hand grasping his wrist. Heavy metal music and hot lead echo through the woods.

There, in the water! Quickly, he swings the weapon to the left, lining the sights, both eyes open, pointing. Bang, bang, bang. The recoil results in a natural tendency for the gun to rise with each shot. This is evidenced as wood chunks from the old boat splinter out and splash into the water. The third shot ripples the water in the pond beyond.

"I want to shoot! I want to shoot!" Vickie cries as she shuffles up behind him. "I have never even held a gun, but I want to shoot it."

"You have to be careful," Robert says. "This is not a toy." He is reluctant at first, but his desire to please her overrides his concern. He grasps the slider and, chucking it back, he ejects a live round. Then he removes the clip.

He turns the gun around, holding it by the warm barrel, and hands it to Vickie, butt first. She takes the gun by the grip. It is heavier than she thought it would be, but not too heavy. She waves it in the air, and it feels okay. With her finger on the trigger, she holds on tight and again waves the gun in the air. BANG. Robert rocks back and falls to the ground. His hands fold over his eyes. Blood flows between his fingers. She quizzically looks at the gun.

"What have you done?" she asks the gun, as though it

had a mind of its own, almost expecting the gun to answer.

"Help!" she screams as she throws the gun down. "Help, somebody help."

Heavy metal music and screams for help echo through the woods.

~~~~~~~~~~~~~~~~~~~~~~~~

To clear an automatic takes three simple steps. 1. Remove the clip. 2. Slide and eject any round in the chamber. 3. Visibly look to make sure there is no bullet in the chamber. The order is important. If the story is true, he ejected the round and replaced it with another when the chamber closed. Then he removed the clip. My daddy always told me, "never point a gun at anything unless you want to kill it."

~~~~~~~~~~~~~~~~~~~~~~~~

"It was an accident," says Lieutenant Harrington, over the telephone. "She didn't know the gun was loaded."

"So," I ask, "does that mean it is okay for someone to point a gun at someone else, pull the trigger, and shoot them between the eyes, as long as they think it is unloaded?"

Later, after looking at the two officers' reports, I call back Lieutenant Harrington.

"Some automatics will not shoot unless the clip is in place. I wanted to make sure that the gun would function without a clip."

"It is a cheap .380," he replies with a little agitation. "The case is closed."

~~~~~~~~~~~~~~~~~~~~~~~~

The next week, I was attending the Justice Court Judges Conference in Austin. A group of eight judges and four wives sat in the hotel restaurant for lunch. As usual, the conversation drifted to inquests.

"Yeah," I said, "I had a stinker, too, last Sunday. Two

weeks in a hot garage. Two hornets' nests were in some old clothes, lying by the body; the poor girl with the funeral home was stung five times while running out of the garage. With the stink and the stingers, I called the Chapel Hill Volunteer Fire Department. They handled it from there."

I noticed that the wife of one of the judges looked nauseated.

"I'm sorry," I said, "When judges talk . . ."

"It's okay." She stopped me with the palm of her hand. "I need to get used to it." Then, the conversations continued.

"I did one the other day," I said, trying to lighten up the conversation, "a gunshot wound right between the eyes. A twenty-one-year-old was shot by his nineteen-year-old girlfriend."

"Was this the one target shooting around Willowmuck?" asked one judge.

"I heard several stories about this one," said another. "They called me for an inquest; when I got there, he was flying away to your county."

"Yeah, thanks," I said. "I ended up with a body with a bullet hole in the head and nothing else to go on."

After hearing my shortened version of the story, the two judges from Zulu County began to comment. My cell phone began its familiar tone.

"Shamburger," I answered. (I try to avoid talking on the phone while eating and visiting with others, but with this job, the cell phone is the traveling office.)

"This is Mrs. Rhine. You did an inquest on my son."

"Yes, ma'am. I am in Austin and was just discussing the case with a couple of Justice Court judges from your county. May I call you back when I get home?"

"Please do," she said, closing the conversation. Changing the cell phone to vibrate, I resumed discussion with the judges.

"There is a new sheriff in town, and he has his own way of doing things," said one judge.

"We have a new district attorney too. He seems to have good a head on his shoulders. He probably needs to hear about this. Keep us informed," said the other.

~~~~~~~~~~~~~~~~~~~~~~~~~

Back at the office, I called Mrs. Rhine.

"It was a drug deal," said Mrs. Rhine, Robert's mother. "I am sure Robert was supplying drugs to them. He was such a good kid, and then this last year he changed friends. The sheriff knows these people, and the officer seemed agitated when I questioned what happened."

"I have ordered the autopsy and called the Texas Rangers. The district attorney has a copy of my case file. Because the inquest was done in Smith County, we share some jurisdiction and venue, but when it comes to turf, each county likes to handle their own," I said. "You do all that you can, then at some point, you need to let go."

"I don't know that I have done all that I can do. Can I have a copy of the autopsy? The girlfriend is five feet and four inches tall, and Robert was over six feet," she said, fishing for anything.

"One problem we have with this one," said the pathologist, "is that it was a post-surgical autopsy. When they operated on him, they used the entry wound and sewed it up when they were finished. There was no exit wound. Did they recover a bullet? I only found some small jacket fragments. Without ballistics on the weapon, I could only guess at the distance of the shot, probably two to three feet, straight in."

I gave him the height of the alleged shooter.

"Was he bending over? On a hill? Squatting down? All of these positions make a difference," stated the doctor.

~~~~~~~~~~~~~~~~~~~~~~~~~

Justice has different meanings to different people, and justice is different according to where the crime was committed. In Smith County, this shooting would have at least gone before a grand jury, with the possibility of prosecution as a negligent homicide. In Zulu County, this case is virtually closed. If the story is as stated, Vickie will have to live with what happened the rest of her life. If it is not the truth, someone may have gotten away with murder.

Murders happen both in the city and in the country, but you expect them more in the city. Somehow, it is different when someone a mile across a big city is shot and killed, compared to your neighbor found murdered in their house, just a mile down the country road.

Inquest #632:
The Dangers of Babysitting

"You need to get up and wash the dishes," Barbara says to her little brother.

"Who died and left you in charge?" Charley asks. "You're not my boss."

"I am the oldest, and Mom left me in charge!" Barbara says, using all the authority she can muster in her twelve-year-old voice.

Mom and Dad went grocery shopping, leaving Barbara in charge of her nine-year-old brother. Their country house is small for a family of four. Standing at the front door and looking to the right, you can see a cloth-covered couch in the den/living room/dining room.

Half sitting, half lying on the couch, Charley watches Saturday-morning cartoons. "Yeah, three years older, but you act like an old woman," he yells above the volume of the television.

"If you do not get up and help, I am turning off the TV." Barbara is getting tired of this.

"I can't hear you!" Charley says, mashing and pointing the remote, turning up the volume to drown out his big sister's demands.

Behind the television is the dining area, featuring an old maple table with unmatched chairs; just beyond is the kitchen. Cabinets line the back wall, and Barbara is standing at the sink.

Standing at the front door and looking to the left, you would see a wall with three doors. Two are bedroom doors. A small bathroom is in the back, by the kitchen.

This is what you would see, standing in the front door and looking into the life of this family.

"Last warning," Barbara warns. "I am counting to three, and if you are not up, the TV is going off!" She pauses. "ONE . . ."

"If you turn it off, it will be the last thing you'll do!" Charley retorts. "Wait 'til this one's over." Charley is focused on the television and agitated by his sister's invasion of his sacred Saturday cartoon time.

"I have been waiting. TWO," Barbara says, realizing she is wasting numbers. "Three."

She drops the damp, dingy white dishcloth on the dining table and struts over to the TV. She bends over, reaches down, and presses the power button. The screen blips and goes black. The sudden vacuum of sound is quickly filled with a verbal protest from Charley.

"I was watching that!" he yells, as though the topic had never been discussed. He does not move from the couch.

As Barbara turns to walk back to the kitchen, there is a click, then a faint electric fizz sound, and Wile E. Coyote is chasing the Road Runner again at full volume.

"Give me that!" Barbara yells, pouncing on Charley and going for the remote control. She has the advantage of the female adolescent growth spurt and easily overpowers him, striping him of his television lifeline and terminating both coyote and roadrunner. "Wash the dishes; then you can watch TV."

"I don't have to do shit," Charley says, getting up off the couch and stalking away.

He does not go to the kitchen to wash the dishes. He does not go to their shared room and throw himself on his bed in a fit of anger or tears. He does not go to the bathroom to look in the mirror and splash cold water in his face in order to regain his composure. If he had gone to any of these rooms, there would be no story to tell—except the eternal fighting among siblings.

"I warned you!" he says, walking into the bedroom of his mother and father.

The shotgun is hidden under the parents' bed. The kids are not allowed to go into this bedroom at all, much less mess with the shotgun. In fact, Charley is forbidden to ever even touch the gun. Dad occasionally fires the gun. He uses it to take down varmints in the yard, and it has been shot up in the air to scare off whatever was out in the woods, hiding in the dark. Mostly the gun is a comfort, ready to protect the family from harm. It is a weapon that gives a feeling of security, especially at night, when strange sounds come from outside and strangers may appear from the nearby interstate.

Nine-year-old Charley reaches under the bed and drags out the shotgun, then hefts it. It is a lot heavier than he thought it would be. It does not fit or feel right; holding one looks so easy on TV. The weight of the long barrel makes the gun point down. He tries to shoulder the stock. It takes an effort to lift and point the gun at anything. Charlie discovers it is much easier to hold the weapon down by his side, like the Rifleman, one hand up front, the other wrapped around the thin part of the stock, finger on the trigger. Without thinking, he walks, determined, into the den and points the 16 gauge shotgun toward his sister. Without hesitation, he pulls the trigger, and then all hell breaks loose. He is surprised. The blast spins him around and knocks him back onto the couch. His ears are filled with the explosion, and he can smell burnt gunpowder as his senses come back to him.

He thinks, "This is nothing like television." He has seen hundreds of gun battles in his life on TV and cannot not remember any portraying the shooter being knocked on his ass. He looks up to see his sister. She too was knocked back, against the table, and she turns to him with a look of wonderment. She does not know what is happening. A hole about the size of a silver dollar is in her T-shirt, between her left hip and her ribcage. They both look at it as though it is not real, or maybe thinking that only the shirt, and not Barbara, is damaged. The hole turns red. Barbara places the dishrag from the table over the wound, and it quickly becomes soaked with blood.

She can say nothing; she can only look at her little brother. Her eyes are fully wide open, shocked in disbelief. The look on her face asks, "What have you done?"

~~~~~~~~~~~~~~~~~~~~~~~~

A shotgun shell is different from a rifle or pistol bullet in that the projectile, or shot, is not a single piece of lead. Most shotgun shells use round pellets, of various sizes. The pellets begin to spread soon after leaving the barrel of the shotgun.

The shot pattern refers to the spread of the BBs or shot when they hit the target, and it depends on the choke of the barrel and the distance to the target. Barbara was approximately ten feet away from the blast, causing an entry wound one and a half inches in diameter.

~~~~~~~~~~~~~~~~~~~~~~~~

Barbara lays the bloody dishrag on the table. She looks at it like she should not leave it there, but she needs both hands to balance herself as she staggers from the table to the chair, to the counter, to the bathroom. This is a mess, and the bathroom is the place where most messes take place, or at least get cleaned up. She manages to open the door and falls against it, holding herself up, looking back toward the front door. She sees the dining room chair lying toppled on the floor and her dazed brother flopped back on the couch.

"Where did I put that dishrag?"

She turns to the bathroom and sees the sink, next to the shower. If she could get to the shower, maybe she could wash all this away, like a cleansing baptism, from which she would walk out anew, feeling refreshed. She has always felt better after taking a shower.

She closes her eyes. Her body feels numb and limp, like the dishrag.

She feels nothing as her body folds and collapses to the floor, lying between the sink and the shower in the tiny bathroom. Her heart thinks it is sending energy, life-giving blood, to her body. The blood flows from her side and pools on the floor.

"I shot my sister," the 911 operator hears. Fifteen minutes, the volunteer fire department arrives. Ten minutes later, the sheriff's deputy arrives, and after twenty-five minutes, the ambulance is there. An hour and a half later, I arrive.

I stand in the front door and look into the life of a family, forever changed. On the couch is a sobbing boy. The skinny nine-year-old is crying because he has just killed his sister. A blood-soaked washrag dangles on the edge of the dining table, and the bathroom door is smudged with red. The TV is turned off.

~~~~~~~~~~~~~~~~~~~~~~

What is the age of accountability? Legally, it varies from state to state. Does accountability involve a fifteen-year-old telling another fifteen-year-old where a gun is? Is it a nine-year-old wielding a shotgun? Or a nineteen-year-old with what she thought was an unloaded gun? What kind of life will Cathy, Charley, or Vickie have with this blemish in their history? I will never know about Cathy or Vickie; they are names in a book filled with names. I did find a criminal history on Charley. The thirty-three-year-old is now in prison for sexual assault. They all still live. Tom, Robert, and Barbara, of course, are dead.

~~~~~~~~~~~~~~~~~~~~~~

No doubt, guns can be fatal; so can paint thinner if it is stored in a typical plastic commercial water bottle that comes into the hands of an eighteen-month-old. The dad, who is a painter, arrives home to find his child properly strapped in the car seat, passed out, the plastic bottle sitting upright in his lap. So can an unfinished septic tank half full of stagnant water, if it comes into the path of an exploring two-year-old. The child is found floating face down in the muck.

Despite all the senseless killings, I am not an advocate for gun control. The "right to bear arms" was an important aspect of our nation's birth and the ability to continue as a free people. It may seem farfetched to think that personal weapons may again play a pivotal role in American society at a time when we depend on law enforcement and a trained military to meet our needs of force. Times do change. I would rather have a weapon and never need it than to need it and never have it. I wish parents and people were more responsible, but you cannot legislate common sense and good judgment.

In Texas, a judge receives special treatment to receive a license to carry a concealed weapon. I took the course, made the score on the firing range, filled out the paperwork, and wrote the check for the reduced judicial amount. The large manila envelope has sat on my filing cabinet for many years now. Every time I start to mail it, I feel uneasy—like this is an invasion of my privacy. If England had had a list of American gun owners during the American Revolution, we might be hearing "God Save the Queen" instead of "Hail to the Chief."

Chapter 19

Electricity Has One Goal

Inquests #3211 and #3212

Just before most guys go to bed, they go through a routine something like this: they empty their pockets, placing keys, billfold, change, and all the pocket accumulations of the day on the dresser or a bedside table, or in a drawer; they whip off their belt from its loops and peel off their pants and underwear, then their socks and shirt, and put them into the laundry hamper. Some shower or bathe before bed, washing away the day's labor. Others wait to wash the sleep off in the morning and face a new day. They may think briefly about what they are going to wear tomorrow, but whatever: the next day's clothes are clean and waiting. As they lie down, their thoughts mostly concern what happened during the day and what will happen tomorrow, along with hopes for a good night's sleep.

Those of us who are on call take off our pants and lay them aside, leaving everything intact in the pockets. The day's shirt is hung in the same place as the shirt the night before, so it can be found in the dark. After a few years of taking midnight calls, we learn to get half dressed before we even wake up. If we shower before bed, we wonder if we will have to shower again before morning. Just like other guys, though, as we lie down, we think about the day and wonder if we will get a good night's sleep.

In Smith County, each Justice Court precinct prefers to

handle its own inquest calls. It is important that we know what is happening within our precincts. This means we are subject to being called anytime, day or night. It seems senseless to have another judge get up and drive forty miles to an inquest two blocks from my house, while I am sleeping or watching television. Still, it happens. The officer hits the key on the mike, which switches it from "receive" to "send," and alerts the dispatcher to call the *on call judge*. The dispatcher will do just that instead of checking to see who the correct judge would be.

One good reason for handling inquests in our own precincts is that we answer to our constituents. They want to know why "their judge" did not pronounce Mother dead and why they had to wait for hours for the county to find someone. Politically, after you assist a family in need, you will have their vote and support forever.

The Smith County Justice Court judges work together to ensure that at least one judge is always available countywide, 24/7. This means every fifth week I can plan on the phone ringing two to four times more often than usual.

I find it amazing when I get a certain feeling that something is happening and then wait for the phone to ring. When that feeling comes on, I usually watch television or listen to an audio book, because sleep will not come. Finally, I give up, undress, go to bed, and doze off — and *then* the phone will ring.

~~~~~~~~~~~~~~~~~~~~~~~~~

Tonight, it is a large thunderstorm that keeps me awake.

I like storms. They show me how insignificant we are and how little control we have over things. Humans like to think we are in control, but nature in the form of a tornado, a hurricane, hail, fire, rain, drought, or a sustained heat wave or cold spell can put us in our place.

I like to stand on my front porch, open to the elements. The spray of the falling rain is cool on my face and skin.

Lightning flashes across the sky, then dives to the ground. It looks close, but I count the seconds before the thunder arrives. Six seconds means it is just over a mile away. Before I can find any comfort in the distance another flash comes, with an immediate BOOM.

The house shakes as the music of the late night thunder rolls. I see tree limbs sway in concert with the wind. Sheets of rain flash into sight as lightning strobes with the heavy beat of thunder. The electricity goes on and off as tree limbs and electric wires make contact. The electricity goes off and stays off when a car crashes into a pole that supports the wires that carry electricity to our town.

~~~~~~~~~~~~~~~~~~~~~~~~~~

Near the community of Sand Flat, the electricity has gone out. A Hispanic family is having a get-together. They moved the outdoor chairs to the porch at 7:00 when the rain started, and the porch was abandoned by 8:00 as the blowing rain made sitting there uncomfortable. Sitting together in a small frame house, they wait out the storm by candlelight. The little house shakes with each clap of thunder. As the wind dies down and the rain drops turn to mist, the visit nears its end.

The lights blink once then come back on. The electricity has returned.

"I think the storm is over. We'd better get on home," Jose says as he gets up from the couch. The men are sitting around the cramped living room, the women are in the kitchen, and the kids are in one of the bedrooms. All are visiting, and now that the storm is over, so is the visit.

"Able, go get your mother," Jose calls out to his son. The boy finds his thirty-four-year-old mother in the kitchen, wrapping up her visit. Maria looks more like twenty–four, with her slender body and long, dark brown hair, some curling over her shoulders to the front and most flowing down her back. Her big, dark brown eyes, set below finely plucked eyebrows, seem like they could look into a man's soul, and her smile can warm a cold stormy night. Tonight, she is wearing faded blue jeans and a loose white blouse with little yellow flowers printed all over it. It is getting late, and tomorrow will be filled with work for Jose and things to do for her, including getting Able off to school. It is a tradition for her and her family to get out of the house on Thursday nights and visit with friends and family, or have friends and family visiting them. The visits are mostly with Jose's family; most of Maria's family still lives in Mexico.

Maria has lived in Texas long enough to have a thirteen-year-old son, Able, born a U.S. citizen, and Jose has his papers, which means that by marriage, she has adopted the United States of America. Her English is passable, but she converses mostly in Spanish.

"Buenas noches," she says as she hugs the evening's hostess at the front door and kisses her cheek.

"Buenas noches," Jose says, waving over his shoulder as he walks to their pickup. He is proud of his truck, an older model GMC. Except for the added chrome, it looks much like it did on the showroom floor, despite having several owners before him and many miles on the odometer. The truck receives a weekly wash and polish, and tonight the white vehicle almost glows in the dark. Chrome bumpers and wheels match chrome-lined doors. Able wonders if one day his dad might hand him the keys to the pickup truck.

~~~~~~~~~~~~~~~~~~~~~~~~~~~

There was a day when owning a pickup truck meant you had to sweat for a living. It was a time when a pickup truck had just one seat, a bench seat, and any passenger was a helper. Desperate teenagers were embarrassed to use the family pickup for an occasional date. The advantage of sitting close to your date was offset by the stigma of having to drive a pickup. If a pickup was the only vehicle you owned, you were considered a defiant redneck, a goat roper, or a farmer, and borderline poor.

Somewhere along the way things changed. A "pickup truck" became just a "pickup" and somewhat fashionable. My

Chevy Suburban looks out of place parked near ten or twenty pickups at the "Cholesterol Feast," a men's breakfast held on Saturday mornings at the church. The bench seat has been replaced with bucket seats, and most pickups now have a back seat. Club cab and crew cab models, designed originally to carry more workers, now carry family. Most teenagers would give anything to have a new four-by-four pickup truck sitting in their driveway.

~~~~~~~~~~~~~~~~~~~~~~~

"Can I ride shotgun?" Able asks, knowing he will be denied, as always. "Riding shotgun" means sitting up front, next to the passenger window. It is a term leftover from stagecoach days.

Mom opens "her" door and then opens the narrow back door. "You know where you belong; climb in." Able dutifully climbs into the narrow back seat.

"Have you done all your homework?" Maria asks as she closes the doors.

Able is a smart kid with lots of potential. His parents have high hopes for this first-generation natural-born United States citizen, maybe even college.

With a twist of the key, the dependable V8 roars to life. The original mufflers long ago were replaced by glasspacks, giving the truck a throaty, rumbling sound. The truck vibrates as they back up onto the blacktop county road, partly because of the manual transmission and disengaging the clutch, and partly because of the mud grip tires on the back.

Jose is in no big rush, but he racks the pipes, and accelerates quickly down the road, just for show. The wet road glistens in the headlights. A foggy mist rises from the road. The sides of the road feature nothing but cow pastures. The main road is only a short distance ahead and is clearly visible in the daytime but harder to see at night and in the fog. As they approach Texas Farm to Market Road 14, Jose looks left and right for headlights. He sees none; the coast is clear.

Suddenly, Jose hits the brakes, tossing everyone

forward.

"What are you doing?" Maria screams, and then she sees the creosote power pole lying across their path.

The truck slides to a stop on the wet pavement, bumping against the pole, and the motor dies.

Jose turns the key, with no response. "It won't do anything," he says.

They sit for a moment, and Jose starts to open his door. He hears a scraping sound. He looks up and sees bare metal wires lying across the top of the truck.

"This is not good. Electricity!" he says.

~~~~~~~~~~~~~~~~~~~~~~~~~~~~

I respect electricity. I do not like to get shocked. I do not like losing control of a muscle as it jerks and jumps to the tingly, pulsing, shocking feeling of alternating current.

A person does not quickly forget the experience of a good jolt of electricity. It makes you more sensitive and alert when you are around electricity. My father-in-law, brother-in-law, and nephew are electricians. They recommend this: "Use the back of your hand to see if the wire is hot. If you grip it, the current will contract your muscles, and you won't be able to let go."

"No, thank you," is my answer. "You can use the back of *your* hand, but not mine!"

I was once standing on a chair, working on a circuit breaker box. The breaker box replaced fuse boxes long ago. The breaker box divides electricity that comes from an outside source and spreads it throughout a house or other building. Each breaker is a kind of controller switch that will turn itself off if too much electricity tries to pass through it at one time. This design is intended to prevent damage to equipment and prevent fires that might result from overheating of wires.

Most metals, especially copper, are good conductors of electricity, but even the best of conductors will offer some resistance. This resistance causes the metal to heat up; electric wiring heats up when enough electricity "runs" or passes through it on the way to the ground. It is strange that pure distilled water is not a good conductor of electricity, but add a little salt and minerals, and it becomes a great conductor. The human body happens to be made of around sixty percent water; the rest is salt and minerals. This makes it a fine conductor, with plenty of resistance. A typical breaker will not prevent a well-grounded person from getting "fried."

The replaceable breaker snaps into the breaker panel, making it "hot." One day, I was replacing a breaker. Having been shocked in the past, I was keenly aware of my position, standing on a chair that was sitting on a box, with a screwdriver in one hand and pushing the new breaker into position with the other hand.

A vibration shook my insides at gut level. I jerked back and flew off the chair, landing on my feet. I stood there stunned but not shocked, questioning what happened. Then the vibration occurred again. My cell phone was vibrating. I stood there like a shocked fool. Like swimming, you should not be alone when working with electricity. This is free advice I do not adhere to myself.

Bad weather often increases the likelihood of deaths and the need for inquests. Usually the deaths come in the form of traffic accidents. Flooding means drowning, rain means sliding down the road, and there should be a law against East Texans driving when there is snow and ice. And what do I have to do? Go out in that same weather to formally pronounce someone dead.

~~~~~~~~~~~~~~~~~~~~~~~~

"Have they called you yet?" It is Fire Chief /Constable Charles Wilson with the Red Springs Volunteer Fire Department.

"What's up?" I ask.

"Judge, we have an electrocution."

"Where?" I ask.

"County Road 311 and F.M. (Farm to Market) 14,"

Wilson says.

I get out of bed to retrieve the pants I had taken off ten minutes earlier. My shirt is hanging where it always hangs. I put on a fresh pair of socks. I do this in the dark for several reasons—the main, one is the electricity is off.

The town is pitch dark without streetlights and the usual leaks of lights coming from houses. The moon and stars are hidden behind the still dark clouds. The wind has calmed and the rain has slowed to a drizzle. As I approach Winona's "blinking yellow light" (that is not blinking) I see the headlights of a police car in "It's a Doll's World" parking lot. I pull up beside the car, driver to driver, and my window glides down.

"Chief Tapley," I say as my window glides down. "Sho' is dark out here."

"Tree took down the power line just this side of the river," he says. "Whole town is dead. It might take a few hours before the power comes back on. I'm just watching and waiting."

"I'm heading to one that wished the power was really off." Tapley looks confused. "Inquest, electrocution," I explain.

"Oh," he says, understanding. "Have fun, Judge."

We move on.

A light sprinkle and wet pavement is all that is left of the storm. I notice the mist rising from the pavement as I drive to CR 311.

Red and blue lights reflect off of the wet pavement. I park by the stop sign at the intersection.

The remains of a wooden power pole are cut into three- and four-foot sections, each rolled to the left side of the road. Two crews from the power company, using bucket trucks, are re-hanging wires. The lifts mounted on the trucks are like giant white metal arms, with elbows to control their movement. At the end of the white arms, the workers sway in the buckets, high above the ground. A white late-model club cab pickup truck sits in the proper lane, twenty feet short of coming to the stop sign where I am parked.

There is no damage to the front of the pickup, something you would expect if the truck hit a power pole. The passenger door is wide open. Officer Robert Johnson with the Texas Department of Public Safety is standing by his patrol car, writing his report.

"Hi, Judge," he says. "I wanted to make sure all the power lines were dead before they called you."

"Thanks. What happened?"

"It looks like the storm blew the pole over and the lines were down. These people," he says, pointing to the truck, "were going home from those people who live just up the road." He motions to a group of five Hispanics standing behind a parked car. "The pole was lying across the road, but the wires ended up lying across the cab."

"This looks like an old pole. Look at the light brown color of the wood," I say, pointing to the heart of what once was a tree. Creosote not only protects the pole from insects but also makes the pole more durable. After years of hot sun the creosote "cooks" out, leaving the pole dry and less durable and also subject to insects, especially fire ants. Then the woodpeckers come after the insects. An old utility pole weighs considerably less than a new one. Poles are supposed to be inspected and old ones replaced before they become hazardous.

The left side of the pickup is clean, a sign either of being washed by the storm or good maintenance. Officer Johnson shines his flashlight at the charred marking on the roof of the pickup, above the driver's side door.

"Looks like this was the main point of contact," he says.

The white GMC is a club cab, meaning that the front and back doors open like French doors. That is, the back door is hinged at the back of the cab, so the doors fan out when opened. The back door can be opened only if the front door is opened first.

We walk behind the pickup and see that both doors on the passenger side are wide open. We can smell burned flesh as well as burned rubber.

"There were three in the truck," Johnson says, "a

Hispanic couple and their thirteen-year-old son. It looks like they did not hit the pole; they just drove under the wires. It appears they decided to get out on the passenger side."

~~~~~~~~~~~~~~~~~~~~~~~~~~~~~

High-voltage lines carry electricity to transformers, where the current is reduced to meet the needs of homes and businesses. The 110 or 220 volts that make it to our house are only a fraction of the voltage going from pole to pole.

Electricity has one goal: get to the ground. When electricity is harnessed properly, we make it work its way to the ground by lighting a room, cooling or cooking our food, spinning a fan, or exciting protons and electrons to give us a picture on the television. By energizing chips, diodes, and whatever is in the computer that I use to write, electricity finds its way to the ground and helps me along the way. Electricity does not think, and it takes the path of least resistance. If you happen to be that "path," you will light up.

A popular item in the sixties was a hotdog cooker. To use this appliance, each end of the wiener is connected to a lead wire that makes the wiener the path. When electricity flows through the meat, it cooks from the inside out. It is the resistance that makes the heat. As the hotdog cooks, the liquid inside it becomes less conductive, until there is no electric flow. A hotdog cooks in seconds using 110 volts. Power lines carry thousands of volts.

The Texas electric chair to which the name "Old Sparky" is applied was in use from 1924 to 1964. During that time, it caused the deaths of 361 prisoners sentenced to die by judicial electrocution. The electric chair was used in many states, and so was the name "Old Sparky." The advantage of electrocution as a means of execution is the speed at which it causes death, if used properly. If there is pain for the person being electrocuted, it is short lived (pun intended).

Besides causing muscle contractions, electricity disrupts the brain. In the novel *One Flew Over the Cuckoo's Nest*, as well as the film made from it, doctors use electricity to change mental patients' personalities and behaviors. Benjamin Franklin did not have these things in mind when he flew his kite during a thunderstorm in 1750.

~~~~~~~~~~~~~~~~~~~~~~~

Maria, Able, and Jose are sitting in the dead pickup in the drizzling rain.

"Able, are you all right?" Maria asks, turning to see Able sitting back in the seat.

"I'm fine. What's going on?"

"Electricity!" says Jose. "It has killed the car!"

"What do you mean?" Maria asks. "There are no sparks or anything. And the headlights still work."

She is right. All seems calm now that the truck has stopped. The headlights show absolutely nothing happening in front of them. All is quiet, and they are doing nothing, nothing but sitting there. The rubber tires prevent 7,200 volts of electricity from reaching the ground.

"I will get help," Maria says, opening the passenger door. As usual, she pushes it open with her foot, and her leg makes its way out the door; then 7,200 volts make their way to the ground through the truck and Maria.

Before Jose can say anything, there is a flash of bright white light, accompanied by a popping sound, followed by a searing, frying sound unique to electricity. Maria's hair is on fire, and smoke rises from her blouse as she jerks and slides out of the vehicle onto the ground.

Jose crawls over to the door and looks down upon Maria. The smoke was not coming from her shirt; it was coming from inside her shirt. There is another cracking noise and flash of light.

Maria's head is close enough to the front tire of the truck that another blast of electricity finds its way to the ground through her head and body.

Jose instinctively reaches for Maria, and another lightning flash takes his hand. The speed of an electric spark or lightning is comparable to the speed of light. If it reaches for you, there is no time to run. Jose falls out the door onto Maria's now-exploding body.

It has been five seconds since Maria met the electricity. Able is in shock. He reaches for the door latch, and the back door swings out. He looks down on Mom and Dad, piled on top of each other, lying on the ground. He sees smoke and steam coming off of them. The burning tire explodes, dropping the truck down to the ground and providing a more direct path for the electricity. This is when the breaker on the transformer blows, freeing the pickup from the hold electricity had on it.

"Mama!" Able yells. There is no response, but he smells burning rubber and something that smells different. His nose twitches. He has smelled it before, when Mom ran out of the house with a burning pork roast. The olfactory sense, the sense of smell, is powerful and creates strong memories. Even though the smell is bad, it takes him to a better time. He blinks his eyes, then shakes his head, bringing him back to reality.

"What do I do? I want to help! I need to get help!" Able think. He slides across the seat and leaps out, away from the pickup truck. He wants to get as far away as he can. He lands five or ten feet away from mom and dad, wondering if he will quickly join them. He stands there a moment, gazing at the bodies of his parents. He thinks to himself and quietly says, "They are dead."

He takes off running back to the house.

"Help! Help!" he cries, banging on the door. "They are dead, Mom and Dad are dead!"

One person calls 911 while the others rush outside. From the house, only two dim red taillights are visible. Some people jump into a car. The tires spin on the wet pavement as they go to the truck. The headlights of their car light up the scene. The white truck sits quietly, with its taillights dimming as the electricity drains away from the battery. Except for the open doors and smoldering tire, it looks as though it is just parked in the road. Then they see the wires.

The wishful rescuers look at one another and do not get near the truck. All they can do is watch. They know about the electricity, how it hides, or looks so innocent, but how it can bite you with a shock, or tear off an arm or leg, or kill you whenever it can. All electricity wants to do is to get to the ground.

~~~~~~~~~~~~~~~~~~~~~~~~~~~

I wrote this chapter a year after it happened. It's strange that upon completion I would receive a call about this accident.

"Judge, thank you for visiting with me," I hear through the telephone. "I am Janet, an investigator for the insurance company representing the electric company. The family has filed suit for fourteen million dollars. May I stop by to look at the inquest record and talk to you about the case?"

The next week she came in and looked at the Inquest Records on the two deaths.

"Can you tell me what you know about the case?"

"Here," I said, handing her a draft copy of the chapter. "The names are changed as well as the inquest numbers. I formed the story from witnesses at the scene and imagined the conversations."

A friend of mine, Able Gonzales, said he knows the family and they received a large undisclosed settlement.

Chapter 20

Things Are Not Always as They Seem

Inquests #4574, #4575, and #1382

Author's Note: This is the first autobiographical story that I wrote, and writing it provided the inspiration for continuing work on what became *Inquests: Living With the Dead.*

Inquests #4574 and #4575

Both hands of the clock are pointing straight up; it is time for lunch.

"Judge, you have an inquest," I hear over the phone intercom from Linda Lusk, my chief clerk. "It's in Owentown."

Death comes when it wants to. It does not coordinate with our convenience. It most often happens at night, or in the wee hours of the morning, on weekends and holidays, and today, during lunch. It is a beautiful sunny day. What a shame someone has to die on such a day.

I punch numbers on my cell phone as I drive down the road. "Southeast Texas Forensic Center," I hear. "This is Crystal."

"Is Doctor Van Dusen in?" I ask the secretary. He is the chief pathologist at the new forensic center in Owentown.

"One moment."

"This is Van Dusen."

"Doc, I am doing an inquest just down the street from

you. Would you like to come?" The forensic center handles autopsies from many of the surrounding counties. The bodies arrive at all hours and usually are put in the cooler. The doctor sees them for the first time when they are rolled into the autopsy room. It is helpful when the doctor can see the victim at the scene and without the smell of formaldehyde or whatever it is that stinks up their building.

"Sure," he says, and I give him directions.

It is a pleasant five miles to the community of Owentown. Springtime seems to bring out the green in things, and today, except for a late lunch, has the potential for being almost perfect.

Owentown sits on the leftovers of Camp Fannin. During World War II, Camp Fannin was a place where young American men became Army Infantry Replacements between May 1943 and December 1945. Most of the barracks and buildings are now only concrete slabs. The foundations serve as reminders of war times. Some of the buildings, still standing, were built to help defeat Hitler and the Imperial Japanese Army; now they are businesses and manufacturing plants. My father was in the Army and trained there with more than 200,000 others. From the hot, humid East Texas training center, he went to fight in the hot, humid Philippine Islands. Thousands who trained at Camp Fannin made the supreme sacrifice, losing their lives while serving their country.

After the war only the Camp Fannin hospital continued to operate. A business transaction between the government and Mister Owen created Owentown. The area has never been incorporated as a city, but it has a population of almost a thousand. Many of the streets are lined with brick houses and picket fences. Occasionally, a historical marker notes the location of an induction center, mess hall, theater, or street.

I drive pass the old Winona train depot. The many coats of lead paint are cracked and curled, and the building now is a dingy, dirty yellow, except for the black letters on a white sign that says "WINONA." Somehow, the old depot, made of petrifying heavy lumber, has traveled six miles down the highway and ended up in Owentown. I remember, as a very young child, going into that Cotton Belt railroad depot in downtown Winona and hearing the clicking sound of the telegraph. Old Mr. Foster had only one arm, but one hand is all you need to tap, tap, tap Morris code, sending a communication down the railroad line.

I take a left on Chapman Road at the Tyler Candle Company, where my daughter, Amy, works, and then turn right on 18th Avenue. I see a yard marked with yellow tape — bright yellow with coal black letters, repeating its message over and over: "CAUTION POLICE DO NOT ENTER." The tape is tied to a tree, then to a car bumper, then to a chain link fence, on which it continues, draped and laced along the top. The tape and the police cars set this house apart from the rest of the suburban neighborhood.

The tape circles a nice brick home with a manicured front yard. On the small front porch sits a few neatly potted plants, and a well-maintained flower bed is in springtime bloom. It looks as though each blade of San Augustine grass was cut precisely to its designated length and all the plants were watered to grow in unison. It is a tranquil setting.

~~~~~~~~~~~~~~~~~~~~~~

I live in a big old wooden frame house built around the turn of the twentieth century that I have occupied for more than thirty years. My family and I have added storm windows on all thirty-four exterior windows, and the huge attic is now a second story. The house has been wrapped in Styrofoam and covered in vinyl to help reduce the cost of the added central heat and cooling.

The remaining stained white shingles are roof number three, since I had torn off the five layers of previous asbestos shingles and wooden shingles. When I told Dad about the house my wife and I wanted to buy, he told me, "You can buy an old house, do a lot of work, and spend a lot of money fixing it up. When you get through, you will still have an old house."

Early on, it was my responsibility to mow the yard. Once someone said they thought they saw a wolf run into the weeds beside the house. When the city asked if I would mow my yard, I told them, "I have designated it as a wildlife refuge!" Now the yard is well kept; my wife keeps it mowed with a riding lawnmower, a gift from Santa. We have a universal grass yard with various types of grasses. And flowers? My wife does her best, considering she has a "brown thumb." Spider lilies came with the house; they still pop up during the appropriate season.

There is not a lot of junk in my front yard. However, on the front porch is a small, rusty old freezer that is older than I am. It has been replaced for primary use with a new, slick, bright, white, more efficient unit. Now both of them sit on the front porch; the old one comes in handy when the new one is full. The front porch also collects the tools that do not make it back to the garage. When I clean out the car or van, everything short of trash ends up in a trash bag, which ends up on the front porch. The gas grill works perfectly under a covered front porch. There is a nice porch swing by the front door. It doubles as a swinging table for things we do not want to bring into the house.

~~~~~~~~~~~~~~~~~~~~~~~~~~

On 18th Avenue, beyond the yellow tape, a concrete drive leads to the two-car garage. Two bicycles, probably belonging to the kids in the house, are parked neatly, side by side, next to a wall-mounted kayak and outdoor camping equipment that is stacked neatly in well-used original boxes. A spotless waxed car sits in its designated parking spot, blocking a dart board hanging on the other wall of the garage. There is no grease or oil on the driveway or the garage floor.

~~~~~~~~~~~~~~~~~~~~~~~~~~

My two-car garage was built back in the day when it was recommended that cars be parked at least fifty feet from the house. Cars in those days were a luxury and a fire hazard. It started out as a two-story building with a room upstairs that doubled as my shop. I remember pulling into the garage when the kids were little and pretending to be at a drive-in theater. I would describe pictures as though the back wall was the screen at a drive-in movie and tell stories to my kids of Godzilla or knights in shining armor.

A falling tree limb took out the roof and top floor and made it a single-story garage. The shop moved downstairs into the garage and took the place of parking.

I spent many nights in that garage building a "kit car" (a 1929 Mercedes). It arrived in boxes and bags of nuts and bolts. A year and many sleepless nights later it became an automobile.

Now a bicycle with two flat tires sits collecting dust in a garage so full of "stuff" that no car will fit. A Kawasaki Drifter motorcycle is parked beside the riding lawnmower. Somewhere in there is a fly rod. I last used it twenty years ago.

A while back, I found a group of mangled, matted plastic worms all stuck together in the bottom of a tackle box that had not been opened in years. It scared me when, by accident, I reached into their hiding place. (Maybe if I leave them alone, they will separate and become usable again, and I will go fishing with my grandkids.) The floor of my garage is made of blacktop. Some call it oil sand; it's a combination of grease and dirt.

~~~~~~~~~~~~~~~~~~~~~~~~~~

I walk through the family's garage into a spotless home: no dirty dishes in the sink or on the counter, no stacks of mail, no old checkbooks or bills. I notice there are no magazines lying around.

A little spiral notebook is lying open on the kitchen counter. There is a note in it, several pages long, in neat handwriting. I have seen many suicide notes. Most start out lucid, with a purpose, and end with scattered thoughts, as though a drunk were forced to write a confession. The notes are of different lengths. Often the last words ramble on as though the writer is thinking, "I am living as long as I am writing." Regardless of the length of the note, by the time it is finished, it looks like the writing of an intoxicated third grader. The stick letters are drawn to spell words that do not exist. The intoxication comes from adrenalin and other chemicals produced by the body and attacking the brain. As stress takes over, reason is blurred in a haze.

This note is different from other suicide notes. The sentence structures are complete and ideas well thought through. The quality of the handwriting is consistent from beginning to end. The note contains directions and apologies—apologies not to the family, but to us who are now looking upon this scene.

The man of the house wrote the note. George was an emergency medical technician and worked on an ambulance. As an emergency medical technician himself, he had seen gruesome scenes before. He knew what we would see and how we would feel.

"This is all my fault—I am just not strong enough," he stated.

This is in contrast to most suicide notes, which sound like they are quoting Homer Simpson: "This is everybody's fault but mine!" This is not a suicide note. This is the note of a murderer confessing a crime.

I was reminded of another inquest, another time, and another note that had similarities to this one.

Inquest #1382:
Another Inquest, Another Time

In the city of Tyler, a large man is found lying outside, face up, between two older brick homes. He has turned himself into a Cyclops by adding a hole to the center of his forehead with a nine-millimeter pistol. His house and yard are the opposite of order and cleanliness. This victim was a compulsive collector of "stuff." The house and yard are jam-packed with boxes full of all kinds of small electrical parts and gadgets. Inside the house, a narrow path winds its way through a maze of stuff. Stepping into the back junkyard, I bump my head on a large, unconnected solar panel and find myself standing among old compressors, tools of all kinds, and even a large wench truck sitting on metal rims surrounded by black, cracked, and rotting rubber tires. Winding my way through the clutter and back into the house, I go to the one room with ample walking space. One wall holds crayon drawings, the kids' proud work.

A computer is running. The screen saver casts strange shadows in the dim room. Floating across the screen is a picture of the man's wife and his two children. The computer is playing "classic Bach" through an elaborate speaker system. His-and-her wedding bands lie side by side on top of a four-page note. The note is coherent and the handwriting constant from beginning to the end. It does not directly confess any crime. It does say he was sorry for what he had done (he had not killed himself yet), and it gives directions on what to do with the children. This causes immediate concern regarding the wife and children. After an hour of working with his cell phone, we find his wife, dead. She is more than 300 miles away, in San Antonio. She was pregnant and had mysteriously drowned in the bathtub two days earlier. Her funeral is to be the next day.

~~~~~~~~~~~~~~~~~~~~~~~~~~~~~~

Now, in Owentown, I stand in the den and kitchen that looks like a picture from one of the home-and-garden style magazines that women look at and drool over, and then tell their husbands what failures they are. A treadmill and workout equipment is neatly confined to one area. Both husband and wife were in the medical field. The wife had recently joined an aerobics dance class and started venturing out to visit with coworkers. Their marriage of fourteen years was coming to a close. She had filed for divorce.

I overhear an officer on a cell phone say, "Mr. Mercer, we just wanted to make sure the kids were all right." "Is that

Bill Mercer?" I ask. The officer nods yes.

"I know him; we served on the school board together." I remember the uproar in the community when his long marriage ended and soon afterward he married a Hispanic lady. We are now at his stepson's house.

"There are two boys that live here. Mr. Mercer is with the younger son. The older teen is on a trip out of state," the officer says. "The owner of the house called Mercer this morning to come pick the child up. He could tell something was wrong."

When Bill had arrived, he found a note on the door: "Call 911."

Alarmed, he went in, found the child hiding under his bed, grabbed him up, and immediately they left the house. He then called 911 on his cell phone as his pickup truck put distance between themselves and the house.

The boys' rooms are down the hall on the left, full of boys' stuff. The rooms are neat and well organized, probably from their upbringing in a house that is the same way. It is unlike most of the boys' rooms that I have seen.

~~~~~~~~~~~~~~~~~~~~~~~~

Entering my house, you will be greeted with music equipment, art stuff, sewing patterns and material (cloth), books, candles, framed pictures waiting to be hung, and baseball caps or hats. Clothes may be piled on the ironing board, waiting to be ironed for the day they will be worn. My kids' rooms are still loaded with valuable "things" they have left behind. Some "things" continue to accumulate. In thirty years you accumulate a lot of stuff. You just never know when printer cables might make a comeback, or even that old stained shirt might come in handy. I could wear it when working on the car or crawling under the house. It would at least make a good rag. So I will keep it, along with thirty other old shirts.

Farther down the hall and on the right in the house in Owentown is the large master bedroom. In it is a walk-in closet. The man's starched and ironed shirts and pants are all are placed upon hangers and neatly spaced a quarter of an inch apart, allowing the clothes to breathe. On the woman's side of the closet, blouses and dresses are neatly lined up. On the dresser there is no pocket change, dust, or clutter; there is a roll of wide clear tape and a roll of duct tape. On the bed is a pool of blood. Closer inspection reveals blood splattered on one wall and the ceiling. Lying on the bed is a metal baseball bat. The call, the note, the blood, and now a baseball bat are signs that something is not right here. All else is as it should be — as though everyone has gone to school or work or on vacation, or maybe even camping.

~~~~~~~~~~~~~~~~~~~~~~~~~~~~

If a burglar broke into my house, he surely would get caught, because it would take him so long to figure out what to take and what to leave; we would get home before the job was finished. It would take two pillowcases and twenty minutes to get the stuff off the top of our dresser, which would include twenty-six dollars and thirty-two cents, all in loose change. It is noteworthy that the change problem did not exist as long as we had kids living at home. We have been burgled: my sons' auto stereo was taken once, a sixteen-foot flatbed trailer was taken right out of my driveway, and once someone siphoned the gas out of Fae's riding lawnmower, then helped himself to my air compressor, chain saw, and tools. Apparently, he needed them more than I did.

~~~~~~~~~~~~~~~~~~~~~~~~~~~~

"Out back," says the detective, motioning for me. The view from the back porch looks like a picture from a landscape magazine. To the left is a patio with an umbrella-covered table, surrounded by matching chairs; next to it is a hot tub. Yard ornaments and flowers grace the yard, which is covered with dark green grass. Large trees canopy the backyard, providing plenty of shade. From the patio, a winding sidewalk leads to the right, to a miniature bright red barn with white painted cross-timbers and a high roof.

~~~~~~~~~~~~~~~~~~~~~~~~~~~~~

When my house was built, it had all the amenities of the day, including a water well beside the back door. After electricity came in, a water pump was installed and the well was covered by the back porch. A toilet and a cast iron bathtub with ironclad claw feet replaced the outhouse. Going to the bathroom still required going outside and crossing the porch. Long before my time, the breezeway turned into a hallway and the back porch was enclosed with windows to become the den.

I have attached a deck to the back door. It is made of wooden pallets—huge wooden pallets. These pallets were made for transporting giant machinery made in Germany. They are made of heavy rough-cut lumber and cut from a rain forest. The wood is soft and absorbs water. The East Texas humidity makes it even softer. Termites love it. On my deck is a Jacuzzi. It sure was nice when it worked.

I have an ornamental crystal ball on a stand in my backyard. The birdbath is used frequently by all kinds of birds. My daughter, Lena Beth, fixed up a nice flower bed, outlined with concrete blocks. A single solar-powered yard light gives off barely enough light to be seen, although it may be the beacon for the many mosquitoes that wait for me to walk out into the backyard. A walnut tree shades the deck; it also lets me know when it is walnut season with the "bonking" sounds made as the nuts fall on my roof.

~~~~~~~~~~~~~~~~~~~~~~~~~~~

On the sidewalk in Owentown, I see the smudged black

track of a wheelbarrow tire as it made its way from the house, to the patio, to the shop. The track forms a black J on the sidewalk that shows where the wheelbarrow was turned around before entering the shop. It must have carried a heavy load.

The shop door was locked from the inside and officers had to force the doors open. When I arrive, the double doors are open wide. The noon sun rays make the opening bright but the inside remains dark. Standing in the light is a stepladder, cocked sideways as though it is falling, teetering to one side. It looks like it is caught in a picture, as though time has stopped. As my eyes adjust to the change of light, I see that a foot is holding the ladder up. The foot is attached to a leg, attached to a body, and all suspended in air.

To the left and right on the shop walls are shelves, tools, and equipment, all in their proper places — except for a drill, an eye bolt, and a nylon rope cut to an appropriate length. These three items were needed for his last honey-do project.

An eye bolt gets its name from the dot over the little i. An eye bolt is a screw with a loop on one end and threads on the other end. The bolt is bent at one end like a closed question mark, forming a nice eye to thread a three-eighths-inch nylon rope through. A colorful nylon rope woven with bright orange, white, and black nylon filament, ordinarily used for water skiing, is threaded through the eye. It came from a neatly coiled roll now sitting on the shelf.

~~~~~~~~~~~~~~~~~~~~~~~~~~

My projects, honey-do or not, start with looking for something: time, tools, and/or materials. During a project, I spend a lot of time looking for something, some kinds of tools and materials. Before and during the project, I take the time to go the store, usually several times, to get the tools and materials I could not find. At the conclusion of the project, and at a later time, I store away the tools and materials, in the process finding many of the tools and materials I was looking for in the first place.

The formula I use for most projects is a 1:3 ratio; that is, for every one minute, hour, or day actually swinging a hammer, screwing a screw, sawing a board, changing a sparkplug, airing up a tire, soldering a connection, weeding the garden, or actually doing something, there are three minutes, hours, or days spent looking for the hammer, screwdriver, saw or board, sparkplug socket, air chuck, solder gun, or hoe.

~~~~~~~~~~~~~~~~~~~~~~~~

Beneath the tilting ladder, on a clean concrete floor, is a small pile of wood shavings, looking out of place. The curly wood filings came from drilling a hole in the wooden truss above, where an eye bolt is placed.

Dangling a foot above the sawdust is another foot, or I should say, a black boot. This booted leg is hanging straight down; the other leg is bent and captured, holding up the ladder. The top of the boot is covered with typical blue jeans, held up with a black leather belt at the waist. On the belt is a cell phone carrying case, and inside it, a cell phone, probably the one used to call his father-in-law. Neatly tucked into the pants and belt is a blue T-shirt. "Give 4 Life; It's A New Day, Donate Blood" is printed on the front.

Both arms are hanging by his side. On one wrist is a white metal bracelet. His shoulders are slumped, his neck is stretched and his head is abnormally twisted to the left. His face is purple, with an agonized expression.

The rope has tightened so that it cannot be seen around the neck, but the knot is visible under his right ear. The rope is tightly stretched from his neck to the eye bolt. The rope slips through the eyebolt and extends 117.25 inches down, at an angle, to the wheelbarrow. There it is, wrapped and tied around the neck of his wife, his victim.

His engineering plans were designed for us to find them hanging by the neck, side by side. She did not move. His 187 pounds of live weight could not lift her 147 pounds of dead weight. Because of the angle of the dangle, his project had failed. She is wrapped in a comforter in a wheelbarrow, and he is hanging alone.

He had used an excessive amount of clear packing tape, wrapping it around and around her head, mouth, and face. Through the tape I can see the violence that took place. Blood-matted hair is visible through the layers of tape. We begin the gruesome task of cleaning up this mess.

The emergency medical technicians on the ambulance had determined with no doubt that they were both dead. The sheriff's deputies secured the area, taking notes of who came and went. The crime scene investigators are taking pictures and gathering evidence. The detectives are putting it all together. The Winona volunteer firemen take him down, and then assist the funeral home in placing her in a body bag and wrapping him in a sheet, to be transported just four blocks to the Southeast Texas Forensic Center for autopsies.

My work here is done. This normally quiet street is now bustling with activity as television crews and media people search for sound bites and quotes. Neighbors stand outside; some sit on their porches; all are looking to see the excitement in their community. When we all leave and the yellow tape finally is wadded up and thrown away, the memory will remain, especially with those who still live there. Some will move on and carry their piece of memory with them. When they read or hear about a murder/suicide, they may say, "I remember when my neighbor . . ."

"This looks like a tough one," says the reporter.

"Yes, it was." I shake my head.

"I heard he beat her with a baseball bat and hung himself. Is that true?," the reporter asks as I am leaving.

"Yes," I say, not realizing I will be saddled with that quote within twenty minutes on the Associated Press news wire, on the Internet, and around the world.

I really wanted to delay that information. I am usually vigilant with the media, but today I let it slip. In minutes it will be on the Internet, then on the news wire, followed by radio and television.

My next few hours will be spent coordinating funeral homes, ordering autopsies, dealing with various news media, and trying to make sense out of a senseless act.

The next morning on the front page of the newspaper is the headline, in big, bold letters: "Man Beats Wife to Death with Baseball Bat and Then Hangs Self, Official Says"

The families probably will be calling during the next few days and weeks, trying to figure out what happened and trying to get some kind of closure or peace of mind. So many "what ifs" and "whys" and "maybe I could haves . . ." Some people think an autopsy will answer all their questions. I try to warn them that the weight of the kidneys and internal organs, test results, and medical terminology will leave them only with more unanswered questions.

The combined autopsy reports consist of twenty-four pages.

SOUTHWESTERN INSTITUTE OF FORENSIC SCIENCES

HER CONCLUSION: The pattern of injury is consistent with five blows. Four were to the left side of the head and one on the left shoulder.

HIS CONCLUSION: Asphyxia due to hanging.

~~~~~~~~~~~~~~~~~~~~~~~~

Even if we could understand, it would not change anything. Death is final, and it leaves the living with unanswered questions. In about ten days I will have signed and certified the death certificates. The reports will be filed in an inquest book, along with a thousand others.

You would think after twenty-five years I would get used to seeing the inhumanity and problems that make up my livelihood. In this case I was affected by the fact that most people would walk through that house and think, "This is the American Dream," or, "I wish my house was this clean and orderly." But how many movie stars, or wealthy or famous people, those who seem to have it all, go off the deep end?

What goes on inside a person determines his or her happiness. I am convinced that most of our personal misery is because someone else is not doing what we want them to do. For some, it is as abstract as not liking the president of the United States or the misery caused by those in authority. For some, misery is caused by friends, family, or spouse, because they will not do or act like the person wants them to. The more the person wants them to change or tries to change them, the more frustrated he or she becomes. A few think by eliminating the offending person, they eliminate the problem, and if they cannot eliminate the person/problem, they can eliminate themselves. Some do both.

~~~~~~~~~~~~~~~~~~~~~~~~~

Death scenes: How does one deal with these situations? As for me, and anyone who works in the criminal justice or emergency medical field, we learn to deal with it or get another job. How could anything positive come from such a violent event?

I am able to reflect on how blessed I really am, and maybe you are, too. As many of us "kick back and relax" in the comfort of our own homes, we need to remember to be thankful. Enjoy the good times. Seek fulfillment even in times when it seems like nothing is going on. When I think times are tough, I am approached by someone with problems much worse than mine.

~~~~~~~~~~~~~~~~~~~~~~~~~

My wife once told me, "You can do wrong if you want to, but if I find out; well, I know where you sleep."

When I get home from Owentown, I kiss Fae, tell her I love her and ask, "Isn't it time we got rid of those old baseball bats?"

~~~~~~~~~~~~~~~~~~~~~~~~~

Three years have passed since I wrote this story. The couple's kids are surviving. I saw them and their grandparents at a Chamber of Commerce banquet as the oldest, a clean-cut young man, received a college scholarship.

The kids have problems but are coping the best they can.

Granddad Mercer came in to talk to me one last time, with a few questions. The visit also cleared up a few questions I had.

"I have wondered about something," he says, mentioning the inquest. "George said he could give a person an injection in the neck that would paralyze all the muscles in the body except blinking the eyes. Could he have given her that kind of a shot?"

"He was defiantly a control freak," I answer, and then look up the inquest. "It shows no drugs were detected in either one." Chances are there would have been a positive find on at least one of the many drugs checked for, although there is a slim possibility that it would not have been picked up. "Worst case scenario, it was over for her after the first lick. He was going for a home run." I quickly thought that was a little callous, but he agreed without a grimace.

The answer to other questions, like "Why two different kinds of tape?," went with the couple to their graves.

"She had filed for divorce and wanted to move out of the house, and her lawyer told her not to move," Mercer says. "She requested certain things in the divorce. George had gone to his lawyer and made sure his petition requested the exact same things. She was served that day."

"I know there had to be a lot of tension there," I say.

"He had e-mailed his sister the night it happened," says Mercer. "Most of it was complaining about his family and his wife. He rambled about how he would take the kids camping and on outings and she would not be with them. It went on and on, and some of it didn't even make sense."

"That explains why the note we found was different from other suicide notes," I reply. "His homicide/suicide note was in the form of the rambling e-mail. The note we read was written several hours after he had killed her."

"And there was another e-mail sent around 2:00 A.M.," Mercer continues. "I just snapped and did the most horrific thing that could be done, the e-mail said."

Receipts for the hardware and rope show they were purchased the morning we found the bodies.

Chapter 21

Hanging With a Towel on the Bathroom Door

Inquest #1457

"Judge we have an inquest at 227 Chapman Road in Owentown. Looks like a suicide."

~~~~~~~~~~~~~~~~~~~~~~~~~

When Fae and I married, we moved into an efficiency apartment at 229 Chapman Road. Our apartment appeared to be converted from a one-car garage and washroom. The bathroom was proportionately large compared to the combo kitchen/bedroom/living room. There was a large, whitish porcelain bathtub with a red-brown rust stain running from the spigot to the drain. I was looking at that stain when Fae almost knocked me unconscious in that tub.

I was in the tub, on my knees, head under the spigot, rinsing my plentiful long brown hair. In the fetal position, I imagined myself beneath a waterfall. My eyes open, I enjoyed the solitude of having my face surrounded by cool running water, my mind resting. My dear new wife quietly approached me in my vulnerable state. What she did caused me to thrust my head up, hitting the faucet with a dull thud. She goosed me! I saw bright stars in a black sky. Other than the night of my vasectomy, this was the most pain she ever inflicted on me.

Ten years later, I am driving back to the wooden apartments made from old Camp Fannin Army barracks in Owentown. The apartments looked as though they have lost in the battle with time. With many coats of paint and several layers of roofing, age has taken its toll. There is always a market for a cheap place to live.

The victim's apartment is larger than the one we had, and it has an actual kitchen area. In the living room/den is an ashtray with a few marijuana roaches. A roach is the part left over, or the butt, of a marijuana cigarette. True "heads," or pot smokers, will use a roach clip and smoke the leftovers into nothing but ashes. Some save the roaches to smoke when they have nothing else. Others say the roach is the best part.

"He hung himself in the bathroom," says the officer as he leads the way.

The bathroom door is slightly open, with a belt buckle hanging over the top. The black leather belt is wedged at the top, which prevents the bathroom door from closing, or, in this fatal case, from opening. I have seen towels, robe belts, and other flexible hanging tools positioned in the same manner.

The victim is squatting and leaning against the door, causing a tension on the belt that makes it difficult to get the door open. When the door finally is opened, the strap lets loose and the victim falls back, just the way he was supposed to, but without our help. Because of rigor mortis the body maintains its squatting position and rolls like a ball, so that the man falls on his back, with arms and legs pointing up. We called this the cockroach position in the Army. The door jamb prevents him from flopping over on his side. He is stiff enough to estimate that at least six hours have passed since he went from erotica to eternity.

The bathroom is small, and he is a large man. The doorway and the bathroom floor are covered with this semi-naked man, who has a towel and leather strap wrapped around his neck, his underwear wrapped around his ankles, and house shoes pointing to the ceiling.

~~~~~~~~~~~~~~~~~~~~~~~~~~

Erotic asphyxiation refers to intentionally cutting off oxygen to the brain for sexual arousal. It is also called asphyxiophilia, autoerotic asphyxia, scarfing, kotzwarraism, or breath-control play. A person engaging in the activity is sometimes called a *gasper*.

A lot of people hang themselves accidentally. They play a sex game and use a safety net that works most of the time. The problem is, the one time it fails, the game is over.

Some do it in the closet, some outside, some in the garage, some in the bedroom, and some in a shed or barn. I do not recall ever doing an autoerotic asphyxia inquest on a female. The goal is to cut off the oxygen to the brain by applying pressure around the neck, or to the carotid arteries, while masturbating. Using a towel as a cushion around the neck helps the airway remain open. People performing this act do not want to choke to death; they really do not want to die. They want to experience a special high. It must be good because many do this more than once, and some do it repeatedly until they die.

The trick is that when they pass out, the noose, or whatever is restricting blood flow, is supposed to turn loose. This can be arranged by hanging on to one end of the rope and pulling with your hands. When you pass out, you let go! The trouble with that is, you let go too early and it spoils everything.

Another way is to wedge the rope, or strap, or towel into the top of a door. Form a loop around the neck using some kind of padding and apply pressure by squatting or leaning forward. Meanwhile, you are doing other things with other parts of your body. When you reach a climax and pass out, you will see stars, ooh and ah, and fall backward or forward, knocking the door open and releasing the stranglehold on your neck. When you wake up, you probably will feel stupid and wonder why you would do such a thing.

Maybe you will say to yourself, "I will never do this again." Then you put the equipment away where you know it will be ready for the next time you want to fiddle around.

That all works if you fall correctly. If you slump wrong, things are different. Your brain stops working. You are breathing and your heart is beating, but the oxygen is not getting to your thinker. You think you need to move, but you are paralyzed and cannot stand up. Instead of stars, you will see a long tunnel with a bright light at the end. You will meet Jesus or someone else to welcome you into the afterlife.

Accidental erotic asphyxiation happens to a lot of teenagers. Word gets out at school, or a movie shows how exciting it is, and the next thing you have is three or four dead kids. No age is exempt. The Owentown man was fifty-seven. I have seen a preteen hanging slumped against a tree with his pants unzipped.

They all look strange, feet on the ground, squatting, leaning, like all they have to do is stand up and live. None are dangling in the air, off the floor or ground, swinging like a real hanging.

I wonder what they thought in those last seconds that seemed eternal — and that were eternal.

I would think: I am going to be found wadded up here with my pecker hanging out, looking like I did not have sense enough to stand up. What are these policemen, firemen and ambulance . . . oh, no, there may be several women gawking at me, cracking jokes and calling me a pervert.

If you ever find me hanging somewhere, it is because someone else put me there.

Chapter 22

Jerry vs. Pam

Inquest #2734

Winnsboro is a nice city, usually quiet, with little going on at eight-thirty in the evening on a weekday. For years "everyone" said Winnsboro needed some nice small apartments, and now Pam lives in one, an efficiency apartment off of Beach Street. There are three single-story buildings with two dusty driveways. There's not much security, but who needs security in a city of less than 4,000?

Jerry's Story

If I could just make Pam understand, Jerry thinks as he walks down the street. My pickup is parked a couple of blocks away at the El Rancho, a local diner. It is best if it is not parked where Pam lives; it might alert her, and I don't want her to get all excited. And, things may not work out according to the plan.

What is my plan? How can I win her back? What can I do to make her see the light? Why won't she talk to me? These questions have been eating at me for over a month. And now, she's blocked my cell from her phone, and the texts I send go unanswered.

Will she talk to me tonight? I will tell her, "I can't live without you." Or maybe, "If I can't have you, no one else will." Surely there is something I can say to make her understand. Why is she being such a bitch? Why is she so irrational? Is she pregnant?

I stand under a streetlight. I need a minute to think. Leaning against the lamppost, I put my right hand into my pocket and feel the cool steel of a .357 Magnum. Why did I bring the pistol? I decided not to bring it, but here it is, and here we go.

Jerry avoids the driveway and steps across a grassy ditch onto the rental property. Her little red car is sitting in front of her apartment. This means she is at home. Or, maybe she is out on a date, seeing someone else.

"Maybe someone else is in the apartment with her right now! Maybe that someone else is the cause of all my misery," Jerry tells his .357, his fingers now wrapped around the pistol grip. But that is impossible. The thought that Pam may not care about him anymore quickly dissolves in his brain. Of course she still cares, and she still loves him; she just doesn't know how much. Jerry's eyes are set on the door of apartment number 104. The only outside window is next to the door. The curtains, made of thin material, are drawn, and there is a flicker of television light.

We dated for three weeks before she moved into my house. For three months we lived together, practically married. Sure we had some rough spots, but Pam, even with her problems, was the best thing that ever happened to me. Then she up and moved into these damn apartments a month ago. She didn't even try to work things out.

"It's over," she said. Just like that. Like she could erase what we had, or have. Like the last three months didn't mean anything.

Three knocks on the door.

"Pam? Can we talk?" Three more knocks, harder this time.

"Pam, come on. I just want to talk."

The next three knocks have a distinct sound, made by the butt of a .357 Magnum.

Pam's Story

It all started with Bill. Or, was it Jim, or Larry? It really doesn't matter. They are all the same. You move in with them, and they think they own you. I actually married Bill, the one before Jerry. We lasted three years, until I caught the bastard cheating on me. I should have known he would do it. Hell, he cheated on his ex, with me!

The trouble women have, leaving a man, is there is no place to go: except to another man. Especially when you are down and out trying to find someone who is willing to help. "No strings attached," they say. Then you move in and the strings get attached.

So-o-o, I was feeling low. Divorce is a terrible thing to have to go through, and Jerry was there to pick up the pieces. Hey, I didn't just move in with him. We knew each other almost a month before he convinced me to stay with him. It wasn't a permanent thing by any means, at least not at first.

Things started out OK. Sex was OK, food was OK, and we went out. Jerry can be a lot of fun. But things changed when I moved into HIS house. It was my clothes in HIS closet; my underwear hanging in HIS shower. What he forgot was it was MY ass in his bed! At the end of every month he would start griping about his ex and the child support he had to pay.

I got a part-time job, and he wanted me to help pay HIS child support!

I saved my money and a month ago leased a nice one-bedroom apartment.

"It's over," I told him. And it is over, for me, but not for him.

He sends texts: "We can work this out," "Why do you treat me this way?," "I hv somthn 4 U," "Meet me 2nite," and on and on.

Why can't guys just get over it? I called the police, and they said they wouldn't do anything. I guess I have to get beat up or shot before anyone will do anything. I blocked his number and I ignore his calls. He uses someone else's phone to get through.

I can't even go out for a drink, because in this small town he'd show up and cause a drama scene. Now all I want to do is sit on the couch and watch TV, and now someone is knocking on the door. Why didn't they use the doorbell?

Pam peeks out the window and sighs with relief. Jerry's pickup is not there. She reaches for the doorknob. Just before she touches it, she hears a voice.

"Pam? Can we talk?" Damn it, it's Jerry. She freezes.

Three more knocks, harder this time. "Pam, come on. I just want to talk."

She stands at the door, holding her breath, pretending she is invisible or not even there.

Three more knocks. That is not a fist he is knocking with.

"Pam, are you by yourself? Open this damn door!"

Jerry's Story

Maybe she is not home. Maybe she left her TV on just to fool people. She likes to fool people, like she made a fool out of me.

"Pam, are you by yourself? Open this damn door!"

If she is home, I will find out. If she isn't home, she will know I have been here. Stepping back, he aims the pistol at the doorknob.

Bam, bam, bam, three shots. Two round holes not even a half inch in diameter, not much bigger than the bullet, appear next to the doorknob. The third shot goes into the lock, and the doorknob and all comes to pieces.

"Shit!" he hears someone inside.

Pam's Story

The wood splinters around the doorknob. Jagged wood chips fly, and then the knob explodes. I feel something hit my thigh. Maybe part of the door. It doesn't hurt, but does it mean that I have been shot?

The door opens easily with a kick. Jerry is standing there, smoking gun in hand.

I look down at my leg and see red blood running down

it and onto the carpet. I put my hand over the wound, but it doesn't do much good. Blood leaks through my fingers.

"You shot me! You son of a bitch!" Now the wound burns with pain.

Jerry's Story

Pam is standing there, bent over, her hand on her leg. She looks up at me. She doesn't look mad. She looks confused. Her hand turns red. Red liquid begins dripping from her fingers and running down her leg.

"You shot me! You son of a bitch!" Now she looks mad.

"Oh, God! I didn't mean to! I'm sorry! I just wanted to talk."

"With a gun? Jerry, what the hell are you doing?" she screams.

Good question. What the hell am I doing? The plan. I must stick to the plan.

"I would never hurt you!" Wait, that is not in the plan. "I love you!" Now I sound like a whiney baby. Come on, Jerry, be a man.

She limps away into the bedroom and opens a drawer. I walk by her to the foot of the bed and turn to say it again.

"I'm sorry. I would never hurt you." But all I see is her butt running out the front door.

Pam's Story

Stop the bleeding; I have to stop the bleeding. Pressure, a bandage. The only thing I have clean is a T-shirt in the dresser. He is between me and escape. The only way I can go is to the bedroom, and close the door. A lot of good that will do. Forget the door, stop the bleeding. I need to call 911. Somebody needs to call 911.

I go my bedroom and open the dresser drawer. I look into the mirror hanging over the dresser and see someone else looking back. It looks like me; she moves when I move, she has the same bloody hands, but I have never seen this woman before. Who am I? Then I see his reflection walk behind me, going to the foot of the bed.

I look out the bedroom door and can see freedom out the front door. I have an opportunity to get the hell out of here. His back is turned. It is now or never.

It is a small apartment, but it seems to take forever to get out. Each step, each limp, I expect to be my last. Talk is over. I get just outside the apartment when —

"Bam," says the .357 one last time.

My Story

If I were cruel, I would end the story here. Who bought the last bullet? Winnsboro is not even in my county; therefore, you can deduce that whoever got shot did not die in Winnsboro. The Winnsboro Police Department responded to the call of a neighbor.

"911. What is your emergency?"

"Someone is beating on the door and yelling next door!"

"Do you think you are in danger?"

"Holy crap! I think I they are shooting each other!"

"Stay on the line . . ."

The police arrive, with the ambulance not far behind. They find the victim alive but ashy in appearance. There is a large amount of blood, and the victim has difficulty breathing. The fatally shot person is quickly transported by ambulance to another location and from there, whisked off by helicopter to Tyler.

~~~~~~~~~~~~~~~~~~~~~~~~~~~

While all this is going on I am having a nice dream. I am on a cruise ship, leaning against the rail on my balcony cabin, looking out over the ocean. The ship is rocking gently, and a cool sea mist spray covers my face. The sea breeze created by the movement of the ship adds even more comfort. There is a certain mystique surrounding where this ship is going. Then the music begins to play, a simple song with no words, just a melody that seems inappropriate to the setting. It isn't even a whole song, only a portion that keeps repeating itself.

It is 1:14 in the morning, and the music is the new sound of my Android cell phone. When I pick up the phone, which has no buttons, I inadvertently kill the call. Squinting my eyes, I find out that the missing call came from Trinity Mother Frances Hospital. I call back the number, expecting to get the PBX operator, who will have to search the hospital to find out who died and where they are. After some phone delays and to my delight, Nurse Carrie answers the phone.

"Sorry about the missed call. I have a smartphone that is smarter than I am," I say.

"I'm sorry to wake you at this hour. This is Carrie, Carrie Young. Do you remember me?"

"Oh, yes, I haven't forgotten my nursing days." I remember tall, dark-haired Carrie. I did her wedding.

Rose Garden Wedding

It was a garden wedding on a warm summer day with a slight breeze. People were gathered to form two lines, a walkway for the bride. Carrie has many friends and colleagues, and forty of the fifty people in attendance were there for her. The trail led to an archway in the midst of the Tyler Municipal Rose Garden, where two young guys were standing. (At this point in my life, mid-twenties is young.) One was casually dressed, and the other was wearing black leather pants and a black cloth tuxedo-style jacket.

"I'm Josh, the groom," said the tall guy with slicked-back, greasy hair. A large silver cross pulled down his left earlobe. He wore a black leather braided bolo tie, complete with a silver moose head that seemed to be looking at me. Why would anyone in Texas be wearing a moose head?

"I am Judge Shamburger," I said, stepping alongside the groom and the other guy, who I guessed was the best man. Both looked out of their element. I was wearing my judicial robe and extended my hand to him, wondering what Carrie had gotten into.

"I am ready to get this over with," he said, ignoring my hand.

"Carrie is quite a girl. You won't find anyone better," I said. I attributed the rudeness to his apprehension, although he did not seem too excited.

"Yeah, she said you were friends," he tartly replied. His reply could have been, "I am a lucky man!" or "Yes, she is special!" or "She is someone I want to spend the rest of my life with."

"We were friends," I said, wondering what to say next. And then something popped into my head: "We spent many nights together."

"Really?" He was obviously puzzled at the comment and turned to look at me. Now I ignored his gaze.

"It was long ago," I said this with an inflection of half "over" and half "longing." When, from the corner of my eye, I saw him start to breathe again, I hit him with, "We've tossed back the sheets and made up many a bed together." Then I turned to look at him.

Sometimes words can hit you as hard as a fist in the solar plexus, which causes you to lose your breath. I remember a Hispanic in jail who needed a translator until I said, "Your bond is $50,000." His knees buckled and he said, "Oh shit!" in plain English.

"You ha-ba-lowed that inglés!" I said.

I really did not mean to hit Mr. Groom so hard with my words.

"I, uh, I find that, uh, hard to believe." Josh started shaking, and his knees began to buckle. He kind of stumbled to maintain his balance. The color seemed to be draining from his face.

"Yes, we worked together at the hospital. I used to be a nurse. She was my charge nurse at Mother Frances." The light came on, dimly at first, but it began to brighten. "We worked the night shift," I said, and he began to breathe again.

OK, I acknowledge it was a mean thing to do. But this

could have been avoided with a simple handshake.

Two months after the wedding, I received a call from Carrie.

"Mitch, do you do divorces?"

~~~~~~~~~~~~~~~~~~~~~~~~

"We have a death at the hospital."

"What do you have?"

"Gunshot wound."

"Actually, I am not on call this week. I was on call last week. Judge Cowart is the judge on call this week." If it would have been a simple inquest, I would have done it myself, but this one has complications. "If you can't find him, call me back, and I'll be glad to handle it."

~~~~~~~~~~~~~~~~~~~~~~~~

"All aboard!" the captain yells. This time I am on a sailing ship and am a working passenger. This smaller ship gets tossed about by the waves. The captain calls the crew on deck for instructions, which include the signal for "All hands on deck." The signal has a buzz-vibrating sound and a familiar melody. Again the signal is given. The third time, I realize it is my Android summoning me again.

"Shamburger."

"Sorry, Judge, he doesn't answer," says Carrie.

"Sounds like a sorry night," I chuckle. "Let me get the paperwork." I use the built-in flashlight app on the Android to find my glasses and a pen, and then the phone's LED lights the long hallway to the kitchen. I have walked down that hallway in the dark a million times, but the phone app is neat. It is handy to have a light when walking down a long, dark hallway.

The Night of My Vasectomy

In 1987, I received a vasectomy. We have three kids, a

boy and two girls, and that's enough for me. If someone tells you a vasectomy is a "painless operation," they are talking about the procedure and not the aftermath. Sure, it is an outpatient procedure, but Fae had to drive me home. Then, as the anesthesia dwindled away, the pain came on. Dihydrocodeine (hydrocodone) and ice packs offered a little relief. For the rest of the day and into the night, all I could do was sit in the recliner, ice in lap, and watch television. I thought that with two more pills, maybe I could go to bed and get some sleep. Fae goes to bed and gets up with the chickens. (That is to say, she goes to bed early and gets up early; we don't actually have any chickens.)

Around midnight I turned off the television, struggled out of the recliner, and waddled to the icebox to grab a goodnight ice pack. I turned off the lights and waddled down the dark hallway to the bedroom. I had walked that dark hallway perhaps only half a million times by that time of my life.

When we bought the old house it was one story; we added an upstairs, with Lena's room. The stairs are in the hallway. Under the stairs is a space just the right size to put a washer and dryer, and we did just that. This centrally located the appliances so that anyone walking down the hall can load the washer or move the clothes from the washer to the dryer.

The dryer door swings out in front of the machine, like a regular door. The top edge is about as high as my belly button. The door is made of steel, and when it is left half open, it sticks halfway out into the hallway. We had all agreed that the door should not be left half open, in the traffic path of the hallway, especially at night.

Although my ambulation that night was more of a waddle than a walk, I did it with purpose, determined to make it to the bedroom with the minimum amount of crotch movement and subsequent pain. I held the ice pack out in front of me, to make sure I did not run into anything. Unfortunately, I held it above navel height.

The edge of the steel dryer door made contact with my severed genitals with a bump. Under normal conditions, it would have been painful. I could only moan as the air left my lungs and would not come back. I fell to my knees. I could not breathe, and I could not get back up. I could see lights, stars, and rainbow colors swirling around. I was on my hands and knees, like a dog, surrounded by darkness. I finally took a breath and let out a louder moan.

I closed the dryer door and proceeded to crawl down the rest of the hallway to the bedroom. Climbing into the waterbed, with the leg stretching involved, was like climbing a mountain. I sloshed onto the bed. Each wave gave a new angle to the pain. The commotion woke Fae.

"What happened?" she asked.

"Dryer door." I could only muster a guttural whisper.

"You know, when I laid down I thought about that dryer door," she said. "You really shouldn't walk in the dark."

I was too weak to kill her.

~~~~~~~~~~~~~~~~~~~~~~~~~~

Sitting at the kitchen table, I ask Carrie the question I have asked so many, many times: "What do you have?" It looks like that dream adventure cruise will have to wait.

"I have a white male, 34 years old. Looks like a suicide; shot himself in the chest, He was flown in from Winnsboro."

"I guess my day begins where his ended."

Chapter 23

Service With a Smile

Inquest #426

She stands behind a counter that is covered with beer advertisements, beer salt, corkscrews, and accessories. She is a happy person, and it is contagious. It is the way she converses with the customers. She is a short, stocky, white woman with dark dyed hair that is ratted out and sprayed to hold it crisp and steady. In her forties, she wears a little too much makeup but has a smile of bright, white teeth which ties it all together. Gaudy chrome earrings lose their cheap look as they comfortably dangle to her shoulders; a large necklace rests on rather large breasts. Her stubby little fingers are almost hidden by large turquoise and sterling silver rings, and long, curled, red reflective fingernails make an audible tapping on the cash register keys.

"That's a bottle of Jack, a six-pack of Coors Light, and, ohhh some high-dollar wine! Are we celebrating tonight?" She smiles, and I return the smile.

"Anniversary," I answer. "She will drink one glass and I will finish the bottle." We both chuckle.

"How long you been married?" she asks with a heavy Southern accent.

"Longer than I have been alive, if you figure it out in dog years. That's probably the best way to figure it. After all, I've been in the dog house more than once."

"Now Judge, you would never get into trouble!" She says this with a mischievous grin and a twinkle in her eye.

"Only with my wife," I say, handing my credit card to the stone and silver hand.

"Hi, Bob." She raises her voice, greeting another customer as she finishes our transaction. "Now Judge, you take care, and come back sooner. It's been over a month since your last visit."

"This will probably last me a long time," I say, justifying the purchase.

Although I will see Linda again, this will be the last time I will see her alive.

~~~~~~~~~~~~~~~~~~~~~~~~~~~

I knew of her rather than really knowing her; she was friendly, more of an acquaintance than a friend. I did not know where she lived. I knew she lived somewhere around Winona, and our paths crossed every now and then. Some people stick in your mind better than others. I am sure her smile and jewelry are pictured in many minds.

A month later, I see her again. Her face is frozen. She is not smiling. This is not the final picture I want to remember.

There are so many retail jobs where people come in contact with people. Successful convenience stores, gas stations, and beer and liquor stores all require people who are able to communicate with a smile and an inviting "I care" attitude. The people going through the checkout line range from millionaires to those living on food stamps. The store employees deal with people with friendly attitudes and some who are having a bad day. A list would include all professions and even the unemployed. Through the doors of the Lucky Leaf Liquor store come cowboys, welders, doctors, bums, housewives, teachers, preachers, judges, and murderers.

~~~~~~~~~~~~~~~~~~~~~~~~~~~

"And how are you today?" Linda asks the male customer. Her bright smile hides the long day spent standing on aching feet.

"I'm OK, just kind of worn out, ready for a Thanksgiving holiday."

"I know what you mean. I'm ready to call it a day myself." Linda lets a sliver of her tiredness show through. "Think I'll have a glass of wine to celebrate the end of a long day when I get home."

"What kind of wine do you like?"

"Cold!" she says and smiles. "Tonight, a Zinfandel."

"A good choice. Nothing like a glass of wine to relax after a long day."

"It may take a whole bottle tonight!" she says, expressing her long day.

"So you have a bottle waiting for you?"

"Chilled and waiting for me at home."

"Where is home?" he asks.

She pauses; he seems nice enough, even good looking in her eyes. He has been in the store before and has shown more than a passing interest in her. Friendly, in fact comfortable, easy to talk to, he is someone with possibilities. She opens the door.

"A few miles from here and a couple of miles across the river." The Sabine River is the county line between Smith and Gregg Counties.

"I've heard a lot of strange things happen in the river bottom." His voice shows concern and sincere interest.

"I live in the Bluff," she says.

Waters Bluff evolved from Walters's Bluff, a community of mostly black folk with genealogies traceable back to slave days.

"What you doing, living in the Bluff? A white girl living in the Bluff!"

"I'm not the only one! Times have changed. Besides, my best neighbors are black."

"Is your husband black?"

"No," she says, "I don't have a husband." There is no regret in her voice.

"Oh . . . that's right," he says apologetically, remembering an earlier conversation. "So is there anyone else?"

"Not really," she answers, looking at a clock that says three more hours to go on her shift.

"So you are drinking your wine alone tonight?"

"Unless something happens." Her voice offers an invitation.

"So, do you have a big Thanksgiving day planned?"

"I have to work tomorrow, but I will celebrate later."

She hands him his change, and they freeze for a moment, looking at each other eye to eye, trying to read the thoughts of the other. The quiet is broken by the sound of metallic grinding, aluminum on aluminum, as the front door opens. Two customers and Rodger — the owner, manager, and her replacement for the night — walks in.

"We'll see," he says, walking out the door as the others walk in.

"Who was that?" Rodger asks.

"You sure are nosey today," Linda answers, and then realizes she has no name for the man.

People begin loading up with beer and spirits for Thanksgiving Day. There are many more smiles and conversations before she can go home. So many flirting men have made so many passes at Linda, making promises they would like to, but would never, keep.

"See you tomorrow," she says to Rodger as she gets ready to leave.

"You are on your own tomorrow! I will be eating turkey!" Rodger answers. "Call me if you need me."

Linda gets into her car to go home, the same way she has done a hundred times before. There is nothing unusual as she looks both ways and drives out on Highway 155 toward Winona, toward the river. Within sight of the "th-thump" bridge, she turns left on Old River Road.

She slows down when she comes to the Old Iron Bridge, a one-lane bridge that was built in 1910. The eighty-four-year-old steel structure looks rickety, especially the aged wooden flooring. The bridge is submerged annually by the flooding Sabine. Creosote boards cross the steel I beams underneath. Over the years, new boards have been laid over old boards, and the old boards suffer from dry rot. Some of the old timbers underneath hang by a splinter; other pieces have fallen to sink or float on down the river. Two parallel paths of timbers of questionable strength line up with the tires of the vehicles that dare to cross. As long as the tires stay on these runners, the cars are relatively safe.

Linda looks 237 feet across the bridge to make sure she has the right-of-way and drives up the wooded elevation to mount the bridge. She enters the bridge from the Gregg County side, where the boards are in need of replacement. Halfway across are the newer boards, which start at the county line. She used to drive slowly across the bridge, looking at many years of graffiti written on the rusted steel girders, listening to the groaning of the rusted hinges and cables carrying her across the Sabine River thirty feet below. One day she realized that the slower she went, the longer she would be on the bridge. From that day on it was just a matter of "is the path clear." In less than five minutes she is driving up to her house.

Living alone does not mean Linda is lonely. She has her friends and a nice brick house in the country. She has lived there for twenty years and frequently visits friends and neighbors. The house is clean and neat, and it features displays of collectibles, memories, and pictures. She is a fan of the Native American Indian, displaying prints, jewelry, a knife, and a tomahawk. Dream catchers hang in several windows. A large beveled-glass coffee table sits in front of an overstuffed couch.

~~~~~~~~~~~~~~~~~~~~~~~~~

All my Thanksgiving Days have one thing in common: I am stuffed. Like Christmas, it is required that we go here, then here, and then to another place, from one feeding frenzy to the next. My wife's family leans toward the traditional feasting: basted roast turkey, country sugar-cured ham, mashed taters and brown gravy, and to-die-for dressing. All this is backed up with four different pies and two giant cakes, at least one being a dark sweet chocolate. The Shamburgers lean more toward "Greens" smoked turkey, smoked ham, sweet taters, oyster dressing, and ambrosia. Both will have cranberry sauce, giblet gravy, all kinds of breads, and everything else that is fattening and high in cholesterol. As for most family gatherings, we worry about what to bring and end up with enough to feed a small developing nation.

Stuffing the jalapeno peppers has fallen on my shoulders. The night before, I will open a gallon of pickled peppers and proceed to cut and gut them in preparation for the goodies I will be filling them with. A good sharp knife makes the work easy, and by bedtime there will be plenty of stuffed peppers for all, even though I will eat several defective ones along the way.

~~~~~~~~~~~~~~~~~~~~~~~~

"Well hello there!" Linda says, opening the door for her unexpected visitor. Most of her neighbors are watching television. Some are in their kitchens, preparing for their own Thanksgiving feasts; I am 4.1 miles away, cutting and gutting peppers. The rest of the night is spent getting ready for tomorrow.

~~~~~~~~~~~~~~~~~~~~~~~~

This Thanksgiving matches the others. I have a cup of coffee for breakfast, then we load up the car and head out to see how much food can be consumed in one day.

~~~~~~~~~~~~~~~~~~~~~~~~

"Linda is not here. I wouldn't complain, but my family is waiting." It is George, waiting for his replacement. He really does not want to get Linda into trouble, because she's covered for him many times. "It is Thanksgiving, after all."

"Not there? It is almost three!" Rodger says into the

telephone. Linda was to take over at two o'clock. "I told her she was on her own today. She is never even late for work . . . and she hasn't called? Something is wrong."

Rodger calls Linda's home phone several times, only to get a busy signal. "I'm going to check on . . . the store," he yells to his wife, trying to avoid questions. "Should be back in a minute."

No one else is on the road this afternoon. Leaves of changing colors are whipped into a whirlwind behind as he quickly maneuvers the winding county road. He drives onto the Old Iron Bridge without looking ahead. The thunder clapping of loose boards drowns out any moaning and groaning the old bridge might have. His tires squeal as he makes the sharp turn at the end of the bridge.

Cars are parked around most of the houses. The neighbors are finishing up Thanksgiving with desserts and/or football. Some are playing outside and some or gathering around the television.

Rodger arrives at a quiet house. Linda's car is not in the driveway. He thinks for a moment that she has skipped out on him, then dismisses the possibility. He pulls into the drive to turn around and notices the nose of her car, parked behind the house. He thinks again that maybe she is skipping out. Why would she hide her car? He finishes his turnaround and parks out front in the dirt drive.

He thinks if this is true, he should fire her, but she is not only the best employee he has, she is also his friend! Besides, nothing like this has ever happened before. At any rate, now is the time to get to the bottom of it.

He walks up to the front door and mashes the ivory button. He can hear the bells chime, but there is no response. He knocks on the door, lightly at first, then louder. He yells, "Linda, are you home?"

~~~~~~~~~~~~~~~~~~~~~~~~

As if the family meals are not enough, we decide to top off the evening at the home of our friends, the Scoggins.

Outside their brick home in the woods is a fire pit. The Scoggins are known for their entertainment of guests, and we have spent many enjoyable fall evenings sitting around the fire, playing guitar, singing, and watching the sparks fly up and away. The real East Texas winter begins around January, and Thanksgiving temperatures vary from hot to cold. This year we had an extended warm season, which I took advantage of with denim shorts and a Hawaiian shirt covered with flowers.

~~~~~~~~~~~~~~~~~~~~~~~

Rodger hesitates as he reaches for the doorknob. Does he really want to go inside? After all, he has done all he can reasonably do. She is probably not at home, but then there is her car. Overslept? But it is past three in the afternoon. He grips and turns the doorknob. It is locked. Somewhat relieved, he steps back. "It's probably nothing," he thinks, trying to reassure himself, but he knows something is wrong. The front curtains are drawn almost completely closed. He makes his way to the little split to look inside.

He sees the right side of the room; everything looks fine. Peering through the slit he can see a glass display case. It reveals Linda's American Indian collection. Panning left, he can see the end of the couch and standing on his tiptoes, he can see the couch is empty. The beveled-glass coffee table is broken, and it looks like she spilled something on the floor — tomato juice, or more like dark ketchup.

~~~~~~~~~~~~~~~~~~~~~~~

As I we gather around the swimming pool my pager beeps.

"It's the dispatcher at the Sheriff's Office," I say to those who are looking at me because of the alert. "I need to use the phone."

I go into the house and make the call. "Judge, we have an inquest in your precinct," the dispatcher says.

"What do you have?" I ask.

"The detectives are at the scene and request your presence."

I know this is not good. I look down at my shirt and shorts. "Where?"

"On County Road 356, the Old River Bridge Road."

"I'm just down the road. I should be there in about ten minutes."

I hope for a quick in-and-out inquest. There is plenty of daylight left, and the only hunger I have is the desire to relax in a lounge chair by the pool. When I arrive, the television cameras are rolling. Reporters are clamoring around the yard, held at bay by yellow crime tape and sheriff's deputies. I have to park a hundred yards from the residence because the street is crowded with onlookers.

"What do we have?" I ask Deputy Ramsey.

"Judge, it looks like a mess," he says and shakes his head.

Inside the nice little house, all looks calm except for blood spatters, a body, and a broken coffee table. She kept her house clean and organized. I see a display case filled with Indian artifacts including arrowheads, bowls, jewelry, and a hatchet.

There is also a wooden display stand, carved with a picture of a bear and the name "Jim Bowie." The stand is made for a Bowie knife, a large, heavy knife with a blade 10 inches long and razor sharp. Although the replica has a shiny mirror finish and is larger than the one the colonel died with at the Alamo, it is a reminder of frontier days. The Bowie knife is not on its stand.

It appears as though the murderer calmly showered and cleaned up when he was finished, neatly folding and hanging the towels. He then walked out the door, disappearing into society. He might walk alongside us on the sidewalk and offer us a warm "Hello." He might be the person who needs a ride, and we drive on, feeling guilty for not giving him a lift. He may be the one in the mall asking your little girl if she is lost.

~~~~~~~~~~~~~~~~~~~~~~~~

SOUTHWESTERN INSTITUTE OF FORENSIC SCIENCES
Pathology Report: Case No: JP2523-94-2662JZ
FINDINGS:
1. Eleven stab wounds of the head and neck.
a. Some stab wounds showing a blunt and a sharp angle.
b. The wound tracks cut important organs that include the muscles, the left internal jugular vein, the pharynx, and the larynx.
c. The deepest wound track measures approximately 4 inches.
2. Multiple incised wounds in the areas that include the mouth, the upper chest, and the right and left sides to the posterior neck, with extension to the right shoulder.
3. Multiple incised wounds of the distal part of the upper extremities. (Defense wounds on the hands and arms.)
4. Stab wound of the back, with no penetration of the thoracic or abdominal cavities.
5. Contusion of the left eye.

CONCLUSION:
It is my opinion that Linda Viramontes, a 48-year-old woman, died of multiple stab wounds.
MANNER OF DEATH: Homicide.

~~~~~~~~~~~~~~~~~~~~~~~~

Serial killers are hard to catch for several reasons. First, they tend to float around, with distance between victims. Law enforcement communication between local agencies is difficult; across county and state lines, it is almost nonexistent. The information highway has improved things, but there is still a long way to go. Second, we try to make sense of their actions, profiling and attempting to nail down the murders to fit into something predictable. The problem is that the only thing predictable is that these killers will kill again. They may favor anyone from little children to old men. They may be dealing with sexual problems, or they may enjoy torturing, and then simply kill the witness. They may beg for forgiveness as they kill or do it with as much thought or remorse as eating a French fry. Victims often are randomly selected, making it difficult to find any pattern, rhyme, or reason. They may not even understand what compels them to do what they do. All they know is they have a mission or desire and the power to end a life.

I believe many serial killers are caught and put away without us even knowing they are/were serial killers. Many murder mysteries will remain unsolved, at the bottoms of the graves of the actors and the victims. We can only hope that their eternity will be appropriate to what they have done on earth. God can forgive them if He wants to, but I find it hard to forgive Henry Lee Lucas, who, with a shotgun, blew the face off of a friend of mine and who probably killed more than 200 others. Nor do I have much sympathy for whoever tortured and took the life of Linda Viramontes.

~~~~~~~~~~~~~~~~~~~~~~~~

The ten o'clock news shows someone walking out the front door in shorts and a Hawaiian shirt. The following day, page one of the Tyler newspaper thoroughly covers the story, pleading for anyone with information to call Crimestoppers or the sheriff's office. Posters began to appear, offering ten thousand dollars for information leading to the conviction of the killer. People just cannot understand why anyone would do harm to such a nice person. The search continues.

Viramontes found stabbed to death in her home on CR 356

Tyler-Smith County Crimestoppers needs your help in solving a murder in Smith County.

On November 24, 1994, Linda Viramontes was found

stabbed to death in her home on County Road 356 in Winona.

The Smith County Sheriff's Office did not find any signs of forced entry.

Police believe that Linda knew her assailant.

The only items found missing from the residence were Linda's purse and keys.

Linda was known to carry large sums of money on her at times.

An unknown older man from the Longview or surrounding area may have been giving Linda the money. Police believe this man may be able to assist with this murder investigation.

Please help us solve this murder.

Remember, we want your information, not your name.

Crimestoppers depends on you!

Call Crimestoppers at 903-597-CUFF or 1-800-575-2833.

Chapter 24

Live by the Sword, Die by the Sword

Inquest #313

"Judge, get here quick," says Gilyn, the chief court clerk. "It is Mr. Willis, and he is stinking up the place!" Gilyn sometimes exaggerates when it comes to smells. She can smell a fart a hundred yards away, and she doesn't hesitate to tell you about it!

James Edward Willis, Jr., is a regular customer in the justice court system, with several convictions for public intoxication. Most of his crimes have been against himself, rather than endangering anyone else. Rumor is that he once had money, but you can't tell it by looking at his car or his worn-out clothes. A shirt that probably will be disposed of rather than washed when he's doing wearing it is tucked into stained khaki pants. A ragged Air Force flight jacket, whose color is worn down to the natural rawhide, drapes across his shoulders. The old lace-up Army boots are laceless and scuffed down to the same color as the jacket.

I enter the small courtroom and quickly realize that the clerk is not kidding. I agree; this man needs to go back outside or to wherever people like him go.

"Mr. Willis," I address him, "I see they are charging you with public intoxication." I take my seat behind the bench. Usually, Mr. Willis would plead no contest and accept nights spent in jail as punishment.

He stands up as I sit down. A ragged stack of papers and envelopes three inches high stays on the seat beside him.

His movements stir air and waft his stench toward me.

"Judge," he asks, "how could they write me up for public intoxication when I was in the comfort of my own home?"

"Mr. Willis, you have the right to remain silent."

"I am a veteran, and I have the right to say what needs to be said."

"Do you want to plead not guilty?"

"No, I just want to get this over with."

"The report says you were in your car."

"Exactly! My car is my home!" He is referring to an old, tan Lincoln town car that has long lost its luster. "I was parked and sleeping under the oak tree in my pasture. Sure, I had been drinking, maybe even drunk, but I wasn't hurtin' anyone."

"I understand," I say. "But someone saw your car and became concerned. They called the sheriff."

"Well, someone needs to mind their own dammed business."

"The deputy that went out on the call couldn't wake you up. That is why he called the ambulance."

"And that is why I refused to get into the ambulance! There wasn't nothin' wrong with me! I was just sleeping it off."

"At four o'clock in the afternoon." I look at him over my reading glasses. "Your car had been sitting there all day. One of these days, we are going to find you sitting in your car, dead."

"Judge, I have lived through a lot. There are a lot worse ways to die."

My nose tells me to wrap this up. "Do you want to plead no contest?"

"If that is what you want to do," he says.

"It is your choice, not mine. You do what you think you need to do." I wonder how a jury would react to the evidence and odor. "It makes no difference to me. I can get another judge to hear the case." (Gladly get another judge!)

"Nah, go ahead and knock this thing out," he says, as if

he were closing the subject. "I want to show you something." He turns to his stack of papers.

I recognize old Army papers. Many veterans hold onto yellow shot records, dark brown medical folders, typed orders with lists of names telling them of their destiny, and manila envelopes stuffed with more orders and pictures. We keep those papers, medals, and ribbons as though if we lose them the memory will go also. It's not just our memory: the little mark we made on the world will be gone forever. The pictures and papers that once directed our lives are all that is left to prove we were ready to lay down our lives for this country.

Mr. Willis was there to show me his proof.

"I am thinking about writing a book. I got it all right here," he says, placing the stack on the bench. "I was in the Navy Air Corps; flew with George Bush!" He pulls out a scrolled black-and-white photo and unrolls it in front of me. A group of men are standing, multilayered, probably on bleachers. Each face is the size of a pencil eraser. They all appear to be happy, probably a graduating class.

"See, that's me." He points with a grimy finger to one of the young, clean-cut soldiers decked out in a khaki uniform. "And there is George. We were both trained to be navigators." He points to another soldier, who looks much like any of the other 200 standing at parade rest. "I served on an aircraft carrier during the 'Big One.' At first I was a tail gunner. Cramped into a little space with a canteen, a sandwich, and a machine gun. My job was to protect the plane. Then, like George, I became a bombardier. We bombed the hell out of those Japs. Ships, compounds, industries, cities, soldiers, people . . . we bombed the hell out of them."

In a way, he spoke as if he had a desire to be back there, flying high above the earth, with the power to turn the enemy below into fire and smoke.

~~~~~~~~~~~~~~~~~~~~~~~~~~~

The events of life make us who we are. Some things happen to us that we have no control over, while other things happen by choice. On December 1, 1969, the first draft lottery since 1942 was held. For the lottery, 366 blue plastic capsules, each containing one date of the calendar year, were dumped into a large glass container. The capsules were then drawn out and opened, one by one, and assigned sequentially rising numbers. Those of us who shared this event remember our number. It was a number that determined our future. As Vietnam was winding down, each male's nineteenth birthday was celebrated or cursed with that number. For more than 70,000 draft dodgers, it meant leaving the U.S.A. For many, a small lotto number meant "signing up," which gave you a choice of the branch of service and a chance to influence the duty or job you might have in the military. For thousands the number meant a long or a short life. My lucky number was 313. My friends envied that number. I was disappointed. The draft was a two-year commitment, and joining up meant at least three years.

I feel there is a need for everyone to serve their country in one way or another. My father served in the Army during World War II. Every now and then, something about his time in the Philippines would enter into conversations. I remember looking at his medals and ribbons with admiration. I watched old war movies and played war as a child; maybe this instilled within me a desire to wear a uniform.

For whatever reason, after a year of junior college I was on my way to Fort Ord, California, for basic training. My six-year military journey began. We saw a film that showed people jumping out of airplanes. It looked like fun, and I always wanted to jump out of an airplane, so I signed a slip of paper two inches high and eight and one-half inches long. A year later I was jumping out of airplanes.

~~~~~~~~~~~~~~~~~~~~~~~~~~

"Mr. Willis, do you think you can stay out of trouble for a while?" I ask.

"Well, I'll do what I can."

"I can get the court cost and fine down to a hundred

dollars. Can you handle that?"

He reaches down into his front pocket and wrestles out a handful of folding money. He then peels off a hundred-dollar bill and drops it by the gavel in front of me with a grin.

I wonder, as he walks out of the courtroom, his papers tucked safely away under his arm, what changed his life. What changed that clean-cut kid from Carthage, Texas, to a seventy-year-old alcoholic living out of his car? Did the things he brags about in the courtroom, later, give him nightmares? Did he come back to an America or a family that had moved on without him, leaving him with only memories of a time when he was needed and he did what he had to do? Now his only need is to get drunk and forget the rest of the world.

As he leaves the Justice Court Center, Gilyn traces his path, spraying disinfectant. She comes back to her desk to find a soggy hundred-dollar bill.

Inquest # 313:
New Year's Eve, 2004

Mr. Willis has made a friend of the owner of the Red Devil Truck Wash on Interstate 20. A few old travel trailers and trailer-houses are scattered around the back of the seedy truck wash. Two beer joints and a liquor store across the interstate are the only other businesses within a mile. The place is known for an occasional drug bust involving a prostitute or two. The owner lets Mr. Willis stay in a small, abandoned room that was once part of a gas station. It is attached to a closed-down restaurant. His bed is an old recliner, where he sleeps in his clothes. A little TV sits on a metal table in front of it. A naked light bulb, complete with a pull chain, swings on a cord, shooting out a hundred watts of brightness and causing shadows to shift about the room as it sways. The light reveals the rest of the room, cluttered with trash and junk, and a trail that leads to an open door in the back. Beyond that door is a dark room with an unbearable odor. Before Mr. Willis, the room was a crash place for crackheads who were following the interstate.

Mr. Willis gets to and from liquor stores by way of "helpers" who, for a few dollars and a drink, will give him a ride. The "helpers" check on him often because they like the money and they like to drink. Sometimes they take his money and leave him to find his way back to his sanctuary. Sometimes it means he has to walk across the interstate. Occasionally he will halfway clean up and go the twelve miles to Kilgore. The cabbies know he is good for his fares, and they will put up with his odor to collect the long fare with a possible tip.

New Year's Days come and go without much fanfare for Mr. Willis. This year, a visit to the Veterans Administration doctors has revealed that his prostate is full of cancer, and he does not know how many more New Years he has left. It has been years since he has connected with any of his family, and tonight that is the way he wants it. Except for his "friends," Mr. Willis is alone.

At 10:30 A.M. on January 2, 2005, two of Mr. Willis's friends pay him a visit.

"I saw him at the V.F.W. in Longview and haven't seen him since," says Jane to her friend, Mary. The Veterans of Foreign War post is a popular and cheap local drinking spot. "That was like two days ago."

"James! Mr. Willis! Are you in?" Mary bangs again and shouts. Mary and Jane are working girls from the truck wash. Mr. Willis helps them out every now and then. In return, they pay him an occasional visit. He is not a bad guy, and he is good for a meal. They fly, he buys. Mary knocks on the front door again and yells, "Mr. Willis." Without hesitation, Mary reaches to turn the doorknob. The door is locked.

"I have the only other key," Jane says, reaching into her purse. The brass key takes some force to move the tumblers, but with a twist and the release of the catch, the door pops open a few inches.

"Oh, shit!" They both yelp and jump back, gagging and shaking their heads as the odor hits them in the face.

"He's done it again!" says Jane. They remember other

times he defecated on himself and the messes he paid good money for them to clean up.

"I'm not cleaning him up," Mary says, still shaking her head. "Not today!"

"Jesus," Jane exclaims. "It smells like someone curled up in there and died!"

They bump shoulders and chuckle as they walk away, leaving the door cracked open.

They show up again the next morning, at 9 A.M.

"Do you think he is in there?" Mary asks as they walk toward the old service station turned apartment.

"We have to look. Anyway, we need to look around in there. There might be something we need. Give me the key, Ms. Chicken." Mary takes the key from Jane, but they find the door ajar, like they left it.

"The light is on," Jane says as she pushes the door open. They step inside. They can hear the shower running in the room in the back, and they look toward the open door and the darkness beyond. It gives them a sense of relief. Maybe he is cleaning himself up, but the place still stinks, bad. He may even walk out of the room naked; if so, they will laugh and run off. As their eyes adjust to the light, they can see dark red spatters on shelves, walls, and ceiling. Then, right in front of them, crumpled across a cardboard barrel, they see the body of Mr. Willis. His stained briefs are all he is wearing. Large cuts mangle his body. His neck is cut to the point that his head is attached by only a small piece of meat.

The girls leave the room and call 911 from the truck wash.

~~~~~~~~~~~~~~~~~~~~~~~~~~~~

"Judge, we have one at the Red Devil Truck Wash at I-20 and Joy-Wright," the dispatcher tells me.

The building looks like many of the closed-down dreams you see along the highways. Investments made in hopes of getting a nice return on their money now stand abandoned and dilapidated. Sun-bleached blue paint and hanging pieces of metal and wood make up the exterior. The fractured plate-glass windows in what used to be a restaurant are so dirty they appear frosted. The word CLOSED is brush-painted across the windows in big red letters three feet tall.

"Judge, you might want to light that cigar for this one," says Officer Stinecipher. "It doesn't smell good or look good in there."

His assessment is disturbingly accurate.

"Damn," I say shaking my head. "Looks like someone used a sword or machete. Any weapon found?" The detective shakes his head no. "I figure this place was a mess before what ever happened here took place."

"Looking at the blood spatters, I would say he put up a fight." The detective points toward the dark red droplets dried on the walls and the shelves scattered about the room. "The shower was running when we got here, probably why he was in his underwear."

"Yeah," I say, "but was the shower for him? Or was it for whoever got blood all over them? This is some cold-blooded shit." I go outside to breathe, but it takes several minutes to feel the freshness of the air.

"Any next of kin?" I ask the officer, who has joined me outside.

The officer nods his head toward a group of modern-day gypsies gathered in the parking lot, observing. "They say it has been years since he has talked to any relatives."

"Let's get him to the forensic center."

SOUTHWESTERN INSTITUTE OF FORENSIC SCIENCES

Pathology Report: Case No: JP2587-05-5649JZ
FINDINGS:

1. Multiple cutting wounds (27) of body.
2. Severe cutting wound of neck that severed the cervical spine and spinal cord.
3. Cutting wound along right temporal scalp with a depressed skull fracture.

4. Large cutting wound along left temporal scalp that fractured the skull from the left temporal area around to the right temporal area.

5. Multiple cutting wounds of upper and lower extremities.

6. Acute amputation of left thumb and tip of left index finger.

7. Acute amputation of distal tip of right fifth finger.

8. Severely decomposed body.

Cause of death: Multiple cutting wounds of the body with transaction of cervical spine and cord, and skull fractures.

DETERMINED BY DOCTOR: Homicide.

Mr. Willis made page three in the papers. There are no big rewards offered, and no public outcries for the violence committed. A few clues lead the detectives nowhere. His body is returned to Carthage, where he is buried. I think about a man who was once called upon by his country to do a job. He was right: there are worse ways to die than being found in your car.

~~~~~~~~~~~~~~~~~~~~~~~~

Three years later and with a new owner, the old station that was Mr. Willis's room gets cleaned out.

"Look, guys," says the boss. "I just want you to clean the place up. Scrap the metal and burn the rest."

"What about these papers?" One of the workers points to a stack of old, yellowing papers and photographs. They somehow look official, different from the magazines and old newspapers scattered around. They are military papers. They include orders to deploy, commendations, promotions, a medical history. Next to them is a small box containing ribbons and metals. Some of the bulk orders have long lists of names, among them James Edward Willis, Jr.

"If you don't haul it off, burn it."

Chapter 25

The Death of Winona Texaco, T.J., and Larry Tidwell

Inquests #1884 and #5221

The Reverend Charles Millikan, pastor of Moody Memorial United Methodist Church, a prominent church in Galveston, Texas, looked over the Sunday congregation. In attendance were many members of other churches, whose churches had been destroyed or damaged by Hurricane Ike. In 2008, that storm blew much of the Texas coast away, including Galveston. To the outsider, three months later, the destruction looked like it could have occurred yesterday.

"We have weathered the storm," he said. "Rooftops are gone. Boats are in the streets. And even though we can see the destruction of nature, all around us we can see the handiwork of God. We see God's people working together building and bringing back a stronger Galveston." Galveston is an island with a prideful history of weathering hurricanes. When the storms end, the land lovers move back to where they came from. The true Galvestonians are not going anywhere; their lungs and blood are filled with the salty breeze of the sea.

Winona Methodist Church had sent fifty flood-buckets to the island. A flood-bucket is a plastic five-gallon bucket filled with sponges, cleaning supplies, rubber gloves, and necessities used to clean up mud, water, and mildew. Thousands of houses and apartments suffered damage along the coast.

"We saw miracle after miracle during the storm: lives

spared, property untouched," the Reverend Millikan continued sermonizing. "And now, we see the real work of God—people helping people, businesses helping other businesses, churches helping churches." Moody Memorial, for its part, opened its doors to pastors and congregations to use its facilities while they repaired and rebuilt their own churches.

"Speaking of miracles," the reverend broke from his sermon with a noticeable change of voice. He was surprised to see two faces sitting among hundreds in the congregation. "I see Mitch and Fae Shamburger, from Winona." He tilted his head to the side and smiled the way only Brother Millikan can do. I heard a murmur quickly arise and spread across in the crowd gathered to worship that day. Little did we know that we had become celebrities.

In the fall of 1968, Milliken entered the Perkins School of Theology at Southern Methodist University. While attending Perkins, he served as youth director for Marvin Church in Tyler. His first pastoral position came in 1970, in Winona, Texas. Whenever you read or hear Brother Millikan's long list of credentials, Winona will be included. Much happened during the time he spent in our little town. Things happened that shaped the life of the man now standing in the pulpit and the lives of those he has touched throughout his ministry. Most significant was his marriage to his lovely wife, Laura. As my pastor, he energized the church in Winona with an active youth program and a visitation program, and he and Laura practically became members of every family in the church. He baptized Fae, married us, and baptized our first-born. Thirty years and six churches later, he was the senior pastor and filling the pulpit at Moody Memorial.

"We as God's people can hold on to the promises that God has given us." The sermon came back to life. I was a little embarrassed about the interruption Fae and I had created.

"We as God's people can depend on the strength given to us through his Son, Jesus Christ. And we as God's people can pause, lie back, and relax into the comforting hands of the Holy Spirit."

The service ended. We were lost in the crowd. Our church of thirty or so differed on a Sunday from this church of four hundred or so. I wondered how we might find our way to the preacher, but I did not wonder long.

"It is so nice to meet you," a stranger said, reaching out and shaking my hand like a long-lost brother, "How are LoLo and the rest of the family?"

"How are the Johnsons and Mr. Sheard?" asked a lady, sincerely looking at me and awaiting an answer. She had heard the stories of Winona from the pulpit. To her the story of Mr. Sheard changing the light bulb could have happened yesterday and not thirty years ago.

"All is well in Winona," I responded, although Mr. Sheard died twenty years ago and Harold Johnson almost ten. Time stands still for people, things, and places when they are locked in a story or a memory.

"Your mom is just short of sainthood here at Moody!" said another.

In this church, three hundred miles from my own, it felt like a homecoming or a family reunion. The difference was that I did not know any of the people who knew me, but they knew me quite well. I began to see them through Brother Millikan's eyes. After all, they were looking at me through his. Soon I felt quite at home and among friends.

"We were so sad when T.J. died," said another, his face slowly looking down and turning from side to side, as in disbelief and sadness. "The stories we have heard about your dad and the Texaco station . . ."

"Oh, Mitch and Fae, I am so glad to see you!" The Reverend Millikan and his wife approached us with a smile that reached from ear to ear. The people parted like the Red Sea, and we all greeted with hugs. Charles and Laura hustled us out of the church so they could have us to themselves. They took us to the local "hot spot" for lunch; it featured little tables, wooden chairs, large seafaring ropes, a seashore ambiance, and the staple foods of Galveston, seafood, in abundance. We sat upon a high deck overlooking the Gulf of Mexico.

"Those days in Winona..." said Charles. He was gazing across the gulf of water and the gulf of time. "Those were the days."

Then, as if waking from a dream, he continued. "Tell us what is happening in Winona."

We did our best to bring them up to date on the town, with both good news and bad. I can see the advantage of freezing memories in time, memories of trips and adventures, memories of those wonderful times, memories when a lesson is learned. We lock these memories into a place in the mind where they will remain forever treasured, subject to recall during darker days, or to recall when seeking advice or direction from days gone by. The world goes on and things change, but the memories can remain the same.

"I remember it like it was yesterday: LoLo and T.J.," said the preacher in wistful tones, smiling and tilting his head, "sitting on that bench at the Texaco station, talking to your dad."

~~~~~~~~~~~~~~~~~~~~~~~~~~

The Thomas Jefferson Shamburger I knew was not a very religious person, at least in the sense of a religion that is "churchy" in the form of organization. Before my time, I am told, he spent a lot of time and energy in the Winona Methodist Church. He continued to tithe and would not work on Sundays. He would not even mow the yard or allow the yard to be mowed on his Sabbath. At one time in his life, he considered being a preacher, and he knew more than I did when it came to the Bible.

During my youth, Sunday mornings often featured gripe sessions between Mom and Dad, with them rushing us kids to get ready and out of the house.

"Go on! Don't be late! Sunday school starts at ten!" we would hear him say as Mom dragged us kids out the door. He stayed home, watched TV, and cooked dinner. Cooking was a delight to Dad, so cooking was not taboo on Sundays.

Sometimes, he would put on a suit and tie, don shoes

shined to a glistening brightness, add his hat, and go to church. He was an impressive figure, standing a portly five feet, eight and a half inches, with his hat, slightly cocked to the right side, covering a hairline that receded to the back of his head. I still see him in the mirror some Sundays when I am headed to church.

Having said this, T.J. was a long, long way from being St. Dad. The man I knew as a child was a rose grower and, in my pre-teen years, a truck driver. He drank, took pills, cussed, and was capable of raising hell and showing kindness with anyone, including and especially Mom. Settling down, at fifty-five, he opened what is now the oldest service station in Winona.

He was as generous with his kindness as he was with his faults. His ability to look into your soul with his deep, dark brown eyes made you feel elevated, to a level where he appeared to be. These attributes are what attracted a young lady, Evie Leola McClenny. She had a beauty that only old black-and-white photos can reveal. Even in her nineties, LoLo maintains the looks and vigor of a much younger woman. They were married in June, 1937, and both came from a culture and time in which divorce was never an option.

Winona (or T.J.'s) Texaco

The station is the oldest remaining structure in Winona, built before the railroad depot across and down the street. Rocks that were red and brown with iron ore, thickly mortared together, make up the oldest part of the small building. When driving across the western plains, deserts, or mountains, you see many deserted little buildings—roofless, hollowed out shells of adobe and rock, worn out by exposure and time. The wood is gone, eaten by insects or rotted away, or perhaps burned away in battles with Indians, leaving the skeleton of rock and mortar. Centered on the front walls of most of them is an empty doorway with windows on each side, like a skull with gaping eyes. When I see such ruins, I think of the stories they could tell.

Perhaps one day, far in the future, someone will ride through the ghost town of Winona on a horse. Horses will be the only transportation available, with trains and cars all but extinct. That future person will look upon the shell that was once Winona Texaco and wonder what stories it could tell.

~~~~~~~~~~~~~~~~~~~~~~~~~~~

Bill Grady gave up the business to T.J. in 1962. Bill moved on to producing the famous Winona Hoedown and later became Constable Bill Grady.

Except for receiving payment in the U.S. Army during World War II, T.J. was always self-employed. He was a businessman, but running a service station is much different from farming or running a tractor-trailer rig across the nation. He ran Winona Texaco by treating customers as though they were close friends or family. This went against his advice of "Never do business with your friends or family. Your friends will desert you, and your family will disown you."

T.J.'s rule was "Never let out on credit what you cannot afford to lose." That policy served him well for twenty years. Customers of all makes and models came to see T.J., sometimes to buy, often just to visit.

~~~~~~~~~~~~~~~~~~~~~~~~~~~

"You know you owe me!" Dad complained to an old black man slouched down in the back seat of a big, old, ragged car.

Large cars built in the fifties and sixties, like Buicks and Cadillacs, were not disposable cars. The heavy monsters were built to last, and they did. Their ability to move down the road surpassed the ability of their exterior paint to fight rust or the interior headliner to stay stuck to the roof. The seats became worn and tattered, and the doors had to be hit with a shoulder to be opened and lifted up to close. Squeaky doors, shocks, and springs are overlooked when the choice is ride or walk.

Every dent and scratch acquired after the third owner will stay in place and will be joined by other dents and scratches. A black car turns dark gray, and a white car turns yellowish. Like hand-me-down clothes, a classy old car would pass from owner to owner until it could be found abandoned out in a pasture or behind an old house that had smoke curling from a stove pipe. This was a yellowish Buick.

"Aw, Mr. T.J., I'm just a po' ol' nigger." The man's slurred speech indicated he had had a few too many. "You just dunning me 'cause I'm black."

Dad was prejudiced in his own way, but he was not prejudiced when it came to business. The fact is, most of his business depended on the black community. Many of the older black people in the area had sweated by his side, budding roses in his fields. They and their families became good, reliable customers and continue to be good political supporters of mine. T.J. would seldom use the "N," word and when he did, it was not necessarily derogatory. This poor black man found out how sensitive Dad was about the whole subject.

"Because you are black?" asked my dad in an agitated voice. He turned, walking back to the shop. He then reached around the sliding door and pulled out a tire tool, a three-foot solid steel bar with an eighty-degree crook at the end. In his quick-step tempo, he was quickly back to the car.

"I'll beat the shit out of you, and I don't give a damn if you are black or white or what color you are!"

By the time he finished that statement, he was at the car window, and the debtor was shrunken down to the back seat floorboard. The driver was not about to move until Dad gave the order.

"Now get the hell out of here, and don't bring him back without some money." The car left, the old V-8 grumbling through leaky pipes and a muffler riddled with holes, the loose gravel crunching on the concrete and asphalt. The tires would have spun out if the motor had had the energy.

~~~~~~~~~~~~~~~~~~~~~~~~

I saw Dad's shrewd business tactics on several occasions; here's another.

There is one major intersection, a three-way blinking light, in downtown Winona. Travelers on Main Street have yellow caution lights, and those coming down the hill have the red one. All travelers going north, south, east, or west must come within sight of the station. When coming down the hill (Dallas Street, or Farm to Market 16), one has to stop and look to the right, toward the buildings downtown, then look left. There is the station, its bench out front, usually with someone sitting there offering a friendly wave. It was not uncommon for Dad to go to someone's house on a cold morning and boost some dead battery. Then that potential customer would drive by and wave at us, and the new batteries we sold, to go to the big city to buy a new battery from a department store. Neighbors want to see their neighbors succeed, but they do not necessarily want them to succeed with *their* money.

When people were late in payment, they would take great pains to stretch their necks, lean forward and quickly look down the street, and not turn their heads so far as to acknowledge that the station existed, as though, if they did not see us, we would not see them. The apparent thought process was that if we did not exist, their debt did not exist. This would sometimes go on months, until an income tax check would come in or some good fortune would enable the debt to be resolved. T.J. was patient, up to a point.

One such debtor, Willy Gee, had accumulated a debt of twelve dollars and thirty-five cents, and for over a year he had successfully avoided eye contact with the station. Before incurring this unpaid debt, he had been an occasional customer, buying when he had to.

One day traffic was backed up at the stoplight. Willy was fifth in line as the cars stopped and waited for clearance. Car one waved to us, as did car two. Car three cut out of line and drove in to the station for a few dollars worth of gas. Car four said "Hello" with a nod. Willy kept his face frozen toward the front as he moved toward the intersection, one car length at a time. He appeared anxious as a car pulled up behind him. He was trapped and at the mercy of traffic and T.J.

When T.J. first saw Willy, he went inside the station, and seconds later he was heading across the street toward Willy. Dad never walked slowly anywhere. His regular walk at the station involved leaning forward and making his feet move quickly enough to keep him from falling forward. This meant he was in a constant form of acceleration when on the move.

The movement must have caught Willy's eye, because he had started to roll up his window when T.J. politely said, "Hi, Willy."

The window stopped with the friendly gesture, and the cars moved up a notch. "Hello, Mr. T.J.," he said reluctantly, unable to avoid the visitor walking up with the IOUs, or tickets, in his hand. "I haven't forgotten you, Mr. T.J., and I am going pay you, uh, when I get my check."

Dad took the tickets in both hands and held them before Willy. Then he ripped them in half, and then he tore them in half again.

"There," he said, "the debt is gone. You have no reason not to be friendly and not to stop by and get a tank of gas every now and then. Don't ask for credit, but you are welcome to trade with us."

Then he handed the torn pieces of forgiveness to Willy, who was now an empty two car lengths from the light and blocking traffic.

Within a month, Willy had paid his old bill and was signing tickets again.

~~~~~~~~~~~~~~~~~~~~~~~~~~~~~

Winona Texaco was a major influence in my life, so naturally it is a major character in this book. The furniture moved around inside the building, but it was always the same furniture.

Inside the rock building is enough room for a large wooden candy display case. Chocolate bars, pink peanuts patties, gum, and many other goodies sit behind beveled plate glass to discourage sticky fingers; wooden doors, on the back side, slide side to side to keep the kids, mice, and rats out. Actually, it is the employees who eat up the profit.

The old cash register that sat on top of the display required a pull of the handle to make it cha-ching. Now, a new electric cash register sits on the counter, powered by a yellow stained Romex wire stapled across the ceiling and tied into the droplight. It still makes the cha-ching noise.

Sitting beside the register is a gallon jar of pickled pig's feet, or pickled eggs, or pickled sausage links — things the kids and employees do not go after. Rusted red wire racks with clips hold bags of potato chips, corn chips, and peanuts.

Hanging from a beige ceiling that was once white is a rack built for the selling of cigarettes. My mornings used to be spent climbing up on a small wooden folding ladder and filling the square tubes with Marlboros, Winstons, Camels, Pall Malls, Kools, Salems, Virginia Slims, Newports, Tareytons, Viceroys, and Lucky Strikes. Some people would buy cigarettes by the carton, but most buy one pack at a time. That is the way they come out of the rack, one pack at a time.

Shelves line one wall, holding quarts of oil in brightly colored tin cans. Those cans can be opened by sticking a knife in the lid, two times with a twist after the second, to make a triangular hole, and one quick stick to vent in air. Or you can use an oil can opener equipped with a spout and everything needed to funnel in one quart at a time. When the tin cans changed to cardboard, they were subject to crunching, and the oil can opener became useless.

Additional wooden cubbyholes above the oil are for tire stems, inner tubes, clamps, and other saleable items. Among the saleable items were a few oddities, new and still in the box, including a distributor cap for a DeSoto and a starter for an Atlas tractor. These were there when T.J. arrived, and they were there when he left. They may be there to this day.

A desk with a large black fireproof box sits next to the

front windows on the right. When the box is closed, the fancy gold writing on the lid indicates the importance and protection of its contents. The front comes down and the top goes up, revealing a lining of asbestos. Inside are hundreds of tickets, or what most would call IOUs. They are the same sales receipts used by the credit card machine that sits beside it. By laying the credit card in position, with the ticket on top, closing the machine, and pressing the handle, the name and number would be forever embossed on the ticket. For us, it was as good as cash. The tickets in the box were not embossed; they were credit. On each is a name, printed or scribed: Sam McFarland, Henry Blaylock, Victor P. Kay Jr., J.W. Billington, Buddy Metcalf, Henry Denton, Anna Coleman, Terry Moore, and Roosevelt Petty. Most of the signatories are dead and gone, but the last names are still around. Some sought credit out of necessity, others out of convenience.

There are two restrooms. Outside and around the corner is the restroom for the ladies, and for whoever did not pass Dad's muster for inside use. In later years, the outside restroom was so abused that we locked the door for good. The men's room is inside. Both restrooms are one-holers with a sink and no hot water.

Next to the men's room, in a small dark hole, is another desk. It is as cluttered and confused as my own. Beside the desk is just enough room to get around. Behind the desk is just enough room for a small secretary's chair with its old foam rubber sticking out through the worn NAUGAHYDE. An electric cord hangs from the ceiling, with a naked, dim light bulb and a pull chain dangling on the end. This is the desk where Dad figures his profits, does his taxes, hides his bottle, and keeps his gun.

An ice cream box sits next to the Dearborn heater. Over the heater is a shelf loaded with stuff for sale. Behind the stuff is a window offering a view of a wooden three-bay workshop for tires, oil changes, and light mechanical work. It provided shade in the summer, but it was cold in the winter. On hot summer days I prefer sitting outside on the bench or on top of one of the gas pumps. During cold days we all seek the comfort and heat of that old Dearborn.

Cold weather would bring in visitors who would buy a candy bar and warm their hands. A rather large number of visitors would appear around Christmas Eve.

The day before Christmas Eve, the annual shop cleanup took place, leaving a tabletop of plywood covered with bottles of everything alcoholic from end to end. Dad furnished much of it. Much of the drink was bought and brought by others, because there was no place in their homes for liquor. Seventy to eighty people, mostly men, would come by for a little traditional Christmas cheer. Many would return two or three times for gas, or to get a little more lubrication, or to get more lubricated.

Many employees worked part-time at the station, including professional people who were between jobs. Sometimes people who just needed a little financial help would push a broom or do something else so Dad could help them out. Many kids grew up with their first job experience working at the station.

Much of my teenage life was spent sitting on the thick wooden bench out front and seeing my friends drive by on their way to Tyler State Park, without a care in the world and without me. I had a motorcycle to pay for.

In front, and under the protection of the drive-through cover, sat the bench. The hardwood bench was worn slick from years of sittings. Three inches thick, it had survived deeply carved initials, dates, and names. The dark grain of the wood has outlasted several coats of paint. It sat unsecured, too heavy and ragged for anyone to consider stealing. Its age is unknown, but no doubt it is very old. How many train cars were counted, by those who sat upon that bench, looking across the street at the Cotton Belt and Southern Pacific trains as they noisily went by? Conversations ceased with the sounds of the air horn blowing and iron wheels hitting quarter-inch gaps on iron rails as the iron horse went through town. The conversation resumed as the clan-kitty-clanks drifted away and the red caboose shrank out of sight down the tracks. Many jokes were told and many decisions were made sitting on that old bench.

Outside the station, next to the telephone booth, is a large white refrigerated box with "Milk" painted in big blue letters across the front. On the other side of the shop area, next to the outdoor vehicle lift, is a little silver ice house, with its thick insulated walls and door. Made of metal, covered with many coats of old flaked and cracked silver paint, the ice house is tall enough for me to stoop and crawl inside.

~~~~~~~~~~~~~~~~~~~~~~~

Working at the station involved more than pumping gas, washing windshields, and checking oil. It included bookkeeping, sweeping, counting minnows, digging worms, changing tires, and handling and busting up block ice weighing three hundred pounds. I also needed to be able to perform oil changes, grease jobs, and minor mechanical work.

We also gave directions to the lost.

"How do you get to Tyler?" someone would ask.

"I would go by car," T.J. would answer.

"That is dumb," the driver would reply.

"I'm not lost," Dad would answer.

We would listen to people's problems, and one day I shared my teenage problems with the Bench Sitters. Dad took me aside soon afterward.

"Mitch," he said, "We are here to hear their problems. They are not here to hear ours."

And we would visit.

"Did you know there were six presidents who lived within fifty miles of here?" asked Sam McFarland. "Mt. Vernon, Jefferson, Pittsburg, Tyler . . ." He would name them off, closing with "and Whitehouse is just down the road." I do believe he was serious, for he was mighty proud to be able to recite this bit of incorrect history. He thought of himself as a wise old black man, wearing, with dignity, his old frayed suit, stained with snuff tobacco and time. He was proud of his old black car and getting one dollar worth of gas. One dollar would buy four gallons, when T.J. first opened, and one third of one gallon when he closed. Mr. McFarland remembered when there were no cars, and he remembered well the times when blacks and whites were considered well-off to own a mule.

~~~~~~~~~~~~~~~~~~~~~~~~~

There were benefits from working at the station. In season, a watermelon would sit in the ice house for several hours and turn into the best ice-cold treat possible on a hot summer day.

When there was nothing to do, which meant T.J. was gone, employees would find recreational projects.

~~~~~~~~~~~~~~~~~~~~~~~~~

"I'll bet you a dollar," said Terry Newkirk. "Throw the quarter up as high as you can, and I will shoot it with my twenty-two." How could you turn down a bet like that? He had already taken a dollar from me a few days before, when he put two arrows inside the little "e" on a Salem cigarette sign. The "e" was an inch and a half tall and sixty feet away. And it was the first time he had shot with my bow!

I waited for a no-traffic time, which was not long coming in downtown Winona, with the quarter in my hand. I walked out to the street and threw the quarter high into the air. POW! One shot, and we never found that quarter.

"No quarter, no bet!" I declared.

"Double or nothing," said Terry.

"You're on, with a nickel this time," I said, thinking *No way.*

POW! POW! POW! "Got it on the third shot," he said.

This coin we found, with a dented edge, and he was two dollars richer.

That was the end of the betting. An additional dime disappeared into the air, and I never bet with him again.

The lesson learned: Never bet on the other man's game.

I decided to paint the rims on my Dodge Coronet 440. Even though we sold mag wheels, I could not afford to buy any.

I parked next to the ice house and removed the un-cool hubcaps. I began to paint the wheels, still mounted on the car. Shake the can and spray; shake the can and spray. When one can was empty, I would pick up another. As I finished the fourth and final wheel, a customer drove up. I quickly stood up and professionally approached the driver.

"Can I help you?"

"Fill her up with regular," he said. He looked at me kind of strange. I wondered why.

I opened the gas cover and removed the gas cap. He looked at me in his outside rearview mirror. Why was he watching me?

I removed the handle from the pump, triggered the lever that cleared the pump, and turned it on. The electric pump motor made a noise as I placed the nozzle into the gas tank. I squeezed the handle, the numbers rolled, and the gas flowed. The driver was still looking at me, like he knew something was wrong. I turned to avoid eye contact, but I knew he was still watching. I didn't know how long this was going to last. I squeezed the handle tight, wanting to get this customer done and gone.

Then it happened. The gas backflowed and splashed out of the tank, up my arm all the way to my shoulder. I jumped back as it burst into flame! It did not hurt, but it was scary as hell! I danced around and shook my arm. I started to try to beat the flame out, and it was gone. There was no fire, and no gas on my arm; the nozzle was still in the tank, and the driver was still looking at me.

I replaced the gas cap and hung the hose.

"That will be twelve fifty. Anything else?" I halfway expected him to say, "Yes, what is the matter with you?"

He said, "No, thank you" and handed me a twenty.

I went inside and wondered what was wrong with me.

I automatically hit $12.50 on the cash register, but $34.80 popped up on the viewer. As I counted the change, I noticed my hands were shaking. At that point, I decided if he did not call the police, I would; or better, I would call an ambulance.

The customer left, and I went to the phone booth.

"Sure Shot" Terry drove up in his little yellow Volkswagen with no brakes and ran into the rock building as his means of stopping the car. This was normal for him; the front of the Beetle was crunched from many such stops. The car served him well and probably can still be found in the watery grave at the bottom of the little lake where he last parked it.

"I am looking for a quarter to call . . . whoever I need to call," I said.

"Man, what's up?" he asked.

"Look at me!" I held out my trembling hands. "And I think I am going crazy!"

His concern showed in the form of a snicker. "What kind of shit are you on?"

I told him the whole story, and he thought it most humorous. When I showed him how I fought the fire, he started laughing. This was contagious; I began laughing, too. I was worried and laughing and convinced that I would be admitted to some loony bin as a basket case.

Terry started singing, "Mitch is a paint freak. Mitch is a paint freak."

"What?"

"Man, you breathe in those fumes from the paint, and it will mess with your mind. I have some friends who really get off on that stuff. They hallucinate and do all kinds of crazy shit and get paranoid like you."

"Well, it is not fun to me, and it will never happen again." And it never has.

Lesson learned: Know what you are dealing with.

~~~~~~~~~~~~~~~~~~~~~~~~~

One quiet summer day at the station was broken by a commotion in the Kay's Grocery Store parking lot. Kay's, like the station, faced Main Street and the railroad. The parking lot and Dallas Street separated the buildings.

I was in the back of the shop working when I heard the sounds. Boom! Boom!. It could have been a car, but it sounded like a gun—a shotgun.

Then I heard someone bumping furniture, rambling hurriedly through the station.

Was I being robbed? I looked up to see Carl Cooper running through the shop door. Carl worked in the meat market at Kay's, and we later served on the school board together.

"That crazy nigger is shooting at me!" Carl yelled. I knew something was seriously wrong because Carl was a black man, but he looked white as he came running up to me.

The first thing I thought was that if someone is after him with a gun, then the someone with a gun would be the next one coming around the corner. If "that crazy nigger" came around the corner shooting, we could both end up dead.

In a split second, I gave instruction. "You need to run that way!" I said, pointing in one direction. He took off running in that direction. I took off running in the other!

I found a vantage point from which I could see that the shooter had left the scene. I went back to calm my friend Carl.

"Damn, Lee Po was shooting at me!" he cried hysterically. "He could have killed me! Call the cops!"

"Relax now," I said. "He's gone. Why would he be shooting at you?"

"Well, uh, I don't know," Carl said, hesitating. "Maybe we had better hold off calling the cops."

"It's over now, and everything is all right," I said, soothing him. "We can call the police if you want to. Remember, he is your kinfolk."

"Yeah, I know," he said, calming down. "I think he shot your van."

"What?"

"I was hiding behind your van on one of them shots."

I ran to my Chevy van to find the side peppered from a shotgun blast. In the center of the sliding door was a slightly dented, three-inch circle now missing most of its paint and showing bare metal. Radiating out from the circle, individual flakes of paint were missing.

"That son of a bitch shot my van!" I yelled "Get the cops out here now!"

The lesson learned: It is different when it is you.

~~~~~~~~~~~~~~~~~~~~~~~~

T.J. had a temper that few got to witness. Every now and then he would drink a little too much — OK, way too much. Occasionally he took a pain pill or two, because of his aching shoulder bursitis, the result of diving into a wave in the Philippine Islands that turned out not to be a wave. The two added together would result in an explosion. I never saw him hit anyone, but one evening at closing time, the sky darkened and I heard a loud exchange of words.

"Get out of here!" Dad said, as though talking to a dog.

It was a cattle rancher, Price Killion. As a child I had gone to the sale barn with Mr. Killion, and he had given me a couple of goats over the years. I did not know of any problems Dad had with Mr. Killion, a prominent cattleman.

"It's a public pay phone!" Killion said. He was drunk and needed the glass walls of the phone booth to keep him upright. The fluorescent light from above helped him see what he was doing. He was sifting through his pockets trying to find a dime. "I need some change."

"You ain't gettin' shit. You need to get your ass off my property!" Dad yelled.

"You son of a bitch, you can't tell me what to do," Killion fired back, as much as a foggy alcohol-soaked brain would allow him to fire back. "Hell, I'll kill your ass." He fumbled around in his pocket, and found a knife instead of the dime and started the laborious task of opening it up. A blade three and a half inches long folded out from the yellow bone handle. The blade was once four inches long. Years on the whet rock had kept the blade sharp and made the blade shorter. The knife had made many a steer out of many a bull. He now waved it at Dad as though he would be the next to undergo that procedure.

"You threatening me?" Dad said, turning and walking away. He went inside, and I prayed it was all over.

"You really need to leave," Mom told Mr. Killion.

"Wait a minute, Dad!" I met T.J. coming out the front door with an old .32 revolver in hand.

"Threaten me!" Dad said, shaking in anger and not slowing down at all.

"It's over," Mom pleaded. She stepped between the Killion and Shamburger mountains. Neither showed any sign of giving in.

"Lord help us." I began to pray real hard.

They both stepped sideways, around LoLo, and advanced toward each other.

"You are a dumb bastard," Dad said, "bringing a knife to a gun fight." He then stuck the pistol into the soft part of Killion's beer belly and pointed it up to his heart. Before anyone could do anything, he pulled the trigger.

~~~~~~~~~~~~~~~~~~~~~~

Now, in 2010, I am sitting here looking at the pistol. "COLT D.A. 32" is stamped on the six–inch, dark-steel barrel. I think "D.A." means double action. Either the hardened steel or keeping it dry has prevented the gun from rusting. The cylinder flips out to the side and holds six .32 LC (Long Colt) bullets. Other .32 revolver bullets will not fit. The hammer has a claw. This means there is no separate firing pin. The hammer drives the claw into the primer of the shell. You do not find such guns anymore. If the gun is dropped and lands on the hammer, it could go boom. Because of this, Dad would always have an empty chamber under the hammer. "Colt's New Police" is stamped in a circle above the wooden pistol grip, with a reared horse or colt in the center. The serial number 2289 means the pistol was made before 1878. More than a hundred years later, it was in my Dad's hand.

~~~~~~~~~~~~~~~~~~~~~~~~~~~~

"Click," said the pistol. Mom screamed. Time stopped. Both the drunks looked at the pistol, as if to ask, "What is wrong with this story?" Killion wisely decided he was outgunned and turned to walk away, grumbling under his breath. Dad held the ancient revolver up, inspecting it. He pulled the hammer back and pointed the gun at the ground.

"Bang!" said the pistol. He pulled the trigger again. "Bang!"

"You'd better run," Dad yelled, pointing the pistol at Killion's back and pulling the trigger again.

"Click," said Colt's New Police.

Dad then pointed the pistol at the ground and popped off another round.

"Come on inside," I called out, motioning, directing, and still praying. He turned toward me with a satisfied grin. "Give me the gun," I said, and he handed it over.

The first thing I did was remove the five shells and pocket them. The next thing was to finish closing the station and go home. That night I inspected the shells. There are three spent cartridges and two with the lead still intact and the primers dimpled — two misfires.

The lesson learned: God answers prayers.

~~~~~~~~~~~~~~~~~~~~~~~~~~~~

I witnessed a few fights at the station. I remember only one really well, and it was the best fight I ever saw.

Herman Starnes was sitting on the bench talking to Speck Burks. The talking developed into an argument that drew the two tall, slim men to their feet, standing nose to nose, with fists at the ready position. Finally came a roundhouse lick, and the fight was on.

Herman lived on Starnes Street, named for his family. His credit was good, and he used it to fill his car up every few days and head over the tracks to inspect his land and go to Gladewater for another bottle. Smith County was a dry county. That meant that nowhere in the county could you legally buy beer or liquor to take home. It is 17.6 miles to the county line, and across that line, beer stores, liquor stores, and a string of honky-tonks lead to the city of Gladewater.

Lofton "Speck" Burks also had good credit. I wrote "L. A. Burks" on many tickets. He would sign, and I would tear off the thin top copy and hand it to him, then throw away the carbon paper and file the thicker card in the black box. There it would sit, along with Herman's and hundreds of others. Most tickets were new and active, but quite a few were many years old and waiting payment.

Speck would come down the hill and stop dead still at the stop sign, which would later be replaced by a blinking red light. The six cylinders of his car would begin to roar as he revved the engine. Over the noise of the exhaust, you could hear the tapping and clanging of loose valves and the knocking of rods. Then he slowly would release the clutch. The motor sounded like a dive bomber as the R.P.M.s dropped, whining as the little white Ford Falcon poked out into the main highway, ready to make the left turn in front of the station. The left blinker remained on as he turned right across the tracks toward Gladewater. Once, he missed the road, causing the poor little Ford to bounce over the railroad tracks. He got stuck. The engine would roar up and down as the clutch went in and out and as traction came and went. The dark red railroad lights began to flash, and the bell started ringing. The gates began to close.

"Call someone!" yelled a customer, pointing across the street. We all just stood there. Smoke billowed from the back tires, and the little car bounced up and across the tracks, with wires and mechanisms dangling underneath.

Speck had taught us by experience. He could make the railroad bells and whistles go off with his car scraping across the tracks.

Both Speck and Herman were more than seventy years old. Both had arthritis. Bent and frozen fingers and disfigured knuckles made clenching a fist impossible. Neither had been in a fight in at least forty or fifty years, and though their sparring minds remembered, their bodies were not all that interested.

Face to face, they moved around like two bantam roosters, waiting for the right time. Finally, the roundhouse thump came, and the fight was on.

Punches often hurt the arthritic hands of the puncher more than they hurt the receiver, so the punches turned into swings, wide circles in slow motion. When a swing landed, it was more like a shove, with no indication of damage felt by the receiving party. There were hollow sounds when chests, emptied by emphysema, collided. Both men were heavy smokers. There was fight in the eye of each, but it did not go any further than the eye. They pushed and shoved, sometimes chest to chest. One fell down. We thought it was over until we helped him up; as soon as he regained his feet, they were at it again.

The fight lasted five minutes and left both men sitting on the bench exhausted and gasping for air. We would have stopped them if we had not been laughing so hard.

Lesson: There is no fool like an old fool.

~~~~~~~~~~~~~~~~~~~~~~~~~~~~~~

Working at the station, I learned many lessons about dealing with the public. I learned much of it from my dad. One thing he taught me was that everyone has value in the world. Something can be learned from everyone, even from old black Sam, who swore to his grave that man never set foot on the moon.

At T.J.'s Texaco, you could fill up your tank, sign a ticket, and come back the next week or the next month to pay. The price was higher than at the new self-serve stations that were springing up along the interstate and surrounding communities, but when people needed help, T.J. was there. Black and white, rich and poor would all seek T.J.'s services and advice.

After my hitch in the Army I spent three summers managing the station. I made enough money, combined with the G.I. Bill, to go to college the rest of the year.

Those summers suited Dad just fine, giving him time to work on the ranch and to travel. Mom and Dad went to Europe, Jordan, and Thailand, journeys lasting a month or more. They would come back from their adventures to country living.

In 1986 Dad retired and sold the station to Pat McCollum. It was one of the last gas stations in the county with full service and credit.

~~~~~~~~~~~~~~~~~~~~~~~~~~~~~~~~

"You need to come to the house and check on your dad," mom said one day. "He is not acting right."

When I got there, I made a quick assessment. "Come on, we need to go to the hospital."

"We need to go?" T.J. said, agitated. "Well, you go right ahead. I need to sit down." He was confused and had been confused and combative all afternoon. He had difficulty standing and leaned to one side, evidence of a stroke.

We got some bad news at the hospital. "The carotid artery on the right side is blocked eighty percent and almost totally blocked on the left," said Dr. Dewayne Andrews. "We need to operate now."

Although he would live another twelve years, Dad never fully recovered. He entered another period of his life, filled with shadows and confusion. Physically, his energy was still there. He was able to get around, sometimes too well. We learned to hide the car keys. He countered by making the three-mile trip to Winona on the bright orange Atlas-Chambers tractor. His son-in-law learned it was useless to plant a garden in T.J.'s garden spot. Dad would "help" by plowing. Unfortunately, he would prematurely plow up the garden before the corn or bean plants could produce any vegetables. The tractor was his last hold on the mechanical world. He enjoyed mowing and would drive the tractor around the pasture and woods with the brush hog blades whirling in the air, in the up position, three feet above the brush and weeds. We tried to keep him fenced in, but occasionally someone would have to drive the Atlas-Chambers tractor back home from Winona. The old tractor is a faded orange now and still serves our family.

After a few years the wear and tear on Mom became noticeable. At nine o'clock at night he might want breakfast, then again at eleven o'clock. At two or three o'clock in the morning he would pester and beg until Mom would fix him bacon and eggs again. My sisters and I started spending nights with Dad.

~~~~~~~~~~~~~~~~~~~~~~~~~~~~

"Mitch, tell Leola to fix me some breakfast."

"Dad, you already had breakfast."

"Mitch, just tell your mom to come in here and I will ask her."

"Dad, it's four o'clock in the morning and we went through this thirty minutes ago." Dad quieted down, but only for a moment.

"Mitch, I got a call from the president. He wants me to go to Africa and straighten out a problem they are having over there."

"Really?" There was no use arguing, and I wanted some sleep, so I figured I would let him talk it out.

"Yes. The niggers are having riots and tearing the place up. He wants me to get some of the good blacks around here and take them over there to straighten them out. I am taking Willy Price, J.W. Billington, Sam McFarland . . ." He named ten others, some dead and some still alive. "YOU can't go."

"Why not?" I asked.

"It's a military operation," he said bluntly.

"I was in the military," I said in my defense. "You are not the only Army veteran in this room." Now I was awake.

"I don't think you could take orders."

"I can take orders," I answered assuredly.

"Then get your mom to fix me some breakfast. I'll take some bacon and eggs."

Inquest #1884:
Dad

Dad's last days are spent in a nursing home, Room 313, bed B. In all my years of nursing I never adapted to the smell of hospitals or nursing homes.

I walk in the room and notice, in bed A, another old-timer waiting to breathe his last breath. It is Mr. Barber, an old credit customer from the gas station. I also had some dealings with him in court. He is barely conscious. I speak to him.

"Leo, Leo Barber, do you know who I am?"

I hear him say, in a whisper, "I know you."

I lean over him to get closer. Talking is a burden to him. "You're the son of a bitch that took my driver's license."

He dies the next day, and Dad dies the day after, January 11, 1998, at eighty-two years of age.

~~~~~~~~~~~~~~~~~~~~~~~

The name Winona Texaco lasted years after the full-service flow of gas stopped. Batteries, oil changes, tires new and used, and a string of managers followed. Pat McCollum sold out to Terry Furrh. Pat became a deputy constable under Constables Bill Grady and Charles Wilson. Terry sold out to Larry Tidwell.

~~~~~~~~~~~~~~~~~~~~~~~

Larry Joe Tidwell (his sister was the one involved in my Pickett Hill suicide attempt), was a man's man. He had a crack problem — that is, his shirt did not meet his pants when he was bent over working on a project or vehicle. He did not care. Winona Texaco became Tidwell's Texaco and finally just Tidwell's. He expanded the operation to include welding, mufflers, hog traps, and wheeling and dealing in most everything, including guns. He made loans, hunted, and loved motorcycles and four-wheelers. He liked to gamble.

The Justice Court Center was next to the station, so frequently I would walk over to buy cold drinks or just get out of the office. Many of the traditions established by T.J. continued, including Christmas cheer and visiting.

For a while Larry took diet pills.

"Larry, I read there is a big law suit against those diet pills you were taking," I said.

"Well, I can't complain too much. While I took those pills, I built all that." He pointed to a new lift covered by a metal awning. Then he pointed to the new cover over the drive through with a sheet metal wall and with a large hinged window. "I would never have done all that without those pills."

~~~~~~~~~~~~~~~~~~~~~~~~

"Larry, I'm going to the boats. Loan me a thousand." I was kidding.

"No problem," he said, reaching into his pocket. He pulled out a roll of bills so big he could not close his big hand around it. He peeled off ten hundred-dollar bills without even putting a dent in the roll. "Is that enough?"

"Never mind," I said, shaking my head. "I don't need credit. I need money." I think if I really needed it, he would have given it to me with no, or very few, strings attached. With Larry, if you were his friend or he liked you, you were *in*. He had many friends, and some were close. The Baptist preacher, myself, and others spent a lot of time visiting with Larry. If you were not in the circle, you'd better watch your money.

When I would come back from the boats, I would moan about losing two hundred dollars. Larry would lean back in T.J.'s old chair, sitting now by the black box, and in his greasy, short-sleeve uniform shirt, talk about winning or losing thousands. He was a gambler, preferring cards. He kept a book, for tax purposes, and would show me some of his winnings and losses. Then we would cut cards for the sodas.

We did not talk about family life. Their house was in the woods, with only one way in and out. His wife could be seen, from time to time, helping out at the station. I am not sure if or where she ever worked outside the home and the station. Their two boys were enough to keep anyone busy, and when they were old enough, they, too, would work alongside their dad.

With the boys grown and gone, she got herself a steady job.

~~~~~~~~~~~~~~~~~~~~~~~~~~

"She is leaving me," Larry said. "I don't think I can live without her. We will never get a divorce."

This was not a Larry I had ever seen, distraught and in tears. In this day and age divorces happen all the time. The possibility of him getting one was really not that big a surprise. Many other marriages, better than theirs, had ended in divorce, and most of Larry's activities did not seem to revolve around his wife.

He tried to patch things up, and she did what she could, but for her it was too late.

A month later I walked into the station.

"Tomorrow, you will find me sitting in this chair with a bullet hole in my head," Larry said. It was a matter of fact statement with little emotion.

"Do you know what a mess it will be?" I lit into him, and he looked at me like I had changed the subject.

"Brains and shit all over the place," I continued. "I have seen too many heads blown apart from doing something stupid like shooting yourself. You have many friends, and I guarantee you that every one of them is going to blame themselves. Are you going to make us feel bad because you can't handle it?"

"Well, maybe not tomorrow," he said.

A few weeks later I received a call from Ted.

"Judge, I am worried about Larry."

A week later the preacher called.

"What are we going to do about Larry?"

Over the next three months there were several more calls. Most said they had talked him out of it. Some actually may have.

"Larry, your friends are worried. I am concerned," I told him again.

"I'll be OK," he said. "There is still a chance."

A month later we were riding motorcycles and I blew a spark plug out of my Kawasaki. I left my bike parked in Lindale, and we rode back together on his new Gold Wing Honda. He seemed in good spirits.

The next month, he was having lunch with his wife, always hoping for life to return to what it was. "What it was" was not what she wanted.

"I am moving out for good," she said. "I am not going back. We need to move on."

"I will be dead within the hour," he replied.

"Don't be foolish," she said.

He gave her his billfold and left.

Inquest #5221:
Winona Texaco, Final Offer

Pat McCollum is the security guard at the Briarwood Grocery Warehouse and Processing Plant. It is a large operation, and Pat is working the front entrance. A little black car stops, centered, in front of the guardhouse. This is not the place for cars to stop. His concern is relieved when he sees his friend Larry climb out of the car. Pat stops by the Tidwell's Texaco and visits Larry occasionally. They talk guns, 4-wheelers and guy stuff. Pat steps out of the guardhouse.

"Larry?" he says, expecting to be told the reason for the visit and then maybe a friendly conversation.

Larry is out of the car, walking away from him to the back of the car. He stops behind the car and opens the trunk.

Pat thinks, "What is in the trunk must be for me." He starts walking toward the vehicle. Larry pulls out a shotgun.

Pat thinks, "He wants to show me his new shotgun." They have looked at guns before. He continues to walk.

Pat stops. The blue-black barrel is pointing up and pressed under Larry's chin. Larry shakes his head from side to side, like he is saying "No."

Pat says, "Larry!" as Larry pulls the trigger.

Nothing happens. They look at each other, as if to ask, "What is wrong with this story?"

Larry quickly chambers a round, points the gun, and pulls the trigger again.

~~~~~~~~~~~~~~~~~~~~~~~~

"Judge, we have an inquest out on Highway 271."

When I arrive, Larry is lying on the pavement, prone and spread-eagled. A pool of blood stains the concrete.

His widow is there. He knew she would be driving that way.

He also knew they would not get a divorce.

~~~~~~~~~~~~~~~~~~~~~~~~

It has been ten years since Dad died. Mom is ninety-one and still running. I asked her once if she ever thought of having another relationship.

"T.J. and I had many wonderful times," she said. "Memories I would not trade for the world. We also had . . . other times. Why would I want to go through that again?"

~~~~~~~~~~~~~~~~~~~~~~~~

"I do," said Larry's widow, as I married her a year later to her new husband. It was a fun wedding, on a dude ranch with a white, horse-drawn carriage bringing her down to a fancy stable, which had been converted to accommodate such events. When I finished the ceremony, Proven Justice (my band) played for the reception and dance. Most of the Tidwell family joined in the celebration. They held no contempt or anger toward her.

"It's a family trait—if you are in you are *in*," said Larry's brother.

~~~~~~~~~~~~~~~~~~~~~~~~

Winona Texaco has not reopened since Larry's death three years ago.

~~~~~~~~~~~~~~~~~~~~~~~~

You may think, from reading this chapter, that Winona is full of drunks and poor folk. There was a time, like in the Mayberry of *The Andy Griffith Show*. Back then, having a town drunk was really no big deal. Most towns had several, and we were no exception.

My favorite drunk story occurred when I was eight years old and exploring around Gumwood Nursery, my father's business downtown. (It later became the Winona Hoedown.) I found Monroe Starnes, Herman's brother, in the alley on his knees, throwing up from the spirits of the night before. I ran back to Mom, very excited.

"Mom!" I yelled. "Monroe done got religion! He is on his knees praying. 'Oh God! Oh God!'"

~~~~~~~~~~~~~~~~~~~~~~~~

I could have written about the many responsible people we have in Winona and all the good things T.J. and Larry did, but it would not be nearly as interesting or as much fun to read—or to write.

We are not all poor. After Victor Kay, Jr., sold the grocery store, he bought a Cadillac. Victor and Lorene, his wife, were dear friends of T.J. and LoLo. He always wanted a Cadillac, but he learned from his dad, Victor P Kay, Sr., that people resented giving their hard-earned money to someone who drove a better car than they did. So he waited. Within a week of passing the store on to his son, Lorene drove into the station in a brand new Cadillac. I gladly fueled it up weekly.

"Ms. Kay, you may want us to order you a new set of tires," I said, hoping to sell a set of four.

"What?" she answered.

"Your tires are getting worn," I replied.

"Well thank you, Mitch," she said and drove away.

The next week I gassed up another new Cadillac for her.

Three times she needed tires, and each time would result in a new Cadillac for her and no tire sale for me.

Chapter 26

Constable Dale Geddie

Inquests #4287 and #4288

Inquests: Living With the Dead is almost complete, but something very important has not yet been told. Hundreds of memories roll through my mind, which has helped in relating the stories so far; still, the answer to a difficult question eludes me: "What was the hardest inquest you have ever done?" Something was hiding far back in my brain, something that may have happened a long time ago. Perhaps it was something that I was trying to forget or keep hidden. The hardest inquest I have ever done was four years ago.

Constable Dale Geddie (August 19, 1960-June 7, 2006): Inquest #4287

Crazy Charley is standing across the judicial bench with other prisoners. He seems agitated and irritated, standing in his jailhouse neon orange jumpsuit. All the prisoners seem to be dressed in oversize clothing, way too big and draping on the bodies inside. Crazy Charley rocks from side to side, not a good sign. He is there to receive his magisterial rights.

An arrested person is given the right to remain silent and many other rights, including having an amount of bond set. Judges are magistrates, and as such read rights to arrested persons. No matter what the charge, the magistrate performing the duty has jurisdiction and retains jurisdiction until an indictment by the grand jury or until the case is filed into another court. When reading rights, the judge also considers probable cause, and a determination is made to detain the prisoner or set him or her free.

"The laws of the State of Texas say if you are going to be

detained for any length of time you will be brought, as soon as practical, before a magistrate or judge, to have your rights read. This is to certify that I, Judge Mitch Shamburger, did, in the capacity of a magistrate, inform to you and each of you, in clear language, who appeared before me here in the Smith County Jail, Tyler, Texas, that you have the right . . ."

All of a sudden, Crazy Charley comes across the bench, swinging his arms. His goal seems to be to take my head off. Leaning back in my chair, I can feel it coming. The bright orange of his uniform and flaying fists are all I can see. There is nowhere for me to go.

Then a grey blur shoots before me. A young jailer quickly, without hesitation, dives in front of me, taking a fist to the eye. I hear the crack and see his head jerk back as he takes the blow that was meant for me. The attacker decides the jailer is a new problem and goes after him. Other jailers join in the fray.

Jailers have to put up with a lot of crap. When a prisoner offers them a good excuse to use force, it is a no-brainer; they will use their training to subdue the prisoner. This may include beating the crap out of him. This prisoner soon finds himself face down on the floor with his own bruises and Officer Dale Geddie on top. Geddie's eye already is starting to change colors and swell.

"WOW! Man, you took the bullet!" I say, looking at a shiner that would put most boxers to shame. Dale looks amused, with a crooked, sheepish grin, and one fourth of his face beginning to blacken. "Just doing my job," he says. There is no mistake: he likes what he is doing and is proud to serve, even if it means working a few days with one eye swollen shut.

Dale Junior is proof that "The nut doesn't fall far from the tree." He got the best from both parents. His soft touch came from his church piano–playing mom, Sandra. His hard nose came from his dad, Dale Senior. Although they shared only the first name, it was still "Junior" and "Senior" or Big Dale and Little Dale. If you knew them, you knew why.

Dale Senior was a deputy and detective for Sheriff J.B. Smith. Once I came across him in his patrol car with a young black man sitting cuffed in the back seat.

"What's going on?" I asked.

"We caught this boy burglarizing his uncle's house," said Big Dale. "We are going for a ride and then we are going to park somewhere out in the woods. And then we are going to clear up some other burglaries." If there is such a thing as an "Oh, shit" look, that kid had it.

~~~~~~~~~~~~~~~~~~~~~~~~~~~~

In 1968 my mother thought my father was crazy, committing to a $380 monthly payment for forty years, for a ranch of 110 acres, a red brick house three times bigger than the one we lived in, and on the income of a Ma and Pa gas station. After paying for a few years, dad sold twenty acres of the ranch. Our new neighbors were the Geddie family. Little Dale was six, and I was fourteen. Isn't it strange how growing up closes the gap between the young and the old? He was just a little kid when we met, and he seemed just a little younger than I when he took the oath of office as constable for Precinct 4 on January 1, 2005.

The office of constable is a carryover from our English ancestry. "Cop" is an acronym for "constable on patrol." The constabulary was established in Texas when it was an independent nation. The Constitution of the Republic of Texas (1836) provided for the election in each county for "a sufficient number of constables." This continues with the Texas State Constitution, where it is established that each justice court precinct will have a constable. There was a time in rural counties when people ran for constable just to wear a badge and tote a gun. As sophistication, law, and demands of the office changed, so have the constables. As an elected official, each constable can work as much or as little as he or she likes. The voters decide who stays on and who moves on. It is the county commissioner's court that decides the budget for the office and what the salary and benefits will be.

A Texas constable has the same jurisdiction and powers of any peace officer. If not a "Certified Peace Officer" when elected, a constable must become certified within a year and then must take continuing education. In Smith County there are five constables, each elected from a justice court precinct. The constable usually serves the justice court by being the bailiff, serving civil process, executing warrants, and providing court security. Some constables in Texas have hundreds of deputies, and others are a one man/woman operation. Often they have their offices close to the justice court. Constables are an integral part of the justice court system. There are different relationships between the office of constable and the office of justice of the peace. Like a big family, sometimes we get along and sometimes we don't.

Constable Bill Grady was waiting for me when I was appointed judge in 1982. He had held the office for many years and fit the picture of an overweight, rough-cut, small-town cop.

"You can outrun me but you can't outrun this little old .38," he would drawl, patting his revolver like he would a small pet dog sitting by his side. You could tell he was levelheaded because spittle from his snuff ran down both sides of his chin. He never let on to me that he had any concerns about my age. A twenty-nine–year-old J.P. was rare in those days. He knew we had met years ago in a chase on one Halloween night. All I did was throw an egg—which threw my arm out of its socket, and I never could throw anything worth a damn after that. Did he pull his .38? I don't know and didn't look back. Now, I was his judge.

Once I ordered Constable Grady to impanel a jury for a criminal trial.

"You want a guilty jury or a not guilty jury?" he asked. We do not get jury panels that way anymore.

Charles Wilson got more votes than Constable Grady and served twenty years as my constable. As a sheriff's deputy he was grounded in law enforcement. He doubled his duty as the fire chief of the Red Springs Volunteer Fire Department.

Wilson is relentless when he takes on a project. A new building for the Justice Court Center Precinct 4 was one of the accomplishments he managed. The new building took us out of the County Barn and a two-room operation to a much nicer facility, located in downtown Winona. In 1987 my job moved right next door to my first job, at the filling station in downtown Winona.

I was warned, "When you get in the car with Wilson, you

better have a change of clothes and a flashlight." It was true. A trip to Dow and Charlotte Graham's Hardware store to play dominos and rub elbows with the old-timers might end up with me holding his extra snub-nosed .38 pistol, hiding behind a tree, waiting at the back door of some house in the woods, hoping that whoever was inside would politely answer the knock of Constable Wilson on the front door. (Note to the Commission of Judicial Conduct: That was many years ago. I do not do that anymore!)

~~~~~~~~~~~~~~~~~~~~~~~~~~

Dale Geddie was my third constable. Although the constable's office was in the same building as the justice court, it had a different outside entrance. To go from one office to another, you had go outside—rain, snow, sleet, or hail, and most of all heat! The key for one office did not fit the lock to the other. Constable Geddie proceeded to literally knock down the walls. The walls he tore away were more than sheetrock and steel; he opened his doors to the court and the community. During the election, he was at every social and church gathering, eating fried chicken, BBQ, and all the trimmings. His contagious smile infected all those around him. After the election it was my pleasure to go with him for presentations to organizations, school kids, or even the Commissioners Court. This opened up a new era for our justice court.

Judges are not encouraged to fraternize with law enforcement personnel. In fact, they are discouraged. There is a difference between the two. The judge says, "You are innocent until proven guilty." The lawman says, "You are guilty and I am going to prove it." The Judicial Conduct Commission desires a not-so-fine line to be drawn to prevent even the appearance of impropriety. It just does not look good when the officer writes a ticket and says, "You want to talk to the judge? He is right there in the car, and he saw the whole thing!" Still, when you work closely with someone, and that someone has the potential to save your life someday, you get close.

I am asked sometimes, "Do you carry a gun?"

"Yep," I say, pointing to the constable. "It is right there on his side."

~~~~~~~~~~~~~~~~~~~~~~~~~~~~~~~~~~~~~

Until a change in County policy, Dale used his personal pickup, affixed with red lights, to do his job. Smith County gave the constables a travel allowance for gas, insurance, and upkeep, to furnish their own private vehicles.

One sunny Sunday after church several of us were standing in front of the Methodist Church annex, The Starnes Building, in Winona. The building was donated to the church by Charlotte Graham (owner of the hardware store). It is across the street from the Hoedown building and what used to be Gumwood Nurseries.

~~~~~~~~~~~~~~~~~~~~~~~~~~~~~~~~~~~~~

The roaring of motors and the screeching of tires make us all look up to see a wild-eyed speed freak taking a turn on two wheels that are squalling like a baby. The car lands back on all fours beside O'Dell's Italian Restaurant and swerves up Church Street directly toward us. The driver has the pedal to the metal and is getting all he can from his beat–up old big-block Chevy. On his tail is Dale, a car length behind, handling his white pickup truck like a sports car. It is a high-speed chase, both vehicles sliding and spinning around the streets of Winona. The chase continues out of town, through the Harris Creek Bottom and up Pricket Hill. The Winona police join the chase, but its car backs off when it starts smoking and knocking, but not Dale. He stays on that Chevy like a tick on a coon dog. The Texas Highway Patrol joins the chase with two cars, and the Smith County Sheriff's Department joins with three more. All these police cars are following a crazed driver and Dale in his pickup. The parade of flashing red, white, and blue lights winds down a two-lane Farm to Market road toward Gladewater. Several of the cars have their sirens blaring and wailing through the countryside, causing horses to run and cows to take a break from grazing and look up to see the fast-moving parade.

"4-0-1 to Smith County," Dale's voice comes over the radio. Constable Precinct 4 has the call number 401. My number is 400.

Radio protocol is for the unit to self-identify, be acknowledged, and then communicate.

"Go ahead, 4-0-1," says the dispatcher.

"We are turning on FM 757 and passing the Starrville Cemetery."

A roadblock is set up, but Mr. Speedo does not make it that far. He pulls over and gives up.

When Dale needs help, it is there for him. All the law enforcement agencies know that if they are in a bind, Little Dale is just a radio call away.

"4-0-1 to Smith County," says Constable Geddie.

"Go ahead, 4-0-1."

"4-0-1. I am en route to the jail with one in custody."

The next day Mr. Speedo is brought before me to receive his magistrate warning.

"What kind of truck was that?" he asks. "Fastest damn thing I'd ever seen. I just gave it up, man."

~~~~~~~~~~~~~~~~~~~~~~~~~~~~

Dale fought through the budget cycle in the county courthouse to get a Smith County Constable car. It was brand new, with a police package: overhead light bar, siren, and radio. It was white with blue and silver graphics (Dallas Cowboy colors) that said "Smith County Constable Pct. 4" within a star.

Sitting in the back seat, you quickly notice there are no door handles. This is to prevent prisoners from escaping. A Plexiglas shield between the front and back seats puts you in a cage with no escape. It is a strange feeling riding in the back seat, knowing you will not get out until someone lets you out. Add handcuffs to the screen separation and lack of door handles and nothing but doom will fill the hearts of most. Others couldn't care less.

Sometimes the perp (short for perpetrator) is so drunk, so messed up on drugs, or just so pissed off he will maneuver himself so that he is lying on his back and then kick out one of the back windows. This will force the police offer to stop in some parking lot and carefully remove the perp from the seat, sliding him over the broken glass. Because the perp is in a supine position, on his back, the police officer must carefully lay the perp on the ground, and his head might make several stops against the car on the way down. The perp ends up lying on his back on the pavement, gravel or asphalt, hands cuffed behind him. Because it is uncomfortable to lie on cuffed hands, the officer will turn the perp over, face down. Then the officer will place enough body weight on his back to prevent him from moving and further hurting himself. They will remain in this position, the officer apologizing for the discomfort and delay, until a unit without broken glass arrives for transport. The cops say, "You can beat the rap, but you can't beat the ride."

~~~~~~~~~~~~~~~~~~~~~~~~~~~

The Smith County Peace Officers Association is composed of all those in the county concerned with the criminal justice system. The group is composed mostly of peace officers, but anyone with five dollars can be a member, and there are quite a few members. In the 1980s, one of the main interests of the association was its annual party.

Peace officers, prosecutors, and judges cannot go just anywhere to have a beer or "Let their hair down." The first party I attended, I saw some of them do things for which they would put other people in jail. These parties have now turned into picnics and family-oriented gatherings. Each month there is food, fellowship, a speaker, and a Smith County–wide law enforcement report. Each agency can disseminate information across turf lines. This month the meeting is on the first Wednesday, June 7, 2006. Dale and I are to ride there together in his new county patrol car.

"They are having fajitas for lunch today at the Peace Officers Meeting. We want to go," says Robin, court clerk. Being a justice court clerk for Smith County requires dedication. Low pay combined with much responsibility can be stressful. We frequently reduce that stress by eating out. "Let's ride in Dale's new car!" she suggests. "We can all fit if the judge rides up front. And someone could ride with Terry." Terry Brunk is a deputy constable, one of several deputies who continued after Wilson moved on. It is not unusual for court clerks to attend the meeting. Today is a beautiful sunny summer day.

"You are welcome to ride along," Dale grins, "but it is hot, and with that plastic panel, no air conditioning will get back to you. I took one to jail yesterday, and he was soaking wet when I pulled him out."

"I need to stop by my house and get my cell phone," I say.

"I'm ready to go," Dale answers. When Dale is "ready to go," he is *ready to go*. He does not like to be late for anything, even lunch.

"Let's take the judge's SUV," the clerks agree as a customer/defendant walks into the building. As usual, someone wants to make a fine payment or file a civil suit just as we are about to leave. Constable Geddie drives away in his new car.

~~~~~~~~~~~~~~~~~~~~~~~~~~~~

Mr. Jim Blaine is sick and tired—literally, he is both: sick and tired. His trip to the doctor the day before did not make him feel any better, and in fact the doctor's advice was little more than an invitation to come back in a week or two if he is not doing better. Pain pills, antidepressants, antibiotics, anti–blood pressure pills, and other pills that do who-knows-what all cost money. He does not have the money to waste on all those pills that "don't do shit anyway."

"I am fifty-two years old, and tomorrow does not look any different from today," he tells his wife. They had been arguing all morning. "I am putting an end to it all."

"Jim," she says, "don't be like this." She has seen him like this before, and she knows he can get violent. When he says he is putting an "end to it," he might mean putting an end to her and the kids staying with them. After all, he blames everything on her, even his health.

"You dumb bitch, you don't understand a damn thing." He stalks out of the room, and she follows.

"Jim," she says, "it is going to get better."

"That's for damn sure," he replies, reaching into the closet.

She knows the closet is the home of the "thirty-aught-six" deer rifle. She goes to the kitchen. That is where the grandbaby is swinging in his little windup swing. Although he is almost two, he still fits in the swing, and it provides amusement. The swing has stopped, and the child is sound asleep, without a care. He is used to all the fighting and fussing; he can sleep right through it. She picks up the phone and hits three numbers.

"911. What is your emergency?"

"My husband." She stops because he is standing in the kitchen door, with the weapon drawn and his eyes focused on her as though she were already dead.

"Jim, don't do this!" She hangs up the phone. She does not realize that two other people from the household have already made their escape and called 911 from the neighbor's house.

He looks at her, realizing that her concern is for herself and the baby. "Don't you worry your little head. I'm not going to hurt you. I'm taking myself out of the picture." He looks around. "Out of this picture."

"We need you!" she cries. "You need to calm down."

"You need my money, and right now I am worth more dead than alive." His insurance is paid up.

~~~~~~~~~~~~~~~~~~~~~~~~~

"Here is your receipt," the clerk says to the defendant-turned-customer. They all walk out the door into the summer heat. I am waiting for them in my Ford Expedition, the air conditioner struggling against an outside temperature of 103 degrees.

"Let's get out of here before someone else comes," I say. Three clerks climb into the Army-green Expedition. One of the clerks reaches for the radio controls.

It is a regular AM/FM radio, not a police radio. She tries to get some music playing before I can turn on my audio book. The station varies according to who sits up front.

It is a short four blocks to my house. When we get there, I leave the engine running for the air conditioning. I head toward the house at a half run, then return to the car, phone in hand. I take notice of my rapid pace. I lean forward, moving my feet quickly enough to keep me standing up, accelerating, the same as my father.

"Judge!" yells Gilyn as we travel down the road. "This is why I don't sit up front!" You would think I could not drive at all unless a clerk or someone else is in the car telling me what to do. The passengers tend to get excited when the "quite capable brakes" on the Ford stop us with room to spare. Occasionally their verbal venom reaches out to include other drivers.

"They're running hot." I point to a Tyler Police unit, red and blue lights flashing, speeding around Tyler's Loop 323. "I guess they will miss lunch."

The Smith County Peace Officers building is a nice one, made of shaped concrete blocks. Constructed with funds donated by both businesses and individuals, it is nestled just outside Tyler, next to the firing range. There is a long driveway across the front; the parking area and main entrance are in the back. As we pull into the dusty parking area, Terry runs toward us. We climb out of the Expedition, ready to go eat fajitas. I notice that Terry is trembling and excited, breathing hard, adrenaline pumping. "Shots fired!

Officer down!"

~~~~~~~~~~~~~~~~~~~~~~~~~~

"Officer down." These words erase any barriers that may exist between police departments. The fraternity of law enforcement congeals when hearing those words, "Officer down!"

Lights and movement swirl around the parking area as car after car speeds away, leaving a cloud of dust.

Terry continues to shake. "Dale is not here! He checked out to assist the Sheriff's Office on a domestic disturbance."

These are two things I do not want to hear. It would be just like Dale to stop and assist on a call. He does not like to be late, but he would put that aside and help a fellow officer without hesitation.

~~~~~~~~~~~~~~~~~~~~~~~~~~

Domestic calls are some of the deadliest calls a peace officer can make. Most of the time, the sight of the uniform and the realization that someone can go to jail will calm the situation—but not always.

"Sorry, Officer, it was nothing," the complainant will say with a busted lip.

After making hundreds of these routine babysitting calls, one becomes relaxed. Then comes the one that results in a radio call of "Shots fired!"

~~~~~~~~~~~~~~~~~~~~~~~~~~

"I shot one," Jim yells to his wife. They are now in the living room. "It wasn't much different from shooting a deer—aim and squeeze, aim and squeeze."

The officer's wound is serious but not fatal. The officer had struggled to safety and hit the emergency button on his portable radio.

Another police car pulls up, across the yard from the fallen policeman. It glistens in the sunlight. It is a new car, painted in the colors of the Dallas Cowboys, with Smith County Constable Pct. 4 written in graphics down the side.

"He thinks he is smart. He parked at the end of the fence," Jim says as he shoulders the rifle. Looking through the scope, Dale appears as though he is only a few feet away. Jim uses the scope view to follow Officer Geddie as he gets out of the car and goes back to the trunk of his car. The lid pops open.

"I wonder what he has in there," Jim says to his speechless wife. "Whatever it is, he will never get to use it."

Dale drops from sight as he goes down behind the trunk and slips on his protective vest. He looks at the loaded rifle in the trunk, lying by the loaded shotgun. Then he stands up, to look around and assess the situation. Jim sees a facial profile fill the rifle scope, a sight picture that the cross hairs make an easy shot. Aim and squeeze, and Dale Geddie is no longer a living, breathing member of the human race. He is no longer a living husband, father, son, friend, officer, or backup.

~~~~~~~~~~~~~~~~~~~~~~~~~~~~~

"Here," I say, tossing a set of about twenty keys to Mindy. "One of them will fit the truck. I'll go with Terry." We run toward his patrol unit. "Do you want me to drive?" I ask him. Terry is already behind the wheel and in a cloud of dust, we are in the procession.

~~~~~~~~~~~~~~~~~~~~~~~~~~~~~

When you do something over and over, you get to where you can do it in your sleep. Your brain goes on autopilot, and you do what needs to be done. It happens when you drive; all of a sudden you are driving down a road, or even pulling into your driveway, unaware of the last twenty miles. It is like a switch that can change your frame of mind from everyday life to the mission at hand. I switch into command mode.

~~~~~~~~~~~~~~~~~~~~~~~~~~~~~

Terry was very close to Dale. It is difficult for me to calm him, since I am fired up myself. Now we are running hot around Loop 323.

"Terry, we won't do anyone any good if we don't get there in one piece," I offer. He is passing the other red and blue flashing lights. A roadblock is up ahead, diverting five lanes of traffic.

"No one goes past here," yells a determined officer.

"I have the judge!" cries Terry, as he slows down with no intention of stopping. We see the command post across the street from the new What-a-Burger. The diner/convenience store parking lot is filled with twenty to thirty law enforcement cars, all with lights flashing.

"We really need to get there in one piece," I repeat. "Slow down."

There is no stopping Terry as he drives through the units to the Command Center, about three blocks from the crime scene. We bounce off the road and onto the grass, then slide to a stop. Uniformed police are standing in ready position. Plainclothes officers are gathered around the front of a dark sedan. One is on a cell phone, attempting to contact the holder of the hostages.

"Judge," reports the detective, "around 11:45 we received a 911 call about a domestic disturbance. Sheriff Deputy Daniel Leon responded. We were told someone was acting crazy and had a deer rifle. Constable Geddie advised the dispatcher that he was in the area and would back the deputy up. Soon after Deputy Leon arrived, there were gunshots, and Leon was hit; he's still pinned down at the scene. We think Geddie got out of his car and was shot. We think there may be another officer on location. We are just not sure right now. The actor has threatened to shoot anything that moves. That's all we know."

"Anything that moves" could include a section of State Highway 271, a five-lane highway within sight of the shooter's house. The traffic is slowed by a traffic light and the roadblock.

The roadblock is moved back, and the intersection is shut down. We are shielded by several small white frame houses that line the streets of an older neighborhood. Most of these homes have been evacuated. Not knowing the distance and not knowing what is going on does not put me in a comfortable state of mind. Policemen with weapons drawn, rifles poised, are ready to do whatever they can, waiting for orders.

~~~~~~~~~~~~~~~~~~~~~~~~~~~~~~

Many policemen live for this kind of situation. They are trained, mentally prepared, and ready to jump into the excitement of an armed standoff. The rest of the job (including low pay, bad working hours, costly education, finding a job, buying equipment, and a high divorce rate) is the price you pay to have life-and-death moments like this.

~~~~~~~~~~~~~~~~~~~~~~~~~~~~~~

"What is Dale's status?" I ask.

"We don't know," is the reply. "He was shot, and he is not responding."

"Then let's go get him! You can use a fire truck as a shield."

"Judge, the guy has a deer rifle, has threatened to shoot anything that moves, and has a clear shot at anyone approaching the area. We are calling in Bubba." Bubba is an armored personal carrier (A.P.C.) with bulletproof plate steel sides. Bubba 1 and Bubba 2 were obtained by the sheriff through Army surplus. An A.P.C. is not fast, but looking like a tank without a turret, it is effective.

"We have him on the phone," another voice rings out.

The negotiator is talking to the shooter on a cell phone. He repeats word for word what he hears. Another officer is taking notes. I am standing next to him, listening to one side of the conversation, feeling useless.

"He says he does not want to live. He just wants to be killed. He does not want to commit suicide. It will mess up his insurance. If he sees anyone, he will kill them."

Time is crawling. I scribble on a piece of paper and hand it to the negotiator. It reads, "Ask if he will let us get our people out."

"We need our people out of there," the negotiator says into his phone. "Will you hold up so we can get them? They are hurt and need help."

"I'm going to stand in front of the window so you can shoot me," comes Jim's reply.

"Shoot the son of a bitch," I say. The order is not taken. "Look, I have a constable down. He has been shot. I do not know his condition. If he is still alive, every second counts."

~~~~~~~~~~~~~~~~~~~~~~~~~~~~~~

Bubba 2 rides on a flatbed trailer and resides at the county farm. Bubba 1 is housed close by, in the jail sally port. It is driven through downtown Tyler and four miles further, just short of the command post. It stops in the middle of the main highway. Steam comes roaring out from the motor section. It is overheated. Buckets of coolant and water go back and forth to the What-a-Burger for what seems forever, to cool it down. The SWAT team is dressed in black body armor. They look like Darth Vader storm troopers scrambling up the ramp and into the vehicle. A medical doctor is on the team. Bubba rumbles by, its steel tracks clanging as it goes down the street and turns right. It disappears behind a house, then only the faint sound of the diesel reaches us. We all stand and wait.

Bubba returns with the wounded officer and the officer who

was pinned down. The wounded officer is quickly placed into an ambulance and evacuated. The other officer briefs the coordinator and command post as to the logistics of the shooter and his evaluation of the situation. He then leans against the car, where I am standing.

"Did you see Dale?" In my heart, I know if he were still alive, he would have been with them.

"Doesn't look good," says the officer, "He took it in the head. There's gray matter . . ." His voice drifts off. My mind shifts gears again. This is no longer a rescue operation; it is an inquest.

Inquest #4287

Bubba's big, powerful diesel engine sounds muffled in my mind, as though it is in the distance. The tracks grind the pavement as it turns around, going back to pick up my constable. The group becomes somber as the news spreads, and Bubba rumbles off.

A few minutes later, Bubba crunches to a halt, coming back to the command post. The back door drops, making a ramp. I make my way to the opening, doing my job. It is dark inside, a contrast to the bright sun where we were standing. It looks like a dark tunnel inside, each side lined with the black storm troopers. A litter, shaking and jerking, rolls out with the broken constable on board. The doctor's eyes meet my own. He has a look of hopelessness, and he sees my look, too.

Dale's protective vest is in place. A bulletproof vest or body armor has saved the life of many a soldier and policeman. Something is better than nothing. We learn later that the shooter had armor-piercing bullets, 150 of them. What kind of deer requires armor-piercing bullets? Unfortunately for Dale, the vest does not protect the head.

Despite his fatal injuries, Dale is quickly loaded into an ambulance that speeds away to the hospital. At times like this, you want to do something, even though you know the situation is hopeless. I watch the ambulance drive away with my constable. He had held office for eighteen months.

We wait a few minutes for the emotional dust to settle. There is no doubt that the inquest will proceed at the hospital. Terry and I get into his car and go. We park in front of the hospital and enter the emergency room.

"He is in the eye room," the nurse says without looking up. The eye room does not have all the emergency equipment, crash carts, defibrillators, or surgical gear the other emergency rooms have. It is a small room with only a sink and the things necessary to wash an eye. Because the eye room is seldom used for eye washing, it is used as a temporary place to hold the bodies of those who do not make it, making room for those who might.

I obtain what little paperwork they have at the nursing station and go into the room. Dale is alone, still lying on the gurney that came out of the A.P.C. He is now wrapped in a blood-stained sheet. I tell myself what I have told so many others: "Just breathe. Slow down. There is no rush." It is different when you're dealing with one of your own.

I find myself pausing as I fill out the paperwork. Each blank I fill in has the added weight of personal knowledge. The name is not just a name; it is Dale Geddie. The date is not just a date; it is a date I will remember forever. It is not like any inquest I have ever done.

"What a waste," I say to Terry, who can stay in the room for only a few minutes at a time. My sadness is not only personal. It reaches out to his family and beyond, to the community. We all lost someone of value. It also leaves my office with a vacuum in the place of Constable Precinct Four.

~~~~~~~~~~~~~~~~~~~~~~~~~~~~~~~~

"Judge, they need you back at the scene," Terry says. I wonder if the officers took advantage of the shooter standing in front of his window.

"Let's go," I say, and we are off.

When we arrive, the command post is gone, traffic is flowing on Highway 271, and things seem to be going back to normal. Someone driving along now would know nothing of the activity of just a few minutes ago. We are now able to drive to the crime scene, the residence where it all took place. The small house is indistinguishable from the other houses around, except for the police cars. Dale's car sits twenty to thirty yards from the house, at an angle, at the end of a chain-link fence forming the front yard. The car looks frozen, like a picture; the driver's side door and trunk stand open. The car looks as though it is stopped in time, waiting for its operator to continue whatever he was doing.

I walk around the vehicle. On the ground is the evidence of what a bullet from a deer rifle can do to a man, blood soaking into the sand. A 12 gauge shotgun is lying in the trunk, ready to assist in Dale's defense. He probably never touched it. Dale had put on his vest. He knew of the danger. He did not know the shooter had put a bead on his head.

"Where is the shooter?" I ask. Names usually get lost when there is a killing. People become "the victims" and "the shooters."

"He is at the hospital. They need you back there again."

~~~~~~~~~~~~~~~~~~~~~~~

Things often get confused at disaster scenes, battles, and crime scenes. This was all three. We drive back to the emergency room. Judge Quincy Beavers is there, ready to do an inquest. Both men were both killed in my precinct, and I had already started the paperwork. Judge Beavers agreed to assist. Before becoming a judge, he served with Dale as a deputy.

Inquest #4288

"Where is he?" I ask.

"He is in the eye room," says Judge Beavers.

I open the door to see both bodies lying there, wrapped in white bed sheets: the shooter and the victim.

One got what he wanted. The other paid the price.

The same SWAT doctor worked on both. Doctors take an oath to keep all people alive. I wondered how much energy he put into the shooter. I still see the SWAT team "doc" from time to time. When our eyes meet, it is though we are old friends or comrades who have been to hell and back.

~~~~~~~~~~~~~~~~~~~~~~~

"He stepped out on the front porch and waved his gun toward us in a threatening manner," says the Captain of the swat team. "A single shot to the chest took him down."

Tough luck on that insurance money. The manner of death is suicide, the cause of death gunshot wound to the chest. We refer to this kind of case as "suicide by cop." Actually, most insurance policies pay on a suicide if the policy has been in force long enough. They consider it a form of mental illness.

~~~~~~~~~~~~~~~~~~~~~~~

"Contact Harmon Funeral home to transport both for autopsies," I say, still on autopilot, doing paperwork, doing my job.

"It's a high-profile case," says Matt Bingham, the district attorney. "Let's send the bodies to Dallas."

I question why the bodies should go to Dallas when a forensic center is just down the road. The cause of both deaths is quite evident. There will be no trial, and there is no real need to know any more than we already know. He insists.

It is a battle not worth fighting.

I am numb. I try to perform as though this is just another inquest and the county would save a few dollars by shipping them together. Also, it crosses my mind that if a supernatural confrontation develops between these two dead fellows, Dale will have an opportunity to slap the shit out of the . . .

"Judge, you're not sending them in the same hearse, are you?" This is the district attorney, again. "Split them up. My office will pay the difference."

Some felt it would be a disgrace or sacrilege to place the bodies of both of these men within one hearse to transport them more than a hundred miles. Law enforcement people are like that. It was not as though they would have to face or talk to one another as they traveled down the interstate. It was more like the idea of being next to someone you really do not like, or even have a reason to hate or wish dead—or worse, since that already has happened. The officers felt uncomfortable with their brother riding to Dallas with his killer.

"Done," I say. "And don't worry about the difference."

The funeral is huge. Law enforcement officers from all over Texas and other states attend the service. With full media coverage and the Internet, the news is carried worldwide, as are the concern and outpourings of compassion. E-mails, cards, and letters come to the office. Calls of condolence come one after another.

Stewart Funeral Home provides the funeral arrangements. Visitation requires a two-hour wait in line to meet, shake hands with, and hug a worn and exhausted family. Everyone agrees that this is a painful tragedy. Each one has a Dale Geddie story.

People from all walks of life come to Green Acres Baptist Church to pay their last respects. Green Acres graciously provides its sanctuary in anticipation of the numbers. Most knew the man, and many come to see the legend.

The service ends with everyone going outside onto the steps and plaza of the church. More than a thousand uniforms with badges, each banded across with a black strip, are gathered shoulder to shoulder standing at attention on the steps, on the sidewalks, and in the parking lot. My staff and I solemnly stick together, hoping and searching, trying to find strength from each other.

The report of seven gunshots in three volleys echoes the twenty-one-gun salute.

The bagpipes slowly play "Amazing Grace." I find myself concentrating on breathing.

A solitary bugler plays taps as a saddled horse is led away. In the stirrups is an empty pair of boots.

Down the winding drive comes Dale's new patrol car. In it is Deputy Terry Brunk. The car stops, away from the gathering, alone on a grassy hillside. Terry opens the car door, climbs out, and stands. The car is parked at an angle, and only Terry's head and chest are visible above the star-marked door. He stands at attention with the radio mike in hand. The black, curled cord extends back to the radio, the lifeline of a cop on duty. He keys the radio mike. The external speaker pops with the volume at full. A metallic voice floats across the airways and into the stillness of the crowd.

"Smith County to 4-0-1." All is quiet. All is still. Time passes. Time stands still. The radio pops again.

"Smith County to 4-0-1." Only the muffled sobbing of a few grieving friends and relatives can be heard.

"4-0-1 is out of service," Terry responds.

~~~~~~~~~~~~~~~~~~~~~~~~~~~~~

There continue to be scholarships in honor of Dale, as well as fund-raisers, memorial markers, and other celebrations and recognitions of his personal life and the life given in service to others.

"Mitch," Dale Senior says a year later, "we appreciate all that people are doing. And Dale would . . . well, Dale would have probably been embarrassed." He took off his white cowboy hat and began to fiddle around with it.

"It's . . . just that, every time we go to a dinner or fund-raiser or festival, to show our support and thanks, we go through 'it' all over again and again. I don't think his mom can take much more." I think he was speaking for himself also.

~~~~~~~~~~~~~~~~~~~~~~~~~~~~~~~~

Five years later, life goes on. A granite marker is outside the office door. "In memory of Dale Geddie" is still spoken every year, as a graduate receives a scholarship in Dale's name or when "Law Day" is celebrated in the streets of Winona.

They say the good die young. I guess "young" is relative to how "old" you are. And now it is "five years later." His picture hangs on my office wall. His memory will hang upon my heart. His story will live on.

~~~~~~~~~~~~~~~~~~~~~~~~~~~~~~~~

If you would like to donate to the Dale Geddie Schlorship Fund in care of the Winona Area Chamber of Commerce send to:

Proven Justice
Dale Geddie Schlorship
POB 232
Winona, Texas 75792

EPILOGUE

Having read this far, you know a fair amount about me. There is much more to my life, of course; for now, it will remain tucked away in the recesses of my brain.

A friend of mine wrote a book about one of my inquests, and one reader commented, "It was more about him than the murder story he was telling." With that in mind, I changed the title of my book from *Inquests* to *Inquests: Living With the Dead.* I've told you quite a few things about myself directly, and the stories of the inquest are, like any written accounts of events, filtered through the brain of the author, so you've seen how my brain filters things. My hope is that through this book, you, the reader, and especially my kids and generations to come will remember and experience my life, and maybe examine your own.

Because these stories are based on true events, I will state again, the stories are told as I remember them. Two people can see the same incident and walk away with two very different stories. I have no doubt that there are variances even among the tales included in this book, all told by me, but at different times and from different perspectives. If my recollections have offended anyone, I apologize and assure you that my writing was done in complete absence of any malice or ill will.

Thanks to those who read portions of the book that involved them and offered their own perspectives. Many of the names are fabricated, as is most of the dialogue, but many names are those of the real people involved in the incidents. I do not take any of their stories lightly, and I appreciate their contributions and suggestions.

Audio books have opened the door for me to listen to many great (and some not-so-great) books read by talented readers. The great books inspire me. One not-so-great book *really* inspired me; it proved to me that even the most common life is noteworthy and everyone, alive or dead, has a story to tell. You may want to check out the audio version of *Inquests: Living With the Dead.*

~~~~~~~~~~~~~~~~~~~~~~

At 92 years of age, LoLo puts on a nice gown, fixes her hair, and goes to bed each night ready to "wake up dead" the next morning. Mom says, "I don't want to go, but I am ready to go."

Performing inquests has taught me several things. Mainly, we should all be "ready to go." Death has no respect for age, status, or any of the things we deem important and are our reasons to live.

Eating proper foods may prolong life, but would a life be worth living without chocolate-covered strawberries or homemade ice cream?

When this idea is stretched to the extreme, some would say the same about climbing a mountain or jumping out of an airplane.

Enjoy the life you have, and live each day to its fullest.

—Thomas Mitchell Shamburger

If you would like to hear me read the book check out the audio version of ***Inquests: Living With the Dead*** +. Included are my comments, aftermath, and corrections. Also, John D Williams tells in his own words of his death experience. The recording was done just days before his funeral!

Available NOW! March 10, 2012

Now 8 months after publication and with the hindsight and comments of others I am impressed and humbled. This book has affected lives. Some comments are: "Thank you so much, it has cleared up some questions," "I never really thought about life and death." "The hardest part was reading about how things used to be. 'Family' seems to be going away." "I realized where I was heading. The book turned me around!" "First thing I thought of was your book and man I knew I had to do something!"

If you would like to make this book available to those who can't afford it, do the "buy a book" program. This also includes the Audio version that I am trying to make available to the blind and elderly who can't read. Make sure you designate that it is a Give-Away Book or I will send it to you and you can give it away.

Proven Justice Inc.
Give-Away-Book
POB 232
Winona, Texas 75792